Spain at the Crossroads

Spain at the Crossroads

CIVIL SOCIETY, POLITICS,
AND THE RULE OF LAW

VÍCTOR PÉREZ-DÍAZ

HARVARD UNIVERSITY PRESS
Cambridge, Massachusetts
London, England   1999

Portions of this book were first published in French in 1996 as *La démocratie espagnole vingt ans après,* © Editions Complexe, Brussels.

Published with the assistance of Analistas Socio-Políticos, Gabinete de Estudios, S.L.

Library of Congress Cataloging-in-Publication Data
Pérez Díaz, Víctor.
      [Démocratie espagnole vingt ans après.   English]
      Spain at the crossroads : civil society, politics, and the rule of law /
   Víctor Pérez-Díaz.
         p.   cm.
      Includes bibliographical references and index.
   ISBN 0-674-00052-8 (alk. paper)
      1. Rule of law—Spain.   2. Democracy—Spain.   3. Civil society—Spain.
   I. Title.
   KKT2020.P47   1999
   320.946'09'049—dc21   99-20486

Acknowledgments

OVER THE YEARS, the research fellows and associates at Analistas Socio-Políticos, Gabinete de Estudios—Juan Carlos Rodríguez, Josu Mezo, Elisa Chuliá, Berta Álvarez-Miranda, and Celia Valiente—helped me to refine and strengthen the points I make in the pages that follow. And certainly events in Spain during the last few years offered many opportunities and stimuli for this book. But it was Marina González Olivares who got me to write it in the end.

Contents

Chronology   *ix*

Introduction: The Historical Process from a
Crossroads Perspective   *1*

1. Spain's Transition to Democracy   *7*

2. The Socialists Rule   *34*

3. The Two Faces of a Generation   *52*

4. Public Drama and the Rule of Law   *70*

5. Unemployment   *103*

6. A Political Shift from Left to Right   *122*

7. The Challenge of Nationalism   *151*

8. Becoming a Civil Society by Trial and Error   *173*

Notes   *191*

Bibliography   *201*

Index   *209*

Chronology

1970. Trade agreement between Spain and the European Economic Community.

1973. Murder of Admiral Carrero Blanco, Prime Minister in Franco's government. First oil shock.

1975. General Francisco Franco dies (November). Juan Carlos becomes King of Spain.

1976. The King appoints Adolfo Suárez as Prime Minister (June). Law on Political Reform pased by referendum in December.

1977. First free democratic elections (June). After UCD's victory (34.6% of the vote), Suárez is confirmed as Prime Minister. Spain puts forward its candidacy for membership in the European Community (July).

1978. New Constitution, passed by referendum in December.

1979. Second general election (June), won by the UCD, a centrist party (35%). Statutes of Autonomy for the Basque country and Catalonia passed by referendum.

1981. Attempted coup d'état (February). Spain becomes NATO member.

1982. Third general election, won by PSOE, the Socialist party (48.4%). Felipe González, Prime Minister.

1984. Unemployment peaks at 20% of the labor force.

1986. Fourth general election (June), won by PSOE (44.6%). Spain becomes member of the European Community and confirms NATO membership by referendum.

1987. Highest GDP annual growth since 1974 (5.6%).

1988. General strike (December). Two policemen involved in the GAL (death squadrons active from 1983 to 1986–87) are arrested.

1989. Fifth general election, won by PSOE (39.9%).

1991. Vice-Prime Minister Alfonso Guerra resigns because his brother Juan is involved in a scandal (January). The FILESA affair comes to light (June). Unemployment is at its lowest (16%).

1992. World Fair in Seville; Olympics in Barcelona; celebrations of the Quincentennial of the discovery of America. The Maastricht Treaty is signed.

1993. Sixth general election, won by PSOE (38.8%). Worst recession in thirty years (GDP falls by 1.4%).

1994. Luis Roldán, former head of the Civil Guard, flees the country (April). Former governor of the Bank of Spain, Mariano Rubio, is arrested (May). The GAL affair resurfaces in December. Unemployment is at a new peak (24%).

1995. Rafael Vera, former secretary of state for security affairs, is arrested (March); former Minister of Interior José Barrionuevo, is prosecuted (December). Both were allegedly involved in the GAL affair.

1996. Seventh general election, won by the PP, a right-of-center party (38.7%). José María Aznar is appointed Prime Minister, with support from center-right nationalist parties.

1997. Felipe González resigns as PSOE's Secretary General (June). Several PSOE officials (including a Senator) involved in the FILESA affair receive prison sentences (October).

1998. Spain qualifies as founding member of the European Monetary Union (May). Roldán sentenced to 28 years in prison. Vera and Barrionuevo sentenced to 10 years in prison (July). GDP estimated growth is at 4%. Unemployment is at 19% of the labor force.

Introduction:
The Historical Process from
a Crossroads Perspective

IN THE PARTICULAR historical and theoretical perspective of this book, I look at the course Spanish politics and society took during the last quarter of the twentieth century, and especially the last ten to fifteen years, from a specific vantage point: the dramatic crisis that shook the country from 1993 to 1996, with its gross political scandals and judiciary proceedings, its spectacularly high unemployment, and its bitter partisan antagonisms. The drama brought out certain features of politics and society, manifest since Spain's transition to democracy in the late 1970s, that might otherwise have been neglected. Also, an examination of the crisis helps to evaluate the events of the late 1990s, marked by a (still protracted) reassertion of the rule of law and a crucial change in political leadership, as well as by Spain's successful entry into the European Monetary Union (EMU) and a deeper understanding of the politics of nationalism. The drama thus throws light at both the strength and the frailty of Spain's past accomplishments and helps clarify its more recent recovery. In addition to tracing the history, I consider these changes through the analytical lens of a theory of civil society. This provides me with the formulations I find most relevant to my particular inquiry, and these may be of use to other inquiries of a more general nature.

For Spaniards, the years 1993 to 1996 were a time of great confusion. After twenty years of democracy, they felt a sudden need to reassess the central characters of the transition, King Juan Carlos and Prime Minister Adolfo Suárez, with a mixture of respect, curiosity, and a dose of anxiety. This curious nostalgia arose out of a need for reassurance. Many Spaniards felt uncertain about trusting their public authorities, and they wondered whether the country had lost its sense of direction.

The serious crisis of public trust erupted in 1993–94, when, after more than ten years of tenure, Prime Minister Felipe González faced some extraordinary accusations: at least of poor judgment, at most of complicity in the criminal activities by state officials against Basque terrorists that had been going on for several years (between 1983 and 1987). Foreign observers who had only a passing interest in Spain might have thought the affair had got out of hand, as they saw González mainly in the light of the ceremonial politics of the European Monetary Union, and generally as a statesman who had contributed to Spain's democratic consolidation. But in fact Spanish public debate at the time was dominated by this issue. The accusations stuck, and a sizable sector of the public did not believe González's denials. Under these circumstances, he was forced to call for elections in 1996 and was ousted from government, though only by a slight margin. Since then, he has managed to evade standing trial, unlike one of his ministers and several high state officials, who have recently been sentenced (in July of 1998) to several years of imprisonment.

Yet this man was the same political leader whom his fellow citizens had entrusted with supreme political power through four consecutive national elections (in 1982, 1986, 1989 and 1993). No wonder the country felt uneasy. If the people had to pass judgment on González and his tenure, they had to judge themselves as well, since they had supported him in power for so many years. If the country's trust in González was in question, so too was the country's self-confidence: that is, confidence in its legal and political institutions, and in its ability to make its leaders submit to the rule of law and to the principle of political accountability.

As I follow the unfolding of this particular drama, I intend to keep my focus on public trust, inasmuch as it is the cornerstone of the relationship between rulers and citizens in a civil society, and on the rule of law and the principle of political accountability, both closely related to public trust. But my focus will not be exclusive. Other crucial choices and decisions had to be made during those critical years, concerning basic issues of foreign policy, the national economy, and the articulation of

Spain's collective identity. Spain had joined the European "club" in 1986, thus fulfilling a long-cherished aspiration. But this club required exacting behavior of its members: lean and open economies, respect for the rules, and careful and realistic strategies. With the setting up of the EMU, the various European countries had to deliver on their promises, not simply put off doing so to some day in the future. They had to get their economies in shape and produce a credible and workable political institutional design that would outlive the present generation of political leaders.

But when the time came to implement EMU's quite momentous decisions, the Spaniards realized that they had done little of the homework needed to implement those choices. It was not only that the debate on the European question had been rather poor; nor even that the government knew that it might have great difficulties in meeting the Maastricht requirements for joining the EMU in the short run. The problem ran deeper.

What the Spaniards had to face was that they had not put their house in order, and the definitive indication of that disarray was the extraordinarily high unemployment rate (about 20%), which had persisted during most of the 1985–1995 decade. No matter how this fact was presented,[1] it immediately deflated all the talk (both in academic and in political circles) about "wise" Spanish economic policies and the "dynamic" economy which had been heard in the second half of the 1980s and early 1990s. In fact, those policies were most unwise in failing to train and deploy Spain's human capital; the country's economy was thus to a great extent static, in that it was unable to generate employment. Moreover, those policies had led the Spanish economy along a path of half-measures, with the result that Spain was in no condition to comply with the macroeconomic criteria agreed upon by the signatories of the Maastricht treaties, even leaving the unemployment problem aside.

Now, this lack of compliance, this seeming inability to play the European game on equal terms with the core European nations, was more than an embarrassment. It signaled a peculiar lack of will on the part of the Spanish authorities that might shed light on another related weakness: their inability to articulate an all-Spanish collective identity that would make room for expression of Catalan and Basque national identities and include them in Spain's government (some tentative moves in this direction were made in the early 1990s, as we will see).

To understand the critical moments of 1993–1996 requires a look back at the previous stages: the transition to democracy and, before that, the period of the 1950s and 1960s, when the character of the political actors was formed. It also helps to look forward, at the *dénouement* (still provisional) of the drama, when a political shift and a generational change took place during the more recent years.

The Notion of Civil Society

Civil society consists of a set of sociopolitical institutions that include: a governing authority which is limited and accountable to society at large; a rule of law that applies equally to rulers and citizens; the development of a public sphere; a market economy free from most violent and corrupt practices; and an array of voluntary associations. It is a precarious construction that takes considerable resources of will and wisdom for people to build, to repair, and to rebuild over and over again. There are no guarantees that it will last. It can be distorted and converted into an authoritarian, collectivistic, uncivil society at any time, if the people living under those arrangements forgo the energy and the determination needed to keep it alive.

If I wished to use an architectural metaphor about building a civil society, I would not take the example of the Egyptian pyramids, made out of stone and intended to stay there for ever, but rather point to the houses of Southern California, built out of adobe and other light materials, likely to collapse under an earth tremor or ready to be remodeled if a change in life style occurs—something that may happen at any time. They are precarious buildings, whose daily permanence is contingent upon the endurance and the ingenuity of their inhabitants in the face of unforeseeable circumstances. Or to use a more dynamic metaphor: civil society would be the story of a process of becoming in reference to a normative goal. It would be a "civilizing process"[2] by which a given society or a number of societies (in the last instance, perhaps the whole of mankind) becomes the bearer of an order of liberty, with general laws, accountable and limited public authorities, markets, public spheres, plural and diverse social fabrics, and a world of citizens in the full sense of the word.

In this book I am less interested in the earlier phases of the construction of a Spanish civil society—the late years of the Franco regime and the period of transition to democracy[3]—than in the later period, from the early 1980s to the late 1990s, which I see as an illustration of the limits and the precariousness of that construction, as well as of some of the mechanisms that may contribute to its permanence and strength.

Two crucial mechanisms to facilitate the task of building and repair work are, first, a sensible design and use of institutions and rules intended to check the abuses of power, in particular by the public authorities, and, second, the development of sociocultural dispositions or habits among the citizens that incline them to reason freely, to speak out, and to participate in the public sphere. Consequently, I will focus on institutions and on the development of civic sensibilities in my endeavor to explain the genesis, the problems, and the current trends of Spanish politics.

Finally, a word on the plan of this book, which has a sort of dialectical structure. In Chapter 1, I provide the reader with the main lines of what reads *prima facie* as a success story: that of Spain's transition to democracy, examined against the background of the economic changes and sociocultural traditions of the later Franco regime that prepared the way for the new regime. At the same time, as a counterpoint to that accomplishment, I take note of some ambiguities and dark areas in the transition that may suggest some of the problems that lay ahead. In Chapter 2, I deal with the period of socialist hegemony during most of the 1980s and early 1990s. This is, again, a two-sided story. On the one hand, it is a tale of democratic consolidation. But there is another side. As I examine the various components of Spanish civil society during the 1980s (government, markets, the social fabric), I find the society suffering from what I call a "low-intensity disorder." The ambiguous patterns observed at that point help fill in the outlines of the principal players, and more particularly that of the main protagonist, the generation of 1956 to 1968. In Chapter 3, I deal with the formative process of this generation, which was to face the bullfighter's "moment of truth" in the shape of the political scandals of the years to come.

In the next two chapters I concentrate on two main topics of the critical developments from 1993 to the beginning of 1996. I take up the political scandals (Chapter 4) and the way they were handled by politicians, judges, journalists, and the public, presenting them as social drama and as a crucial test for the rule of law and for the Spanish public sphere. Unemployment is examined in Chapter 5, in which I look into the institutional and sociocultural roots of the problem and its links to economic policy.

Chapter 6 traces the political shift from left to right that took place in

Spanish politics through the mid-1990s, largely as a result of the previous developments. I follow the way in which politics reacted to the mounting crisis of those years, and I make suggestions about how the events came to bear on the electoral resolution of the crisis in 1996. Then I follow up the unfolding of it into the late 1990s. I do not try to pass judgment on an ongoing process, but attempt rather to delineate the ways in which some of the issues (such as the rule of law and the public sphere, the economy and the European Union) are handled in a new political landscape, under the rule of a center-right government and a new generation of political actors. Finally, in Chapter 7, I take up the issue of the accommodation between central and peripheral nationalisms (mainly the Catalan and Basque). I explore the opportunities for reconciling the several nationalities that inhabit Spain and for civilizing the manifestation of their conflicts. This leads me, again, in two opposite directions, to the past and to the immediate future. Thus I cover some historical ground and comment on the most recent attempts to put an end to terrorist violence in the Basque country.

I conclude, in Chapter 8, with a brief discussion that ties up the different lines of my argument and outlines the tasks that lie ahead. My wish was to provide a useful example for explaining any country's process of becoming a civil society as a process of trial and error, of coming to a sequence of crossroads where politicians and citizens may take the correct road or make the wrong turn, only to face a new choice along the way. More particularly, I suggest that the lessons to be drawn from the Spanish experience may be applied, to a point, to Central and Eastern Europe. Indeed, I hope this experience will be of some use to other European (and perhaps also non-European) countries embarked upon the complex and hazardous route of establishing and nurturing their own civil societies, day in and day out.

CHAPTER ONE

Spain's Transition to Democracy

FEAR AND HUBRIS are the moral and emotional foundations of authoritarian governments. Their rulers do not have to answer for their actions, and they justify their rule by claiming that their subjects are unable to govern themselves. General Francisco Franco, Spain's authoritarian ruler for almost four decades, declared he could be held to account only by God and History, not by his fellow citizens. He took power, he claimed, to put an end to nearly three years of fratricidal strife—a bloodletting which showed that Spaniards distrusted and feared each other too much to rule themselves. To achieve a lasting peace, the country needed a strong ruler.

No liberal democracy can be built on such foundations. Hence at the heart of the Spanish transition to democracy lay two interrelated experiences: making the government accountable to the citizens and subject to the rule of law, and overcoming the memory of the Civil War. These developments were part of a wider process of the emergence of a civil society, which in turn prepared the way for the transition, made it possible, and made it lasting. The changes in the style of governance and in the relationship between the political elite and the general public were stressful. The politicians discovered the limits of their ability to handle problems and found it difficult to accept political responsibility for their failures; the citizens demonstrated limits to their civic involvement. The consequences of these limits and difficulties will be fully discussed throughout the book.

The Emergence of a Democratic Society

Spain's transition to democracy during the 1970s has been told as a success story. In the 1980s, it inspired democratic transitions worldwide (in Eastern Europe, Latin America, and Asia). At home it gave birth to institutions which have been in operation for more than twenty years, and by now a whole generation of Spaniards has been brought up in a liberal democracy.

This success was largely unexpected. Spanish intellectuals, journalists, and politicians still persisted in looking at events through the lens of the Spanish Civil War of the 1930s, which had made such a lasting impression on collective and individual memories. Hence they watched and interpreted the last-minute compromises within and outside the Francoist establishment, and paid close attention to the personalities of the political players. Despite the significance of these factors, however (including outside pressure), the success of the transition to democracy lay neither in the contemporary circumstances, nor in the charisma of the protagonists (which was notoriously lacking), nor in the old memories. Rather, the key to it was to be found in socioeconomic and sociocultural developments that took place between the mid-1950s and the mid-1970s.[1]

These developments can be summed up as the gradual emergence of a "civil society"—a concept open to diverse interpretations. For my purpose, the idea of a civil society largely corresponds to that of a nomocratic order (as opposed to a teleocratic one: Hayek 1978): it is a sociopolitical configuration defined by formal and abstract rules that frame the activities and interactions of autonomous moral agents. The system has five *institutional* components which are interrelated: the *rule of law* which applies equally to rulers and citizens; a *public authority which is limited and accountable* to citizens; a *public sphere* where citizens meet and debate their common concerns; a *market economy* as a system of spontaneous coordination among autonomous units, subject to the rule of law; and a vast array of *voluntary associations* (including semi-formal organizations such as social movements and other, softer forms of sociability). At the same time, civil society does have a particular *community basis:* it is anchored in a particular social unit (say a nation), with its own identity, and with boundaries that separate it from, and establish the forms of relations with, other societies. And, finally, it contains a crucial *cultural* dimension. Most, or at least a critical mass of the members of a civil society must hold civic (or civil) beliefs that will advance the implementation of the institutional design and ensure that it works properly. As cornerstone of this sociopolitical system, the critical mass of individuals must learn to play two roles: that of citizens who stand up to their rulers and debate common concerns; and that of individuals engaged in free exchanges in various domains, within the framework of the law.[2]

By the 1960s and early 1970s, elements of civil society in Spain were numerous and quite strong. People had become used to patterns of activities and interactions that provided the institutional and cultural instruments for challenging the authoritarian regime, and for building a liberal one. Among them were some legal institutions in place already which checked (to a significant extent) the ruler's discretionary powers. On another level, various forums of public debate, diverse markets, and several associations existed which allowed individuals to conduct their activities with a large degree of autonomy. As a result, many people developed habits of thought and behavior that made them ready and able to challenge the rulers as well as to interact, trust one another, and organize themselves, and thus to prepare themselves for democracy.

It took time and a special set of circumstances to allow these sociocultural traditions (that is, the blend of institutions and cultural dispositions) to emerge, since the starting point was a teleocratic (authoritarian) order to which the economy, society, and cultural life submitted. After the Civil War, the Spanish state was organized along authoritarian lines. General Franco held supreme power with the support of the army, the Catholic Church, and a heterogeneous coalition of businessmen, peasants, and sectors of the middle class. These supporters had an influence on governance, but they could not make Franco accountable for his political deeds; even Franco's ministers used to give no more than perfunctory accounts of their actions to a rubber-stamp Parliament.[3]

The Francoist state sought to organize the economic and social life of the country along corporatist lines, foster a homogeneous Catholic society under the aegis of a conservative church, and pursue a policy of isolation from the rest of the world. In order to continue to promote these goals, however, it needed a neutral (or favorable) international environment. In time, changes in this environment combined with domestic transformations to block their fulfillment.

The relative isolation of the country (and the forced submission of half the population after the Civil War) allowed the Franco regime to pursue its dreams of a strong authority and autarky for a while. But with the defeat of the Axis, Franco was forced to look for some accommodation with the Western democracies. A few years after World War II, the Francoist state received Western support (in 1953 Spain signed a number of pacts with the United States and a concordat with the Holy See), but this support was conditional: Spain had to open up to the international capitalist economy and allow a degree of pluralism in its society, particularly regarding the church and Catholic organizations. These conditions proved eventually to be decisive catalysts for far-reaching transformations of Spanish life in the years to come.

International links contributed to domestic problems. In the 1940s, Spain had been an agrarian society with half of its labor force employed in the agricultural sector. In the 1950s, protectionist and import-substitution policies gave an initial boost to industry, but by the middle of the decade industrial growth was running out of steam, and the Spanish economy faced a serious balance-of-payments crisis. The government then decided to put an end to its import-substitution policies and forgo its dreams of autarky. No sooner did Spain begin to head toward an open economy integrated into the international markets, than capital, commodities, and people started to flow across its borders, bringing with them, or followed by, institutional and cultural transformations which led to a general relaxation of government controls.

Peasants and farmers became industrial or construction workers and urban residents, leaving the countryside depopulated. By the mid-1970s, labor force in the agricultural sector had fallen from 50% to 15% of the total. Millions of tourists flooded the coasts of Mediterranean Spain, and hundreds of thousands of Spaniards went northward to work in Germany and France; at the same time students went to study abroad, entrepreneurs imported machines and production techniques, foreign investors poured capital into the economy, and consumers got used to foreign-made goods.

Impressive economic growth followed, and the economy grew at an annual rate of about 7% until 1973. By the time Franco died in 1975, Spain was a modern economy that ranked tenth among capitalist economies worldwide. It had a booming service sector, a broad industrial sector, and its agriculture was undergoing rapid transformation. Economic development had created a working class recently uprooted from its rural origins and eager to reap the benefits of increases in real wages, as well as an incipient welfare state (which had begun to develop in the mid-1960s). Toward the end of the 1970s, the standard of living of the average Spanish worker was about one-third lower than that of the average French worker and quite close to that of an Italian.

Opening the economy went hand in hand with a general opening of the country to outside social and cultural influences. The impact of the new stimulated a resurgence of old tensions. As soon as the state lost its ability to keep the gates of Spanish society closed, and the goods, the messages, and the people flooded through, the latent old domestic conflicts flared up, putting pressure on the existing institutional framework and forcing people to experiment with new institutions.

Economic changes, for example, brought changes in industrial relations regarding collective bargaining, strikes, and workers' associations. Driven by the economic development of the sixties, collective bargaining (allowed since 1958) spread throughout industry and generated some recognition of workers' representatives as well as increasing tolerance of strikes. As a result, days lost to strikes rose from approximately 250,000 per year in 1964 to 1969, to 850,000 per year in 1970 to 1972, to 1.5 million per year in 1973 to 1975. By the time Spain entered its democratic transition, the working class had accumulated more than ten years' worth of experience of mass strikes, collective bargaining, and semi-clandestine representative unions.[4]

At the same time, the Catholic Church and religion itself were subject to profound transformation. The church was challenged from all sides. The Second Vatican Council came as a shock to most Spanish bishops, while priests and laymen seized the opportunity to press the older generations of bishops and leaders of the religious orders to modify the church hierarchy, revise their conception of the role of the church in society, and rethink their alliance with the Francoist state. It did not take long before the Spanish church ceased to be proud of contributing to Franco's victory in the Civil War and was asking the Spanish people's forgiveness for having failed to avoid the war. Meanwhile, the country had begun a process of moderate secularization in the widest sense, and popular interest in the dogmatic and moral teachings of the church had declined dramatically.

The 1950s also marked the emergence of a student movement, and a new generation of university students found its generational identity in opposition to Francoism. By 1975, the year of Franco's death, Spanish universities had developed a political culture hostile to the political regime of the day, and the initiation rites of the entering classes consisted of acts of protest and unrest against the political and academic authorities. The consequences were not limited to the universities. As they graduated, these new lawyers, journalists, doctors, engineers, and economists extended their university values and demands to share power and check social and cultural authorities to their spheres of professional activity. And it was members of this generation who went into oppositional politics and filled the ranks of an emerging political elite.

As a result, by the mid-1970s the economic, social, and cultural institutions of Spain were getting ever closer to those of Western Europe, and the moral perceptions of Spanish people were becoming similar to those of other Europeans. As the exchanges with the outside world increased, Spaniards were exposed to other institutions and cultures. Their freedom of movement increased along with their opportunities to get ahead, and the scope of their civil rights widened. Expectations of government accountability, of access to open markets, of self-organization, and of free debate of common concerns were becoming ingrained habits. The next step was to find the political language that would suit this world view, and the difficulty here was how to overcome the memories of the Civil War.

Putting the Civil War Behind

A civil war is the most glaring contrast to a civil society. In a civil war, violence takes the place of legal institutions and the rule of law; rulers of the opposing camps demand uncontested authority; markets, free speech, and civil associations are suppressed or subordinated to the conduct of war; and the foundation of it all, the community of fellow citizens, disappears and is replaced by two rival communities.

In Spain, it was not easy for many years to translate the public's new social attitudes into political terms, precisely because the country did feel haunted by the memories of the Civil War (1936–1939), the civil unrest that preceded it, and the political repression that followed it. Once the war ended, the Francoist state perpetuated the enmity of winners and losers. The community was divided, and mutual fear and resentment persisted in both camps. The Franco regime did its best to fuel the fires. It used every excuse to celebrate the war; and every war celebration was a reminder of victory for them, defeat for others.[5] The government presented the war and the Francoist victory as the key events in modern Spanish history, the culmination of a centuries'-old battle between competing versions of Spain's identity: between two Spains. In turn, also for many years, the opposition was adamant in defending a reverse mirror image of Spanish history, similarly pitting two opposing images of Spain against each other.

Yet by the mid-1970s the intense ideological conflicts of contemporary Spanish history had abated considerably, and sentiments had on the whole mellowed. Both the right and the left were inclined to accept a peaceful compromise with their opponents and to adopt more moderate attitudes. More importantly, the great majority of Spaniards, better educated than in the past, had been out of touch with ideological politics. Instead, they had been taking part in the functioning of the economic, social, and educational institutions of civil society. Many gained experience in negotiating, acquired confidence in their own judgment and ability, and appreciated the rewards of pragmatic strategies and compromises. They had little desire to participate in ideological battles: their world view had been enriched with countless rituals of peaceful dialogue, and they looked for a political discourse that would fit their dispositions. The new language would be that of a modern, Europeanized Spain which had left behind, once and for all, the drama of the Civil War. By implication, this would have to be a post-Franco, democratic Spain.

The mellowing of the late Francoist era provided the new generation with the sociocultural basis for a reinterpretation of the Civil War. Heretofore, both the right and the left had demanded that Spaniards take sides in an ongoing historical-metaphysical struggle between the forces of good and evil. This invitation sounded less and less appealing to people who had engaged for a decade and a half in a pattern of peaceful compromises. Hence a less Manichaean, more ambiguous argument gradually gained ground among large segments of the Spanish public. According to this version, although the fascist and military forces that rebelled in Spain in the 1930s did wrong, they did so in response to large sectors of the population that were justifiably alarmed by the radical threats of the extreme left and by the indecision and incompetence of the moderate left. Moreover, the domestic confronta-

tion was compounded by international intervention. On the eve of
World War II, German and Italian fascist regimes, Soviet Communists,
and Western democracies played out their imminent conflict by med-
dling in Spanish domestic politics.

This somewhat complex argument, with some variants, finally prevailed in the collective memory of the generation growing up under the
last stage of Francoism. Large numbers succeeded in distancing themselves from the traditional posture of the combatants of the war, and
refused to take sides. As a result, the Civil War took on, in retrospect,
an aura of "tragic inevitability." This conclusion—that the war had
been a tragedy for which both sides and foreign powers were to
blame—had enormous implications for political discourse. The share of
guilt and responsibility then had to be more or less evenly distributed
between the combatants; the total amount of guilt and responsibility
also had to be reduced, since each side was merely responding to threats
from the other; moreover, they had been treated like pawns in the
larger game of world politics that overwhelmed them. Finally, if a tragic
reading of the war was extended to include postwar developments, the
(remaining) guilt could be expiated. While the losers had already expiated their guilt through suffering and repression, the winners could
expiate theirs through losing most of their social and political powers as
a result of a democratic transition. In other words, democracy offered a
possibility for putting an end to the disturbing saga of the Civil War
once and for all.

And so the democratic transition took place in a domestic climate
that favored change and the readiness to leave war memories behind,
with the additional advantage of a hospitable international environment
(Whitehead 1986). Political maneuvering and bargaining allowed the
transition to proceed forwards step by step. The new King, Juan Carlos,
and his Prime Minister Adolfo Suárez moved fast and decisively, with
the support of the majority of the population. The government bu-
reaucracy learned to adjust to the situation under the public's close
supervision. The parties proved able to accommodate themselves to the
mood of the country, which pushed them relentlessly along a path of
reform, moderation, and peaceful compromise.

Public pressure was decisive at three specific moments. During the
period between November 1975 and June 1976, for example, popular
agitation and general restlessness were critical in influencing the King's

decision to appoint Suárez as Prime Minister. Conversely, when Suárez took the initiative for political reform, in the fall and winter of 1976, the people made it clear, by their participation in the referendum of December 1976, that they trusted Suárez's intentions and political judgment. The victory of a center party, Unión de Centro Democrático (UCD), in the elections of June 1977 demonstrated the public's general inclination toward a position of political moderation, at the expense of the extreme left and of the extreme right. These elections dispelled many politicians' expectations and preconceptions, fears and hopes, about the potential for radical politics or for a continuity with the past. They set the tone for the tasks of writing the Constitution and working out other compromises.

The political elites were successful because they were able to learn from the public. An additional stimulus to pay close attention to the public mood came from the army. Perhaps surprisingly, the army stood for a commitment to a peaceful transition, and demanded from the politicians respect for national unity and good order in the functioning of the state apparatus. As a result, the political class was enjoined to write a Constitution and establish policy patterns that emphasized from the very beginning the integrative role of politics. The new political system was built on the cornerstone of the 1978 Constitution. In it the framers tried to avoid the pitfalls associated with the earlier Constitution of 1931. The new Constitution symbolized national reconciliation and accommodation between right and left, between the church and secular culture, between capitalism and social reform, between the center and the national aspirations of the periphery. Thereafter, the integrative role of politics was emphasized as much in the design and functioning of Spanish institutions as in the political discourse. The monarchy gradually emerged as a unifying symbol of the nation. National elections routinely served as forums to proclaim the virtues of a democratic system that abhorred political violence; and campaigns based on images of moderation repeatedly demonstrated their success at the polls.

So far, so good. Yet there is a flaw that will bear heavily on the rest of the story. While the new democracy was getting established, assassinations by Basque terrorists became more frequent. At first this was treated as an anomaly or the result of a misunderstanding. But in fact it grew out of a peculiar local development which had taken place during the last ten to fifteen years of the Franco regime. For reasons I will not go into here, while sociopolitical conditions *softened* in most of Spain, they *hardened* in crucial parts of the Basque country; and while memories of the Civil War faded away or were reexamined and toned down in Spain everywhere else, sentiments ran in quite the opposite direction among the Basques. In that region of Spain a group of clerics, nationalists, and Marxists drew up a tally of political oppression, economic exploitation, and cultural aggression by the Spanish state against the Basques. This accounting fired up a segment of the youth and served as justification for terrorist violence.

Basque discontent expressed itself through an array of rituals that got to be routinely performed: displays of flags, street manifestations, assassinations by car bomb or gunshot, press communiqués, wall paintings and graffiti, and lavish funerals for the fallen local heroes. In glaring contrast with the solemnity displayed in public celebrations of the Constitution, the pacts and national elections, and the display of monarchical pageantry, these rituals were not social dramas (Turner 1986) that served the purpose of healing and restoring the community. Just the reverse: their main intent was to create a chasm between the Basque community (or rather, the nationalist Basque community) and the rest of the country.

Leaders and Political Parties

With the democratic transition a new political class emerged, a composite of disparate elements gathered partly from within the Francoist milieu (the King included) and partly from the anti-Franco opposition. At the center of the stage stood a new party, the Unión de Centro Democrático (UCD, or Democratic Center Union), composed of moderate ex-Francoists and assorted democrats from the right, center, and center-left of the spectrum, former members of small parties organized around single leaders (for instance, the Social-Democratic party of the followers of Dionisio Ridruejo).[6] They all came together at the last minute, on the eve of the 1977 elections, under the leadership of standing Prime Minister Adolfo Suárez. They had no time, then, for refining their political differences and competing claims to the political spoils. And, for a while, all internal tensions among the various components of UCD took a back seat to the pressing task of helping the government to make the transition to democratic rule by designing the institutions and gaining widespread support for them. This work pushed the government and its party into a course of action aimed at achieving a large political consensus while giving proof of its ability to govern.

The new rulers had to prove themselves and the new political institutions by their ability to solve or manage some of Spain's basic, most urgent problems. Their style of governance reflected a tendency to incorporate other parties and to share political responsibility with domestic economic and regional elites—and, if possible, with supranational European institutions. One of the results of the new governance style was the establishment of a "mesogovernment"—government by consensus, so to speak—in which the government and the opposition parties got together with business, unions, and regional politicians to handle economic and regional policies and share responsibility for them.

The democratic transition took place at an especially difficult moment in Spanish economic history. Between 1960 and 1973 the economy had grown by 7% per year and exports by 10%, and the labor market had reached full employment. The economy took a downturn after 1974, and went into a decline after Franco's death. By mid-1977, inflation peaked at around 26%, and unemployment already affected 6% of the labor force. The government, aware of the problems, postponed major decisions until after the June elections of that year. Then it got together with opposition parties, acted as if it had a mandate from unions and business (still disorganized), and reached an agreement based upon a moderate anti-inflationary policy. Workers were persuaded to make their demands for wage increases on the basis of a projected rather than past inflation (thus avoiding the Italian-style indexing of wages).

The Moncloa Pacts of 1977 were followed by a near-continuous series of "social pacts" or agreements among disparate parties, usually involving the government, business organizations, and one or both the main unions (UGT, Unión General de Trabajadores [General Union of Workers], and CCOO, Comisiones Obreras [Workers' Committees]); these remained in effect until 1986. These and other agreements, in particular the Workers' Statute of 1980, formed a pattern of consultation between the government and its social partners. The result was a modicum of social peace (despite an incidence of strikes higher than in most European countries); moderation of real wage increases; and employment protection for the already employed, possibly at the cost of a steady rise in the rate of unemployment (see Chapters 2 and 5 below).

The state of the economy was not the only problem the new democratic regime had to handle. Democratic Spain inherited from Francoism a highly emotionally charged and complicated regional problem, particularly with respect to Catalonia and the Basque region. In the late nineteenth century, industrial development in those two regions attracted immigrants from all over Spain. This influx provoked a powerful reaction by a sizable portion of the resident population. Given the culture of the times, the reaction took the form of nationalist movements, which developed strongly in the decades that followed. By the mid 1930s, the army and much of the population of Castile and other central parts of the country thought that such peripheral nationalist movements were a serious challenge to the unity of Spain. Franco's victory in the Civil War put a temporary end to them, but Catalan and Basque regional aspirations came back invigorated after Franco's death.

Prime Minister Suárez and his UCD party arranged a compromise that was finally accepted by all parties concerned. They set up a quasi-federal system of regional governments with a large degree of autonomy (Comunidades Autónomas), not only for Catalonia and the Basque region, but for all seventeen Spanish regions. This required devising a complex web of pacts and agreements concerning provisions in the Constitution and regional statutes. Sometimes the wording of these agreements was deliberately ambiguous. The Constitution recognized only one unitary Spanish nation, the constituent agent whose sovereign will was expressed in and by the Constitution itself. The agreements, however, spoke of Catalan and Basque (and Galician) "nationalities"— and this wording, which most Spaniards read as a lapse or a rhetorical concession, was read as a recognition of a separate national identity by the peripheral nationalists. On the other hand, in the division of rights and jurisdictions between the central and the regional governments, the agreements granted so-called exclusive powers to both (in fact and *de jure*)—thereby leaving the Constitutional Court to face, in the following years, the endless political bargains and legal appeals caused by the inevitable misunderstandings about this issue.

Learning to work out compromises in the face of such ambiguities did not come easily. In 1979 and 1980 Basque terrorism increased, along with growing assertiveness of regional and nationalist movements all over the country. The apparent willingness of the Socialists to use the issue in their party strategy (and to support Basque nationalists' call for self-determination) increased the level of anxiety in the army. Not that this army was similar to that which had fought the Civil War. Many generals and most of the officer corps had shared in the common experiences of most civilians; by 1970 two thirds of the army officers in Madrid had a second civilian job, and by 1974 one third of the army officers had a university education (Puell de la Villa 1997: 140, 160). It may then be argued that most were willing to accept the new constitutional framework. However, one of the implicit understandings underlying army support for the new Constitution was that the unity of the fatherland would be kept (and that law and order would be upheld). Thus for part of the military the turbulence of 1980–81 provided a good enough reason for the military coup of February 1981.

Immediately, the King denounced the coup, and the bulk of the army supported him and put it down, again acting with the implicit understanding that the politicians would manage to keep nationalist and regional problem within limits. The scenario was set for continuous bargaining among the parties, ending sometimes in compromises, sometimes at an impasse. Everything hinged more and more on conventions and traditions to be worked out in time. Meanwhile, political and economic institutions such as the King, the Constitutional Court, and the markets, along with countrywide organizations such as business associations and unions plus the major political parties, helped to contain the system's centrifugal tendencies.

One issue on which almost every political and socioeconomic group agreed from the very beginning was Spain's application to full membership in the European Community (by contrast with the second thoughts of Greece and Portugal at the time of their own democratic transitions: Álvarez-Miranda 1996). Spain had almost integrated its economy with Europe's, and had got a favorable status of association with the EC in 1970. The country was thoroughly familiar with the experience of Spanish workers in Europe and of European tourists in Spain. The people had a clear self-image of being a Western European society. By the time of Franco's death, many Spaniards felt that joining the EC was the culmination of a long journey into modernity. It was unthinkable not to do so. Though negotiations with the other European countries, and last with the French government, took longer and were much more difficult than expected, there was never any doubt in the Spaniards' minds about the end result. At last an agreement was reached in 1985, and Spain joined the club in 1986.

From the very beginning, the Spanish public supported the new Constitution and the party system. Though elections were frequent, voter turnout was fairly high. The public showed almost no support for anti-system parties, and had a marked preference for parties which abided by the principles of democratic politics and of civil society. The electorate's support for moderate foreign and domestic policies was consistent with the public's prevailing stance in the left-to-right ideological spectrum, and, more importantly, it corresponded to voting patterns and even to electoral shifts.

In the last twenty-one years, Spain has held seven national elections (in 1977, 1979, 1982, 1986, 1989, 1993, and 1996; see Table 1), besides a number of local, regional and European elections. Despite this state of semi-permanent elections, the voters have shown few signs of fatigue or disaffection. Turnouts were fairly high, and few votes went to anti-system parties (with the exception of a number of Basque sympathizers of terrorism: around 10 to 12% of the Basque electorate). Support for democracy as expressed in polls has been strong and steady across the years.[7] Spaniards concentrated their preferences on a few parties ranging from moderate left to moderate right—parties which supported some mix of market economy and welfare state, civil liberties, toleration and pluralism, and (most of them) a pro-Western foreign policy.

Continued support for these policies and institutions was reflected in a remarkable continuity in the voters' location along a left-to-right ideological spectrum.[8] On average, on a scale of 1 to 10, the center stood around 4.7. It was 4.8 in 1980; 4.3 in 1983; 4.4 in 1989; and up again to 4.6 in 1993, and 4.8 in 1998. The smaller number documents a swing of political mood away from the center-right government (of UCD) toward the center-left (the Socialist governments), and back again to the center-right (the Popular Party government) in the mid-1990s. We should probably take into account that people in Spain, as in other southern European countries such as France and Italy, seem more inclined to perceive (or express) themselves as closer to the left of the spectrum (Spain 4.6; Italy 4.7; and France 4.9 in 1993) than people in central and northern parts of Europe (United Kingdom 5.4; Germany

Table 1. Spanish electoral results in national elections from 1977 to 1996

Parties	1977		1979		1982		1986		1989		1993		1996	
	% of votes	% of seats	% of votes	% of seats	% of votes	% of seats	% of votes	% of seats	% of votes	% of seats	% of votes	% of seats	% of votes	% of seats
PCE (IU since 1986)	9.4	20	10.8	23	4.0	4	4.5	7	9.1	17	9.6	18	10.5	21
PSOE	29.3	118	30.5	121	48.4	202	44.6	184	39.9	175	38.8	159	37.6	141
CDS	—	—	—	—	2.9	2	9.2	19	7.9	14	1.8	—	—	—
UCD	34.6	166	35.0	168	6.5	12	—	—	—	—	—	—	—	—
AP (PP since 1989)	8.8	16	6.1	9	26.5	106	26.3	105	25.9	107	34.8	141	38.8	156
PNV	1.7	8	1.5	7	1.9	8	1.6	6	1.2	5	1.2	5	1.3	5
CIU	2.8	11	2.7	8	3.7	12	5.1	18	5.1	18	4.9	17	4.6	16
Other	13.4	11	13.4	14	6.1	4	8.7	11	11.0	14	8.9	10	7.4	11
TOTAL	100	350	100	350	100	350	100	350	100	350	100	350	100	350

Sources: Castillo, 1994: 62–63; *Anuario El País* 1997: 62–63.

5.6; the Netherlands 5.4; Denmark 5.6),[9] though this Mediterranean bias to the left is more manifest in terms of rhetorical or symbolic politics than in support for actual left-wing governments (and even less for actual policies).

In Spain, voting patterns and electoral shifts have been consistent with continuing political allegiance to democratic institutions and support for moderate policies. Electoral results in 1977 and 1979 looked similar enough to induce some observers to talk of a "pattern." UCD obtained about 35% of the votes, and Alianza Popular (People's Alliance, AP), about 8/7%: this gave the right around 43% of the total vote. The Socialist party (PSOE, Partido Socialista Obrero Español) got around 30% of the vote, and the Communist party, around 9 to 10%; hence the left had between 38 and 41% of the total vote. Then the government crisis of 1980–81 and a strategic blunder by UCD resulted in a momentous electoral shift in 1982.

The crisis was caused by a mix of external and internal factors. The aftereffects of the 1979 oil crisis weighed heavily on the Spanish economy in 1980–81. Terrorist activities flared up and unrest heightened in connection with regional and nationalist movements. The crisis culminated with the military coup of 1981. Under pressure, Suárez, the gifted tactician of the democratic transition, seemed to have lost his nerve. At the same time, an endemic organizational weakness of the party (Hopkin 1995) gave rise to competing claims for leadership. The aspirants were supported by a variety of local and personal loyalties and reflected diverse, though vaguely defined, ideological sensibilities. Amidst this disarray, some crucial strategic mistakes were made which added to the tension.

Given the electoral results of 1977 and 1979, UCD could have decided either that it had enough political clout to govern with a centrist minority government, with the (reticent) support of AP and Convergència I Unió (Convergence and Union, CiU: a coalition of Catalan nationalists), or that it did not enjoy enough support and should try to form a coalition with AP. Suárez favored the first option, but was defeated by those who thought otherwise.[10] Many who did so dreamed of a British-style two-party system, in which conservatives and socialists alternate in power. But the defeat of Suárez turned out to be a strategic blunder that gave the PSOE fourteen years of uninterrupted government (and a comfortable majority for more than ten years).

Thus the electoral shift of 1982 is to be understood partly as the result of problems in governance, and partly as a suicidal move by the centrist party in government, of which the PSOE made good use in its political campaign. In 1982, PSOE got 48% of the vote and the Communists only 4% (possibly 6 percentage points went to PSOE). The centrist parties (UCD and CDS, Centro Democrático Social [Democratic Social Center], a party that split off from UCD and was led by Suárez) got just 9% (PSOE probably got some 10 percentage points from the centrist electorate), while AP obtained 26%. In the following years, the PSOE went down to 44% in 1986, 40% in 1989, and 39% in 1993. The newly formed IU (Izquierda Unida [United Left], a coalition shaped around the Communists in 1986) rose from 4% (in 1986) to 9% in 1989 and 1993 (back to the Communists' results in the late 1970s). IU's rise reflected the cumulative effects of the 1986 referendum on Spain's membership in NATO (the Socialists reversed the position they had taken in their electoral platform, which had strongly hinted they were for getting out of NATO; now they recommended staying in). In addition, the general strike of December 1988 (when the Socialist government was challenged by the unions) alienated some of the PSOE supporters on the left.

PSOE was able to stay in power so long as it kept its hold on centrists who had little inclination to vote AP. Between 1982 and 1989, AP had a ceiling of about 26% of the vote; then it changed its leadership, its image, and its name (to Partido Popular [PP, People's Party]). As it began to lean more to the center, it garnered 35% of the total vote in 1993 (absorbing most of the debris left by the sinking of Suárez's CDS, which had managed to get 7.9% in 1989), apparently attracting most of the centrist voters who switched to PSOE in the 1982 debacle. The latest election, in 1996, saw PP's victory over the PSOE by a slight margin (38.7 to 37.6%) and the recovery of IU with 10.5%, that is, up to the highest percentage of votes once enjoyed by the Communist party (10.8 in 1979; see Table 1).

Thus far the story of Spanish electoral politics looks familiar and reassuring: a tale of political (and policy) stability with a few dramatic electoral shifts and continuous tactical maneuvers to gain the center ground of the electorate. Yet one disquieting point is the low level of party membership, which could indicate the public's lack of interest in civic matters. Before this can be confirmed, however, three important qualifications must be made: (1) Spanish voters generally tend to support the political parties without joining them; (2) this position is compatible with continuing interest in political and civil matters; and (3) this trend applies also to most Western European democracies (Mair 1998), not just to the Spanish case.

The data, gathered from different sources for the last two years, show a party membership rate of 3% for Spaniards aged 18 and over.[11] Comparing this figure with those of Western European countries, we find them moving closer and closer to the Spanish rates. Between 1985 and 1990, membership rates in the United Kingdom went from 5.9 down to 3.3% of the population; in Germany, from 4.5 to 4.2%. And despite its higher figures, the trend was similar in Italy (from 10.5 to 9.6) (Gunther, Montero 1994), while the French data look like the Spanish ones (Machin 1990; Ysmal 1989). But let us not exaggerate the trend. There may be a floor to it. Between 1984 and 1991, PSOE and PP gained members: PSOE went from 153,076 members (97,320 in 1981) to 309,401 (Tezanos 1993; 1992); and PP, from 163,062 to 300,988, although these increases may have been offset by loses in other parties such as the PCE (from 84,652 in 1983 to 44,775 in 1991) (Gangas 1995).[12]

Moreover, low party membership does not necessarily mean little interest in civic and political matters. The Spanish public exhibited both strong attachment to democratic institutions and high voter turnout (despite frequent elections) during the entire twenty-odd-year period. And though the Spanish rate of participation in voluntary associations seems low (see Chapter 2; see also McDonough, Barnes, and López Pina 1999), this should be weighed against other factors. For instance, union membership rates, around 10 to 20% of the salaried population in the last ten years, are rather low by international standards, but unions command considerable worker support. This is evident in the electoral turnout and results at the time of elections to workers councils, and by the workers' response to the unions' call for collective bargaining or strikes (including general strikes). Business associations are also important, and the church's influence remains very significant. At the same time, we observe clear indications of the growing vitality of nongovernmental organizations (NGOs) in all spheres of life—consumer, environmental, neighborhood, cultural, sports, and many other areas. To this we should add the "soft" associational or *pandilla* (peer-group) networks, which make so much of the lively informal interaction among the Spaniards. These *pandillas* are not tertiary associations that meet rarely and whose members hardly know each other (Putnam 1995); on the contrary, they promote intense and frequent contacts among the members of the group. The fact that this social life goes unreported is no reason to ignore it: any reasonable and detached observer of Spanish everyday life will confirm its vitality. The density of these networks (the so-called social capital) correlates with the growing centrality of the family and the extended family to which the nuclear family is attached (see Chapters 2 and 4). Altogether, the combination of formal and informal associations plus family life gives us a far different picture from that of an anomic, atomistic, mass-consumer society of self-absorbed individuals.

The role of parties in contemporary politics is changing, and the Spanish case exemplifies a general trend. Low party memberships are becoming part of normal democratic politics. They signify a gradual redefinition of the parties' roles worldwide, and, more generally, of the relationship between politicians and citizens. The distance between the public and the parties, evident in the reluctance of voters to join the parties they vote for, may be seen as a consequence of a general perception that the parties have lost some of their original or previous roles or functions, and particularly their leadership role. They may be worth supporting and may even be indispensable, but still not attractive enough for people to join or to be guided by them, at least not in the traditional way.

As we look at the Spanish democratic process as a whole, what we see is the gradual coming of age of parties. These, at various times, aspired to lead the nation and control its fate, but later considered themselves lucky when they were able simply to adapt to circumstances, even if so doing changed their original character beyond recognition. Moreover, in the process of being so changed, they were partly educated or civilized and partly destroyed, whether because they disappeared, or because they had to go through a painful catharsis and be reborn.

These vicissitudes were common to the main Spanish parties. The UCD exemplified both the virtues and the limits of a political metamorphosis that turned Franco bureaucrats into the prime movers of the new democratic regime. But once the task of the transition was accomplished, the leaders were overwhelmed by the circumstances. They lost their way, and UCD collapsed. The PSOE began by changing its ways drastically in order to accede to power. Once a Marxist party that preached the scriptures of class struggle and that was apparently eager to build a socialist economy and to get Spain out of NATO, it was reborn as a conventional Western European social-democratic party, eager to manage capitalism and to be a reliable partner in the Atlantic Alliance, all in approximately four years. But after a few years in government, at the zenith of its power, the Socialist party too went through a period of loss of direction, internal tensions, and malaise. It confronted an economic crisis and a pattern of law-breaking activities (within the state and the party), both of which it failed to manage—and this led to bitter defeat, soul-searching, and (still) inconclusive attempts at self-renewal. Finally, even the conservative party had to change its leadership, its program, its electoral tactics, and even its name (from Alianza Popular to Partido Popular) in order to become a credible alternative to the Socialists; after all that, it gained power only by entering into an alliance with the peripheral nationalist movement parties, a move that reversed its political stand on this issue.

As the Spanish parties went about their business in the years after the transition, they constantly took the public and each other by surprise—since it was universally taken for granted that parties had neat, fixed identities and knew once and for all what they were and where they were going. Some Spanish politicians had indeed entered the game believing, or pretending to believe, in their own propaganda, which included the fairy tale that they had long prepared themselves for the job and were ready to cope with all contingencies. Most were deluded by the apparent ease of the transition to believe that they had produced it, that it was the result of their political work—and that, in any case, at least the Constitution was of their own devising. The political protagonists shared the current conventional wisdom that the only job of political parties is to contest power and carry out their programs.

The point is that in Western societies parties had traditionally attracted new members mainly because they played a multiplicity of roles. A fairly long list could include the following: (a) electoral machines, (b) instruments for political mobilization between elections, (c) instruments of governance, (d) instruments for aggregating socioeconomic interests, (e) producers of ideologies, (f) producers of policy programs, (g) producers of collective identities, (h) sources of civic participation,

(l) sources of civic education, (j) sources of legitimacy for a political regime, and (k) symbols of historical events which were a crucial part of civic memory. Today, however, and already at the time of the events we are discussing, all these activities are less important than they were in the past. Moreover, in performing these roles parties must now face strong competition from other organizations.

As electoral machines, parties are less necessary in the television age, when much political campaigning is done through this medium. The political process changed character when everybody had a TV set at home. Since then, political campaigns have tended to focus on the relationship between the political leaders and the public, even though the parties still play a significant role in reinforcing and echoing the leaders' pronouncements—in Spain this was most notably the case with the Socialist and the Catalan parties, but it held true even for the conservative PP.

Parties have been, in the past, extremely important mobilization machines between elections. At present, however, if parties are still needed at election time, they may slip almost into irrelevance in the periods between elections—although, fortunately for them, Spain has been in a state of permanent campaigning due to the proliferation of national, local, regional, and European elections (all of which have been interpreted, at least in part, as national contests). In the period between elections, the parties are forced to compete with public-relations machines run by close advisers to the political leaders. These provide inspiration, political slogans, speech-writing, and rhetoric. In a paradoxical way, the personal entourage is especially active when the party is in control of the government. For instance, in the case of PSOE, the party apparatus of Ferraz St. (where the party headquarters were located) had to compete with, and usually played second fiddle to, the advisers to the President in Moncloa (the location of his office).

Parties are instruments for governance and for filling political leadership and government positions. But it is a well-known fact that there is usually a tension between the requirements for public service and the requirements of party loyalty. Political leaders have to engage in a delicate balancing act between the need to attract independent professionals from outside the party, and to reward party loyalty and take into account all of the extended political "family." In the Spanish case, parties showed a slight inclination to put nonmembers in top positions in the sectors of the civil administration dealing with economic policies. At all events, parties have been a quarry for political personnel; for instance, 72% of delegates to the 33rd PSOE Congress in 1994 had official positions, up from 67% in the 32nd Congress in 1991; this matched the public's perception (30%) that the main work of that Congress was not to elaborate a program, but rather to distribute official posts (45%).[13]

Parties are instruments for the aggregation of interests, but they can be partly replaced in that capacity by professional associations or lobbies that bypass them and deal directly with the administration. To the extent that both the PSOE and PP took the turn toward becoming catch-all parties (already clearly noticed as a general trend at least since the 1960s: Kirchheimer 1966), their ties with particular organized interests loosened. Mutual detachment and (partial) alienation between PSOE and UGT, the Socialist union, and between PCE and CCOO, the Communist union, illustrate this trend.

Parties are sources of ideological identification and producers of ideologies. That is, they are sources of world views, and markers of ideological location (that is, location in an imaginary ideological space from the extreme left to the extreme right). In general, most political parties are no longer seen as the bearers of comprehensive world views. For most of the population, the era of absolute politics is gone, though a degree of nostalgia for it remains among some political enthusiasts (charismatic churches in the United States, Islamic fundamentalists, some brands of post-Soviet Marxism, nationalist extremists, and so forth).

In Spain, instances of political fundamentalism were marginal, and the prevailing mood was one of moderation and pragmatism. On the other hand, political parties still played an intriguing though basic role in keeping the so-called ideological space alive, placing people in an imaginary left-to-right half-circle.[14] This may be one of the very few functions left to them, for which they have very few competitors. In the long run, however, the parties focused their efforts at political persuasion upon the portion of the electorate which places itself near the center. From this it follows that the politicians have played down their ideological messages and have avoided elaborate ideological arguments in order to emphasize general ideas and values which are compatible with a variety of ideological discourses—even though, at critical moments, they tried to handle embarrassing situations (for instance, to sidetrack a legal prosecution or win a close electoral contest) by resurrecting some of the symbols of an ideological past (see Chapters 3 and 4).

Parties may also be producers of policy programs, whether in the form of promises (in electoral campaigns) or platforms to be implemented (in power). Most commonly, however, parties are in the delicate position of being the consumers of the ideas and the know-how of middle-class professionals, most of whom are not party members but rather civil servants or independent experts, operating as individual consultants or as members of expert networks or think-tanks. But in today's world (and this includes Spain), both civil servants and think-tank experts tend to get around the parties and go to the top leaders, the organized interests, and the public, if they are smart enough and know how to handle the media. The parties may then also try to translate the program into the media-friendly language and introduce the mix of clarification and confusion which accommodates a variety of speech routines, political sentiments, and interests.

Parties may certainly be producers of collective identities. Nationalist parties may be able to (half) invent nations (as in the former Yugoslavia, where they transformed an ethnic potential into several aggressive and mutually exclusive brands of political nationalism). Some of the Spanish parties (most notably the Catalan and the Basque nationalists) have played that role in the last decades. The complication in this case is that if these ethnic enclaves are themselves divided between nationalists and non-nationalists, and if, moreover, the nation of which they are part is itself a member of a supranational entity, then the role of the nationalist parties may become blurred in the long run and lose its edge, and their enthusiasm may generate only fatigue among their followers. This may explain some of the complexities and uncertainties of the Basque and Catalan nationalist parties. Likewise, parties may (half) invent social classes, usually in a context of party struggles or compromises. This is what most Western European socialist and communist parties did or tried to do for a period of time with regard to the working class. But that is now past history. Today, the Spanish parties that inherited socialist and communist traditions may keep some symbolic remnants of the past, but their talk is of "the people" or "the nation" or some other variant of an interclass community.

Parties may be sources of civic participation and forums for debate. Clearly, however, the parties' bid is contested by an ever growing number of competitors: to begin with, by a variety of social movements or nongovernmental organizations—pro environment, peace, feminism, "gray panthers," and other causes. These movements had a certain vitality just around the time of the Spanish transition. The parties tried to control and colonize them (and succeeded in doing so in some cases). But at present the parties' ability to control movements and social organizations has diminished, in Spain as in other Western countries.

Parties are supposed to be sources of civic education. In principle, this could be a most important role. But certainly in the Spanish case, the record is mixed. Some of the parties did live up to this task during the Spanish transition, while others have rather promoted an uncivic (or uncivil) education. Here, a distinction should be introduced between words and deeds, verbal and performative statements, propaganda and practical examples. In Spain and in liberal democracies in general, most parties are eager to rival each other in expressing their public allegiance and respect for the Constitution. But in actual practice they may well behave in an uncivil way, trying to overstep the limits of their authority and showing disrespect for the rules of internal debate, even ignoring it altogether. For instance, parties may be organized as oligarchies whose leadership maintains itself in power with no time limits, co-opts itself, and gets approval for its actions by a rubber-stamp congress that meets every two years—as has been the current practice of Spanish parties. Or they may violate party financing laws, try to insulate their leaders from institutional controls (including judiciary control), and engage in smearing and intimidating tactics against the persons and institutions which try to make these controls work—in fact, it may (and will) be argued (see Chapter 3) that this is what the Spanish Socialist party did when confronted with political scandals in the 1990s. Likewise, in their internal dealings parties may repress or hinder open debates and currents of opinion and thus discourage independent thinking. Alternatively, they may try to open the party to militants or even to mere sympathizers, as the Socialists have tried to do (still with uncertain results) when they decided, in 1998, to initiate primary contests within the party to choose some of their candidates for the next local, regional, and national elections. In short, sometimes the actual performance of political parties contradicts their rhetorical defense of the tenets of a civil society. When this happens, they become uncivil organizations with respect to the accountability of party authority, respect for the law and the rules of the game, and the openness and richness of their internal debate.

Parties may be sources of legitimacy for the political regime. They are supposed to reinforce the legitimacy of a liberal democracy, as they provide the routine-like operative mechanisms that give institutional expression to a liberal regime and show how public business and public debate are to be conducted. It is widely believed that "without parties there can be no democracy"—a statement which has been subscribed to by two thirds of the public in survey after survey during the last decade and a half.[15] Yet obviously parties fail to do their job if by their actions (and sometimes by their propaganda) they erode the public's trust in the political institutions of a liberal democracy. Besides, other people and institutions may play a similar role, complementary or taking the place of parties. In Spain, the King played precisely such a role, rather successfully, for a period of time; the courts and a critical mass of concerned citizens (party members or not) may play it too.

Finally, parties may be symbols of historical events that are crucial to a country's civic memory. They can inherit a legacy of gratitude for having brought national independence, imperial hegemony, freedom, democracy, economic prosperity, or so-called social conquests to the country at some point or another of the past. This is not so much the case in Spain, where the present parties' historical role has been substantially more limited. They did contribute to the transition, but only as part of a very complex constellation of factors—and the party that did most, the UCD, is in fact no longer part of the political landscape. Spanish parties have had to attract followers mainly on the basis of their present performance and current benefits.

In summary, it may be argued that the Spanish parties were formed under circumstances which allowed them to play a complex role in Spain's civilizing process. On the one hand, they were key players in the transition and the political changes in government since then. They helped the population to handle the complexity of the political game and to identify and relate to their political leaders. They articulated the discourse that gave form to the public's interests and sentiments as it entered the political arena. On the other hand, the parties were subject to the limitations just mentioned, and partly for this reason could not offer high enough incentives (whether select benefits or contributions to collective goods) to attract many members.[16]

Indeed, both electoral shifts and low party memberships can be explained as part of normal involvement with the problems and opportunities of democratic politics; they may even be seen as an indication of a process of consolidation of democratic institutions. But if everything was normal in Spanish politics, this normalcy hides the usual paradoxes of democratic politics. Thus no sooner had the Spanish people freed themselves from political bondage than they began, as a matter of course, to drop the burden of political responsibilities and to invest their political leaders and parties with the powers and the capacities to rule them. Obviously, this was simply the working of representative democracy as enshrined in the Constitution. The unspoken part of this representative mechanism was, however, the distance the citizens put between themselves and their responsibility for their own fate. Because of this distance, problems could and did arise when the citizens needed to take their rulers to account for the failures of their performance (see Chapter 3).

Maybe it was also part of the new democratic normalcy that once the democratic leaders got into positions of power, they found new ways to displace sizable portions of *their own* responsibility in every direction, down and up. They made, first, the very sensible discovery of the limits of the central government's ability to govern, followed by the (unexpected) discovery of what I have called the mesogovernment solution of power-sharing with socioeconomic and regional elites, to be applied to economic and regional problems. This was a way to handle socioeconomic affairs for a decade (1977 to 1986), and it had both benefits and disadvantages. This was, also, a way of living with the fairly complicate problems aroused by regional differences in Spain, and the assertiveness of Catalan and Basque nationalist aspirations.

The limitation of central governance in domestic politics took place also in foreign policy. First, there was an immediate and near-unanimous drive by both politicians and the public to join the European Community, and therefore to give up some of the powers and capacities for self-governance so recently acquired, as if the Spaniards had felt that political freedom was a burden better shared with others than placed squarely on their own shoulders. Second, the Socialist governments of the second half of the 1980s were later to discover that a good way to handle domestic problems they could not solve was to link national issues to those of a larger supranational community. The government could then always go back to its citizens and say, *à propos* of this or that policy: "Let us be realistic. There is not much that we can do. Once we are in, say, the Western community, we are obliged to abide by their rules and carry out their policies: to participate in NATO (in 1986), or to adjust our monetary policies to those of the European Monetary System/Bundesbank (in 1989)." In a sense, this apparently shrewd move resembled that of Ulysses when he tied himself to the mast (Elster 1986) to resist the sirens' song: for the Socialists, the temptation was to follow their original sentiments favoring neutralism in foreign policy and populism in economic policy. The only thing missing from this scenario was the initial act—that is, a straightforward and honest attempt to persuade the public of the virtues of placing government policy in a no-choice situation.

Not surprisingly, democratic normalcy had a reverse side in the ambiguities and paradoxes of democratic politics, and in the ambivalence of politicians and the public toward full-fledged political responsibility and political involvement. Everything was, then, normal in the Spanish democracy: and this "everything" included the possibility of its distortion.

CHAPTER TWO

The Socialists Rule

THE CONSTRUCTION OF a civil society is not an easy undertaking. An institutional framework is not enough; it needs to be put to its proper use. The job requires the combined efforts of professional politicians and ordinary citizens. After the democratic transition, Spanish citizens and parties established an uneasy relationship which we will examine more fully as we look into the state of politics and society during the long period of Socialist hegemony. From 1982 to 1993, Felipe González presided over a series of Socialist governments which were supported by absolute majorities in Parliament.

By the early and mid-1980s, Spain's liberal democracy appeared well consolidated. But it had a dark side, which becomes better defined as we look more closely at the workings of the different elements of civil society—the rule of law, politics, markets, the social fabric, and the public sphere. Another crucial factor in the functioning of the democratic society is the character of the group which occupies the center stage, and which therefore bears the main responsibility for the lights and shadows it casts. I do not mean just the Socialists, but rather a loose generational group which included them but extended beyond any political party—I mean the elites belonging to the generation of 1956–1968, people who were shaped by formative experiences under Franco, played a major role during the transition, and then came to occupy positions of authority in the 1980s. That decade was largely of their making, and it reflected their strengths and weaknesses.

Let us imagine, for a moment, that this Spanish generation was a character at the start of a fictional adventure. Herman Melville's *Moby Dick* begins with the hero eager to board a ship and go to sea. Restless, Ishmael begins to stroll through New York and reaches the furthermost point of the island. He realizes that he is not the only one: many others like him stand on the shore and look at the enormous distances with longing. Open spaces and the sea attract a certain type of people, those who are free and jealous to safeguard their freedom. They stand by their promises and require others to do the same; they are self-confident yet open and interested in the outside world. In the story, Ishmael accepts the call of the sea and finds like-minded souls. In our case, the Spanish generation would follow its inner voice and the call of others, the community of Western European nations to begin with, to establish a society of free men.

Ishmael soon reaches the sea. He is resolute, and the Island of the Manhattoes is neatly laid out: by walking down most of the streets, parallel to each other, one reaches the water. For the Spaniards it is not easy to reach the sea—to achieve a civil society—from their inland cities of baroque design. They live in another sort of country, where many do not trust themselves and shun open skylines; where the urge of some to be free runs up against the urge of others to reconstruct new forms of old and familiar servitude. In the course of their wandering they may come to realize that their own goals and desires are confused, their fate undecided, and even their identities are far from fixed.

Public Policies

After almost forty years of an authoritarian regime, the Spanish people needed time to develop the feelings and habits of living together in the framework of a liberal democracy, so that a cultural artifact could become a living tradition. It took time also to realize that democracy was a natural way of being in the world: as natural at home as in the rest of Western Europe. Over the years, while Spain lived in a full-fledged democracy, the public had many opportunities to vote in national, regional, and local elections, and did so in large numbers. Getting used to various institutions went hand in hand with getting used to certain types of public policies, and the constancy of habit tempered the restless inclination of many Spaniards toward change. Since the 1960s, when a large part of the population felt the urge to change its ways (Pérez-Díaz and Rodríguez 1997), society settled into a more conservative mood.

In a paradoxical way, the Socialist-led governments were witness to this conservative disposition, profited from it, and reinforced it. In the 1982 elections, the Socialists used the slogan "for change"—as if electing them meant not just an ordinary change (of administration) and a few reforms, but change *par excellence*; a historical or qualitative change that embodied some longing on the part of the people for a deep, structural, and wide-ranging transformation of society. This was partly true and partly a mirage. It was true with regard to symbolic matters of psychological importance, since the country needed some way to disguise the deep structural continuities that survived the transition from Francoism. New faces and new life styles were needed at the forefront of the political spectacle.[1] However, in all but a few symbolic matters, it soon became clear that the public's dominant desire was to preserve the status quo and regain a sense of normalcy.

In 1982, the greatest threat to the status quo was a visibly exhausted ruling party, bitterly divided and with hardly any leaders to provide a sense of unity and direction. The UCD had marginalized Adolfo Suárez, who left it and founded a new party (CDS). The new UCD president, Leopoldo Calvo-Sotelo, lacked the will and the political know-how to unite the diverse factions and to stop the defection of party members, whether to the right (like Miguel Herrero, to AP) or to the left (like Francisco Fernández Ordóñez, to PSOE).[2] Calvo-Sotelo gave the impression that political power was a burden he wanted to get rid of, the sooner the better. He called for new elections in the fall of 1982, and gave up leadership of the party.

The public observed the self-destruction of the UCD party between 1980 and 1982 with astonishment. Fear of a political vacuum pushed a great many voters into the arms of the Socialists, whose slogan "for change" was substantially qualified by more reassuring ones, such as "we will put the country to work," "we want things to function," and "we want modernization," all of which augured a fundamentally prudent and conservative strategy that appealed to a large portion of the population (including former UCD supporters).[3]

Responsive to this conservative mood, the Socialist government and its supporters decided to retain the basic guidelines of existing policies (of the centrist governments), but put on a new face of youthful determination. The formula was successful enough to win the support of an absolute majority in Parliament in the elections of 1986 and 1989 (see Table 1). With regard to foreign policy, the Socialists took an oblique track that ended with a reassertion of Spain's commitment to NATO (Pérez-Díaz and Rodríguez 1997). But on the domestic front, they opted for a more straightforward approach. The constitutional tangle of Spain's autonomous regions was to be managed ad hoc. The economic policy consisted of pacts which gave priority to the fight against inflation (while maintaining or increasing real wages), but it neglected supply-side measures. The Socialists followed a gradual, cautious, and uneven policy of liberalization of product markets that attempted to suit the interests of the respective sectors;[4] they implemented some partial measures and reforms of the labor market. The administration's readiness to live with an unemployment rate of considerable proportions accompanied an incremental growth in the welfare state, following the trend that had begun in the 1960s and accelerated under the UCD governments (Pérez-Díaz, Chuliá, and Álvarez-Miranda 1998). This hub of pragmatic and gradual public policies preserved the fundamentals of the status quo and facilitated the public's support for the Socialist rule.

A generally cautious policy of muddling through applied to regional policies. These evolved in a rather predictable way, soothing to a public that had become apprehensive after the shock of the military coup of 1981. The regional governments got into debt, but not much more so than the central government. At the same time, they showed greater concern for local affairs and greater accessibility to the public. In the Basque country and Catalonia, nationalist parties tended to enjoy comfortable minorities or slight majorities, which helped them get used to exercising power; in turn, people in these regions became accustomed to living in a political climate that included a dose of symbolic dissidence, more shrill in the Basque country than in Catalonia.

Dealings between these peripheral nationalist parties and the Socialist government became particularly important in the Basque country. In the early years, the Socialists took the fateful decision to permit the use of death squads and other illegal means to fight terrorism. This decision was little noticed at the time, barely discussed in public forums, and neglected by the public attorneys and judges. The dirty war was carried out between 1983 and 1987—though it became a source of embarrassment for the government and a public scandal only in the 1990s, when it came to dominate the center of the public debate (see Chapter 3). But in 1987, the Socialists and the Basque nationalists (with the Socialists as junior partners) formed a coalition government for the Basque country which lasted (with a brief interlude of nine months in 1994) until 1998. This rather long collaboration brought a modicum of governability to a region otherwise afflicted by terrorist activities and grave political unrest. It also produced some workable compromises in highly controversial matters (for instance, in the sensitive areas of language and educational policies). In addition, Socialists and nationalists acquired habits of reciprocity and mutual responsibility in the tasks of government, and developed the ability to patch things up and to live and let live.[5]

In general terms, during most of that period (and until political competition became more acute in the 1990s), the political parties seemed to tolerate one another, with some difficulties and occasional stridency, but without major dramas. The Socialists were well entrenched in power and felt they could afford some concessions, while AP, frustrated at the invisible ceiling to its ability to grow, experimented with a variety of political leaders (Manuel Fraga, Miguel Herrero, and Antonio Hernández Mancha, then back to Fraga, and finally choosing José María Aznar in 1989).[6] The parties remained in competition, but they all seemed to accept the framework of the rules of the game of Spain's liberal democracy. People witnessed the rows and deals of parties with curiosity and with the usual mixed feelings characteristic of most democratic countries; they supported them without identifying with them or joining them. To the public eye parties were controlled by hierarchies whose members took sides and formed factions, and which preferred to keep their rank-and-file members at a prudent distance, but people understood that this was to be expected. They looked around at the rest of Western Europe and thought their parties were similar to others (and probably more serious than the Italian ones, for example, at least until the wave of corruption scandals hit Spain in the last few years).

So far so good. But this spirit of accommodation also contributed to tolerating the development of vested interests and client networks in and around government; these originated in the state apparatus and at the very roots of the traditional forms of social life. Thus particular groups (parties, civil servants, or coalitions of public and private agents) tended to appropriate the state's resources and means of administration. Despite its rhetoric of modernization, the Socialist regime favored this development for reasons of its own internal logic as well as external circumstances. On the one hand, the Socialists were hungry for power and held on to it with determination. They also believed they had a mission to fulfill that required putting party loyalty first and technical competence second. In general, missionary ideologies tend to justify the missionaries' arrogance; the belief that one has a mission in life tends to be associated with the idea that one has the right and the duty to fulfill this mission by all means. Moreover, it should not be forgotten that many of the Socialist leaders and some of the cadres acquired authoritarian habits during their political adolescence in the school of revolution. Long after revolutionary ideas have vanished, reflex responses may linger on, just as the symptoms of hysteria continue after the original trauma is forgotten.

As much as they wanted to rule, the Socialists found that people were eager to be ruled, partly because they were used to it after almost forty years of Francoism, but also partly because many Spaniards (among the elites and ordinary citizens alike) shared a traditional, semi-collectivistic view of public affairs: the state knows best how to look after the citizens' welfare.[7]

In 1982 people voted for the Socialists largely because of their *horror vacui*. In need of governance, they fled from the spectacle of rulers who apparently wanted *not* to rule and lacked not only the will to power but even the instinct for survival—while some of the UCD barons destroyed their leader, Adolfo Suárez, others joined the PSOE, and the rest gathered around a rudderless government that had no course to steer. This time the country wanted real rulers, and it got them. Although some sensitive souls soon grew uncomfortable with the Socialists' *prepotencia* (arrogance and abuse of power), for most it was precisely the Socialists' apparent determination and desire to rule that proved to be one of their main attractions, as the public underscored repeatedly by reelecting them.

For many individuals, this attraction to the PSOE was also linked to reasonable calculations of interest. As a catch-all party, it appealed to the interests of all social classes. Indeed, the economic establishment soon opened its doors to the Socialists. The middle-class professionals understood that their careers depended on not antagonizing the powers that be; the employed core of the working class was content to receive employment protection; and the lower classes, welfare benefits.

The newly formed ties between a network of special interests and the near-patrimonial state were strengthened indirectly by the turmoil within three key institutions which normally endeavor to keep a distance from (and sometimes to check) party politics: the judiciary system, civil administration, and the universities. Each one of them was subject to extraordinary structural strains, due in part to changes in the external environment. The judiciary experienced a marked increase in litigation—people became more sensitive to the defense of their private rights, as usually happens in a democratic polity. The demand for secondary and higher education increased considerably, while the administration had to cope with many problems of adjustment to the new quasi-federal system. These problems were compounded and aggravated when the government introduced critical changes in the internal functioning, the composition of the personnel, the rules of entry, and the criteria for career opportunities in all three areas, with the political intention of controlling the system of justice and the administration, and neutralizing a possible source of political conflict (at the universities). As a result, these institutions became subject to endemic conflicts arising from redistribution of power and mobility of personnel, which consumed their energy for many years, reduced efficiency, and probably blunted their capacity for control and criticism.

Particularly important was what happened within the judiciary. The mood of the Socialists early on was one of elation. They found themselves with a huge absolute majority in Parliament, in control of most regional governments and all the important cities, with a large following in the countryside, and no credible opposition. It seemed to them that they had a mandate with a strong backing of public trust, for a program with very little actual substance. The slogan "for change" left ample room for interpretation—in fact, taken literally, it made very little sense: just enough to mark the Socialists off from their self-defeated adversaries. So the party ideologists believed it was up to them to bring the slogan to life by means of their own intellectual resources and profound convictions. However, just at that moment they had no tradition to follow, and that for a very good reason. Only a few years before the 1982 elections, the Socialists had made an ideological U-turn: having enshrined Marxism in their statutes in the mid-1970s, they took it out following their defeat in the 1979 elections—an outcome which had convinced González of the need to push the party toward the center. By the time of their accession to power, the Socialists espoused a vague social-democratic outlook of a pragmatic kind (that term, "social-democratic," was not politically correct then, but it was appropriate all the same, since it meant that they were keen on increasing the public sector and prone to regulate and to intervene).

Their approach to the judiciary was to make sure that it did not become an independent branch of government that might check, control, or put a brake on what they intended to do. To that effect, Vice-president Alfonso Guerra was inspired to claim that "Montesquieu [was] dead," a statement that meant to extend a (somehow premature) death certificate to the division of powers in the Spanish arena. Acting with this intention, the government early on put pressure on the Constitutional Court to endorse a highly controversial decision to expropriate a private conglomerate (the RUMASA affair: see Chapter 3). And the same purpose governed the changes (in 1985) of the rules for selecting members of the General Council of Judiciary Power (Consejo General del Poder Judicial), which monitors the functioning of the judiciary system and holds the key to awarding judgeships. While in the past the members of the Council had been selected partly by the Parliament and partly by a mechanism of co-optation within the judiciary bodies, from then on selection was exclusively in the hands of the Congress and the Senate—which in the political circumstances of the 1980s meant the hands of the Socialist government.

The state soon discovered the uses and customs of opaque and uncontrolled management. The principal instance of this opaqueness was the budgetary process itself. The practices of extraordinary loans, additional credits, budgetary items that could be increased afterwards, reforms in the public works budgets, and many other devices transformed the budget from a sober accounting into a poetic metaphor of the state's real spending. Between 1985 and 1993, the state spent on average 33% over the approved budget every year (Edo et al. 1994). Control by the National Audit watchdog (Tribunal de Cuentas) was ineffective, since it took place many years after the fact and produced no real sanctions. The most worrisome item was the so-called reserve funds, the last recourse of the state's labyrinthine *arcana imperii*. Indeed, the government claimed it had to give no account whatever for the use of these funds once it had declared them "secret"—apparently not even when they were used to commit crimes (see Chapter 3).

Yet it was in the character of this government that it did so little, having so much power and discretion. The word "government" comes from *gubernaculum*, rudder or helm of a ship: to govern is to be at the helm. But sometimes, rather than pursue a charted course, governments do little more than move cautiously trying not to antagonize its supporters (financial institutions or unions, among others), or merely drift with the tide. Often they operate through discretionary measures which grow into an accretion of disparate agreements, while they promote a great deal of respect for existing traditions for fear of upsetting these complex equilibria. It is important to cultivate relations with friendly groups while keeping a careful eye on those opposed; this ebb and flow of client relations takes up a lot of the state officials' energy, attention, and intelligence. Whatever rhetoric of change the government may have once espoused is redirected to a continuous redefinition of the terms of the status quo—even though, in the process of keeping things as they are, some pragmatic measures may lead to significant developments.

During most of the 1980s, the Spanish state behaved in a cautious, ad hoc, and often confused manner. When it did act purposively, it was with great timidity, as when it undertook the liberalization of the capital markets and a partial liberalization of the labor market (in 1984). These measures produced a protected core of about two thirds of the labor force, and an unprotected periphery consisting mostly of young people and women. In other situations, the state's sense of direction was wishful thinking: policy just drifted, as in the case of the growth of expenses.

Overall, the growth of the welfare state was the consequence of the perceptions and expectations of both the public and the political class at the beginning of the transition. Despite vague background assumptions of some sort of collectivism, the Socialists were reluctant to go too far along the path of regulation and intervention in the economy. Early on, by contrast, by the middle of the 1970s, most of the country believed that public spending and the corresponding tax burden should increase, so that a welfare state could be developed. Nobody had opposed the UCD's political measures along this line, which merely advanced an already existing trend (fairly strong in the fields of public health and public education since the 1960s). Europe set the pace, so Spain increased its public spending to narrow the gap: between 1985 and 1993 public spending rose from 40% to 48% of GDP (before the transition, in 1975, it was 27%), while in France it grew from 53% to 54% in the same period, and in Germany from 48% to 51%. Correspondingly, the tax burden increased between 1980 and 1992: 48% in Spain, 5% in France and 2% in Germany.[8] Given the differences in GDP between Spain, France, and Germany, the Spanish government's strategy was to narrow the gap by betting on substantial increases in public spending oriented to public consumption. This could only happen at the expense of savings and investment and, given also the speed of implementation, was later seen as the wrong move in the long run.

Most government spending went to pay for growth in public sector employment (which grew from 1.5 million employees in 1982 to 2.2 million in 1992) and for social expenses. Unemployment subsidies rose along with the growth in unemployment (which peaked at 24% in 1994). Pension payments increased extraordinarily, and were augmented by subsidies for temporary disability, early retirement, and rural underemployment. The health system expanded moderately; education more intensively. The percentage of children between the ages of 3 and 5 in preschool went from 47% in 1975 to 84% in 1992 (CECS 1994), and the number of university students increased from 0.8 million in 1985 to an estimate of 1.5 million in 1995 (Ministerio de Educación y Ciencia 1995).

Very little of all this spending was investment oriented. Public as well as private efforts to promote research and development were modest, so that Spain's spending on R&D continued to be much lower than in other European countries (0.7% of GNP in 1989–91, compared to between 2.3% and 2.9% for France, the United Kingdom, and Germany).[9] Investment in telecommunications was low, and state expenditures in infrastructure were remarkable only in the few years preceding the landmark events of 1992 (the Olympic Games in Barcelona and the World Fair in Seville).

Thus for many years political stability seemed to accompany a sensible economic policy that allowed the gradual integration of Spain's economy into the European and world economies. That policy, which the government presented as the only alternative, combined a cautious monetary policy with a lax budgetary policy, and a tax policy with few incentives for saving and investment (and limited redistributive effects). This combination, which appealed to voters, had some success in controlling inflation and did attract foreign capital after the spurt of growth in the second half of the 1980s—though it did little to stimulate the exports sector and settled for increasing trade deficits. With time, such meager successes grew too costly. First, there was the price to pay in terms of unemployment (always above 16% of the labor force and reaching up to 24%; see Chapter 4); second, much of the economic activity was the result of cheating.

But here again a word should be said about the Spaniards' views of the rules of the game. According to the positivistic tradition in Spanish legal and political thought, reflected in the prevailing mentality, the state was not meant to be the guarantor of respect for the laws, understood as formal and abstract rules which the state itself was to follow. Rather, the state *pronounced its will* in the form of laws. At the same time, Francoism had got people used to a state which was in control of the executive, the legislative, and the judicial branches. The state made the rules and laws, and implemented them by means of continuous and specific interventions in the social fabric. Like God of the Old Testament, the state does not have to abide by own rules or reward those who follow abstract principles. It rewards those who follow specific mandates—and behind these specific mandates there were often fairly precise interests: generally private interests in collusion with the interests of civil servants and incumbent politicians.

These collusions—sometimes hidden, sometimes presented as reasonable understandings between state (or party) officials and business groups (or unions)—were common practice in Spain (and in many other so-called regulated capitalist countries following the continental European model and Japan), and they worked rather well until quite recently. In the early 1990s, under increasing globalization of the economy and a change in the political-moral climate of many countries, such collusive practices were no longer easily tolerated. But the political-financial scandals that erupted in Spain in the 1990s referred to behavior that was commonplace in the public and private sectors during the 1980s.

In 1992, the governor of the Bank of Spain since 1984, Mariano Rubio, was accused by a parliamentary commission of illegally enriching himself while in office, and was suspected of tax fraud and of insider trading (in favor of an investment banking conglomerate, IBERCORP, headed by his old friend Manuel de la Concha, former chairman of the Madrid Stock Exchange).[10] Several large corporations (banks, private and public companies, and multinationals) were caught in a web of illegal financing to the Socialist party (the FILESA affair: see Chapter 3). The disclosures gave rise to inventive, huge, and systematic efforts to contrive accounting tricks, but they did not prevent collapses, bankruptcies, and allegations of fraud or various wrongdoings. BANESTO, one of the three biggest banks in the country, was said to have had an unreported financial shortfall estimated at $4.3 billion by the end of 1993.[11] Another case, the SEAT car-making subsidiary in Spain, was accused of deliberately under-reporting losses to its parent, Germany's Volkswagen: it reported a $85 million loss instead of $1.3 billion. Nearly 20,000 Spanish workers feared the loss of their savings in a $500-million real estate scandal involving the UGT Socialist union. The Kuwait Investment Office lost some $4.5 billion in ventures organized by its Spanish representative, Javier de la Rosa. All these activities involved lax financial and management controls.[12] The scandals shed light on the dubious nature of many dealings in the financial and corporate establishment, and on its relations with the government. At the same time, there was a thriving underground economy, estimated by some at 20 to 25% of GDP,[13] fraud in unemployment benefits and social security contributions, and tax dodging estimated at Pta 3 trillion (in 1994).

This lack of respect for the rules of the economic game paralleled little respect for the law in general in other spheres of political and civil life. Most notably, Spain grew accustomed to terrorism: a worrisome totalitarian phenomenon which, in the Basque country, draped itself in the ideology of nationalism. Because terrorism concentrates on specific objectives, the temptation for the majority of the people is to wash their hands off it, and to end up thinking that normalcy includes the additives of fear and terror. Thus many people, particularly in the Basque provinces, became used to living with an annual average of 34 people killed between 1981 and 1992, down from an average of 80 between 1978 and 1980. For many years too, street violence linked to terrorist activities has been a near-daily experience in some parts of the Basque country.

Nonpolitical violence also spread. Though Spain's rate of criminal offenses is low in comparative terms, there was a rise in crime (the yearly average number of crimes against the person rose from approximately 9,000 to 16,000 between 1984–1986 and 1990–1992, and attacks on property from 600,000 to 900,000, an increase which probably reflected growing drug addiction and drug traffic). The jail population almost doubled between 1982 and 1993 (up to 46,000 inmates). As it got more difficult to operate the justice system efficiently, there was a tendency to keep as many as possible of the suspected criminals in jail before they were brought to trial (in 1992 around one third of the prison population in jail in 1992 had not yet been tried).

Building Social Capital

For a long time it has been a commonplace that Spain lacked a social fabric strong enough to promote economic growth, social cohesion, and cultural creativity. Left to themselves, the centrifugal and destructive forces of Spanish life (the "inner demons of Spain," as General Franco put it) would prevail and bring disaster to the country. What it needed, according to the old-fashioned conservatives, was a strong state that would provide growth, social stability, education, and cultural guidance—a strong state together with a watchful church.

Not only conservatives subscribed to the view of an unstructured society (*invertebrada*, to use José Ortega y Gasset's expression; 1959a [1921]) in need of energetic elites as a unifying force. A similar diagnosis was offered by the liberal intelligentsia and the radical movements of the twentieth century. Anarcho-syndicalists and Socialists alike dreamed of a complete overhaul of society, and they could think of no other way to do it than through willful exertion by dedicated revolutionaries or, in the case of the Socialists, by professional politicians, officials, and unionists eager to use the state as the Archimedean point to move the world off balance.

Considerably toned down by ideological changes and historical experience, remnants of these dreams of state activism received a new impetus during the transition and found their way into the Socialists' rhetoric. The weakness of organized associations (as seen in the decline in church attendance and affiliation to unions and parties) gave some plausibility to the idea that, once again, the Spanish people experienced the classical predicament of an unorganized, atomized society facing a strong (Socialist) government. The government therefore felt it had to play the role of enlightened despot *malgré soi*, because it faced this dilemma: if society remained unorganized, it could fall prey to authoritarian politics in the long run; if the government undertook to organize society, it could turn authoritarian itself. The Socialists never went so far as to take this very seriously, but they toyed with the idea of choosing the second alternative—of applying the Gramscian approach to civil society, which boils down to the enlightened politicians' systematic attempt to shape and control as much as possible of the country's social and cultural life.

The Spanish social fabric was more resilient than expected, however, in ways that took many observers by surprise. It may even be said that a good deal of the social cohesion of the country was due to the workings of neglected forms of sociability, which helped the country to handle some quite difficult social problems. Let us take, for instance, the case of unemployment.

At the time of the *beginning* of the transition, the unemployment rate was minimal. But in just a few years it went up to 6 or 7%, and then jumped to double digits. Spain could have suffered an explosion of social conflicts, with masses of unemployed questioning the legitimacy of the new regime. None of these fears materialized. The danger became so distant that already during the 1980s Spaniards were acting as if unemployment rates around 20% of the labor force were natural; a feature of the landscape one could live with indefinitely (provided that, on occasion, one said something a little lugubrious like "how ghastly, how awful," and then moved on to another topic). Much of the political and academic debate and most of the influential press tiptoed around a situation that was a clear anomaly in the Western world. We may contrast the greater capacity of the United States to create employment with Europe's, but even so, Western Europe's unemployment rate was half the Spanish one (even though Spain's participation rate in economic activities was lower than the European one, due to the later recruitment of women into the labor force).

Why was Spain able to live in these conditions for such a long time without a social explosion? Among other reasons, it was the experience of living in what I call a "four-corners society," the name of a Spanish children's game. This game, similar to the one called "musical chairs," is for five players. Four children occupy the four corners of a space and run to trade places, while the fifth one stands in the middle and tries to get to an empty corner first. In real life many people, particularly the young, learned to play an imaginary four-corners job game: holding a precarious job (or one relatively unprotected by labor laws, under several formulas established in 1984 for short-term contracts); a job in the underground economy; unemployment with some kind of benefit or other that could be called "working on the dole";[14] hopefully landing in a stable job; or indeed being left out and standing in the middle, watching out for opportunities.

Many young people, once they came out of the educational system where they had been between the ages of 6 and 16 (or, in more serious cases, between the ages of 3 and 23), spent the next few years job-hunting and job-switching. From this they did not learn more than survival tactics and the virtues of resignation and endurance: training programs were few and of poor quality; career advancements were blocked by the older workers; and even higher-quality work of better-trained young people did not guarantee them a future in companies, because the rules were such that when a firm had to restructure, they were the first to go.

For this system to endure, young people's expectations have to be reduced. Yet somehow the individual and social costs of their aimlessness and uncertainty must remain bearable, and some way must be found to gather and share compensating resources. The institution that met these needs was the Spanish family. It took care of adults and young people who experienced these conditions. The family redistributed its available resources among its members: money, mechanisms for access to social security, information about job opportunities, and living space at the home or homes. It did everything so that its unemployed members did not lose their self-esteem or cease to feel part of a group and the object of its concern. The family did this without serious internal conflicts, thanks in part to the gradual loosening of family authority over the past thirty years. The current generation of adults, the first beneficiaries of this softening, had transmitted this standard to the following generation and created a climate of live-and-let-live. The network of these extended families enabled a generation to survive, and it was also the chief factor responsible for the creation of small and medium-sized companies throughout Spain.

The vitality of the family was extraordinary, and its upsurge, spontaneous. Its success in sustaining Spain's social cohesion and developing its social capital went far beyond what it accomplished in alleviating the problem of unemployment.[15] As has been amply documented, Spanish families have given crucial assistance, services, and emotional support to old people. They have also supplemented health and education services. In short, they have been, and still are, one of the basic pillars of the welfare system.[16]

With the family as the hub, other "soft" forms of sociability (networks, informal organizations) arose in the context of the free time and the limited professional horizons of the young, frequently around leisure, culture, or sports-related activities. These types of sociability were traditional and had always been important in Spain: we find them, from a very long time ago, in the groups involved in organizing the Holy Week in Andalusian cities and *pueblos*, the giant firework displays *(fallas)* in Valencia, the clubs *(peñas)* in Navarra and other places; but in the last ten to twenty years newer groups, clubs, and informal gatherings blossomed in cities and villages, and the greatest impulse for local *fiestas* came from them (and from the subsidies they got from local governments). The communal and voluntary character of many of these fiestas intensified—as happened, for instance, in the celebrations of the Holy Week, when hired hands (whose prices had gone up) were replaced by volunteers. They competed with each other for the privilege of carrying the ornamented *pasos* (scenes from the passion of Christ and the Virgin Mary)—and were even eager to pay for it.

Not all of these soft associations appear in official statistics. Even so, the statistics disclose a striking surge in voluntary associations after the mid-1970s. Between 1970 and 1976, a yearly average of 1,200 societal associations were inscribed in official registers. These were nonprofit voluntary associations, *excluding* mercantile or ecclesiastic associations, political parties, trade unions, and associations of professionals and of civil servants. From 1977 on, the yearly average of new registrations quadrupled (around 4,800 between 1977 and 1987; up to 6,100 on average in 1988–1990). Membership surveys of associations show an interesting disparity in the evolution of these societal, less formal associations, and that of the more formal political, union, professional, and religious ones. Interest in cultural, sporting, recreational, and single-issue associations (consumers, human rights, ecologists, neighborhood, etc.) is marked: membership grew from 14.1% to 41.3%. By contrast, membership in political parties was reduced by half (from 6.6% to

3.4%); in unions it decreased slightly (from 8.7% to 7.5%); in professional associations it stayed the same (3.5 to 3.6%), and in religious ones it grew a little (from 5.2 to 6.6%) (Prieto Lacaci 1993).

The data show that far from being an atomized society, Spain was replete with active family networks, soft forms of sociability, and increasing interest in many kinds of societal associations. Even the more formal organizations were open to a good deal of networking and informality at the local level. For instance, the slight increase in interest in religious associations reflected a more popular turn in the evolution of religious feelings and associations in Spain. The media used to pay attention to the declarations made at the episcopal conferences. But these were the least interesting aspect of what was happening in the Catholic Church. In Spain (as in most countries), what mattered was the multilevel interaction among lay Catholics whose interests were diverse, and this often took place at some distance from the pastoral work of the clergy.

Something similar was happening to trade unions and business associations. On the one hand, the importance of these formal organizations should not be underestimated. It was said disparagingly of trade unions that they had just a handful of members (and indeed union participation rates came down to some 10–15% of the workforce by the end of the 1980s), and of business associations that they formed a superstructure of self-coopted leaders surrounded by a bureaucratic apparatus, having scant contact with the world of business. The reality was not exactly like that. Trade unions were able to mobilize a large part of the population in the general strike of December 1988. In elections to works councils, the two largest trade unions usually obtained 80% of the delegates; and they were consulted and listened to in public matters. Their counterparts, the large business organizations, held a *de facto* monopoly of representation that nobody disputed, and were accepted by the business world as well as diverse sectoral interests. On the other hand, it is true that many important matters were handled by the local unions and companies rather than at organizational summits. On this level there were signs of tension between the upper echelons and the local chapters of the unions about certain issues, such as the proper level of collective bargaining.

Spain's social fabric proved to be alive and strong, even if it was not in the form and of the type that the bulk of Spanish observers, social

leaders, and opinion makers may have wanted. They would have preferred a civil society in which an elite of enlightened people influenced
and penetrated a network of associations and guided their thinking.
People who used to be progressive intellectuals or subscribed to the
classic conservative tradition felt comfortable with this vision. Their
dream was of large socialist (or conservative) constellations at the core
of society—a reasonably oriented society that would follow their lead.
They might be happy with class struggles or with corporatist experiments. They were certainly not happy with these bland and vague social
fabrics or civil societies in the Spanish style, where control and power
escaped them.

CHAPTER THREE

The Two Faces
of a Generation

A LIBERAL DEMOCRACY would cease to be one if society delivered to a political class, together with its vote, its capacity to debate and decide public matters. Under these circumstances, a civil society of free citizens would be reduced to an uncivil society of nominal citizens, subject to political alienation (in the classical sense of agents losing control over the outcome of their activity). But in fact, in most civilized societies people do not deliver their political capability in this way; they do put limits on the state; and when they delegate their power, it is within strict bounds, always reserving the option to intervene. As citizens, they see themselves as permanent participants in public affairs and consider the political class not as their masters, but rather as their servants.

From this normative understanding of democratic politics follows the view of democracy as a process of opinion-formation, in which politicians and citizens continuously debate common problems and their solutions. Each decision, far from being irreversible, may be reexamined in the light of its consequences, changes in circumstances, and changes in collective feelings—in the "civilized conscience" of any particular society (much in the way common law is believed to evolve in common law countries). From this viewpoint, the opinions of civil servants and politicians who speak in the name of the state, as well as those of the leaders of parties, churches, unions, business, and the media, are on a par with the relevant opinions of the citizens themselves: all are engaged in a sort of continuous civic conversation.

In Spain a certain type of civic conversation began to emerge in the 1960s, taking advantage of the softening of the Franco dictatorship. The interlocutors were churchmen, students, professionals, artists, journalists, politicians, and many others. The polyphony of voices brought out projects for change, worries, diagnoses, and fantasies. In this early period certain habits of discussion, rhetorical style, and stereotypes were established. The transition to democracy amplified this conversation and required people to make the connection between talk, political activities, and political responsibilities. Public debate had been limited and restricted in a thousand ways by the previous authoritarian regime. Democracy brought with it the guarantees and the incentives for a more intense and extended debate. But some of the habits already formed earlier persisted in the new era.

Although public conversation grew increasingly lively and wide-ranging, it suffered from imprecision and confusion. This had negative consequences on how the protagonists identified their own interests and those of others; how they were able to negotiate; how they understood the circumstances of these negotiations; how they understood the feelings and orientations which made these exchanges meaningful; and how they learned from the experiences of negotiations in other contexts. These flaws of expression—lack of precision and confusion—may have stemmed from poorly developed habits of discussion in schools, which have not been geared to educate students for debate. Likewise, the traditional formulas of Spanish sociability do not train people in the art of listening. At social gatherings (like the *tertulia*) everyone speaks in monologues. People do not listen: they just wait for their turn to present their own points of view; at the same time, each interrupts the other. In order to overcome the resistance to listening, voices are raised and people speak emotionally; this emotional emphasis is achieved by identifying everyone either as a friend or an enemy. As a result, the practice of sitting around in groups and talking strengthens the condition I call tribalism, which has been and still is very influential in opinion-making in Spain.

In conversation, emotional considerations are rarely separated from the merits of the argument itself. The normal thing is to identify the person writing or speaking as belonging to a particular "tribe." This is an effort-saving device, whereas thinking requires considerable effort and attention. By resorting to stereotypes, however, many economical Spaniards save mental energy. The most worn political stereotypes are those of left and right and those of nationalism. They are still used, partly for nostalgic reasons. People do not want to stop being young—nor did the Spanish generation of 1956–1968 (which included most of the Socialist leaders)—so they cling to the fiery slogans of youth, although real public or private life may have little to do with them. There may also be a calculated interest in it: some debates can be won by falling back on the tribal shout.

Symbols and Reality

To be sure, the level of a country's discourse can improve significantly through the habit of critical realism (or critical rationalism), the discipline of carefully observing and scrupulously registering facts and learning from experience. But this is not easy. At times people prefer to substitute words for reality. Accustomed to the darkness of Plato's cave, we fear the light; we think that in using words to manipulate the shadows, we deal with the things themselves.

A reliable sense of reality is acquired or lost, sharpened or softened, as the result of experience, and it depends on many factors. In Spain, a considerable inclination toward magical thinking has persisted in certain intellectual, church, bureaucratic, and professional circles (though not among peasants). For example, the world of Madrid's royal court and intellectuals in the seventeenth century was one of (partial) self-delusion, and some of Spain's best literature of that age (Cervantes and Gracián) supports such an interpretation.[1] To give a more recent example, the passions that led to the 1936–1939 Civil War can be understood as driven by strategy and delusion. The very shock of the war could have impaired the capacity of many Spaniards of the generation of the 1930s to cope with reality: the survivors, many broken and demoralized, lived through the harsh conditions of the 1940s and the early 1950s in an official climate of grandiloquent (and possibly self-deluding) rhetoric.

While not wishing here to engage in a history of the mentality (and hence of the sense of reality) of the generation of 1956–1968, I do think it is worthwhile to point out some of the unrealistic tendencies of the university-educated segment of this generation, which was to lead the country in the 1970s and 1980s. From the start, their encounters with reality occurred in a more protected climate than they wished to recognize. Their families protected them from economic difficulties, but not only from them. Because they were children of a middle-class generation respectful of the Francoist state, their dissidence was largely tolerated in its initial phase by their perplexed, irritated, erratic elders. The young people also benefited from the protective circle constituted by the halls of residence *(colegios mayores)*, Catholic organizations and cultural networks, and even political and cultural spaces organized by a net of dissenters who had a measure of protection by some circles of Falange (the Spanish Fascist party).[2]

In its youth, the generation of 1956–1968 got used to manipulating symbolic reality and imagined that this activity affected empirical reality. According to this way of thinking, the agrarian reform of the 1930s and the imminent crisis of capitalism were still live issues. Playing with words, using the part to mean the whole, members of this generation believed, or acted as if they believed, that having a few proletarians in their political organizations was the same as being one with the working class. Such games initiated them into the arts of political dissimulation, dissembling, and duplicitous language, and the youngsters found consummate masters in these arts among the previous generation—Enrique Tierno Galván, for example, a well-known intellectual and a remarkable teacher and Socialist leader (in time, his teachings became an important influence on PSOE). Tierno managed, for several decades, to project an aura of ambiguity about his ideological positions as well as his political tactics and goals. Possibly overtaken by habitual make-believe, he also embellished his personal and political biography so much that even a straightforward question about his place of birth and his social origins was too much to ask, apparently, as he kept giving false responses to these rather trivial questions. Maybe he just decided, early in life, to work up his image and appearance into a series of masks, in order to deflect criticism and prosecution and to suit the situation he was part of, and which he tried to control.[3]

The purpose of these anecdotes is simply to speculate on why Spaniards of the 1970s and 1980s found it very difficult to face up to the reality of things and call them by their right names, and tended to use rhetorical devices not to face up to the truth but to work up a "better" reality made out of the stuff of words, if not of dreams—a sort of functional-imaginary world that might not correspond to reality but helped to manipulate it.

Political leaders too sought to evade their responsibility through symbolic manipulations. Later in the 1990s, when the head of government was confronted with a massive pattern of either gross improprieties or unquestionable illegalities on the part of the administration and the Socialist party (see Chapter 4), he (Felipe González) could say, "I assume my political responsibility," meaning, "I assume the responsibility of saying that I assume the responsibility." Moreover, this kind of trifling with the rules of reasonable communication was taken by influential journalists silently or with a smile, as a clever trick.

The economy experienced similar unreality problems. Those directly concerned refused to recognize that much of the economy was underground, and that the root of the problem lay in the very rules of the official economy. But not naming the problem did not make it disappear. Likewise, the business leaders involved in the above-mentioned scandals systematically broke the rules of financial activity and still expected to gain time or cover up their activities by cultivating the press for years (investing heavily in the media in order to divert attention from the huge losses in their financial operations).

All these "conventionalist stratagems" (to use an expression of Karl Popper's) or evasive maneuvers might "please the imagination but did not advance our knowledge."[4] But they could be, and were, successful in the short run. During the Franco years, most politicians had learned to deal with bureaucratic infighting within the state and political maneuvering of the opposition. But they had no experience of the hard life of political responsibility: of making risky political decisions, facing the consequences, and learning from their mistakes. At the same time, there was a sort of glass wall between events in Spain and events in the rest of the world, as a result of a long history of inwardness and relative isolation which had been reinforced by the consequences of the Civil War. Consequently, there was a lag in time in which changes in the world reached the Spaniards and were properly understood by them.

Most of the youngsters who became interested in politics in the 1950s and 1960s started off with the assumption that the world was moving in the direction of socialism, or at any rate toward socialist-democratic, state-directed economies and societies. Having been impressed by one variant or another of Marxism, they took it for granted that liberalism was fading away. Another group was influenced by a Catholic-Jesuitic, "prudential" way of thinking that approached public affairs with remarkable equanimity and pragmatism (not to say cheerful opportunism). The important thing was not so much to pass judgments according to some absolute standards of truth (life being so complicated, and God's ways so mysterious), but rather to anticipate the direction in which the world was moving—which suggested a blend of corporatist ways, old and new, allowing for some touches of bland "personalism" here and of fiery talk of social injustice and people's liberation there.

Most of the time, most of these young people focused on events in Spain, having only a "subsidiary awareness" (Michael Polanyi's term) of what was going in the world outside. There, the promises of a socialist alternative to the liberal and capitalist order became ever less plausible, even though the 1968 events in France and elsewhere seemed to conjure up, like a mirage, new hopes for the old dreams. But the Soviet Union stagnated; and as role models, the socialist countries of Central and Eastern Europe looked increasingly dubious. Yugoslavia's cooperatives were insignificant local experiments. Janos Kadar's pragmatic government in Hungary could not do enough to erase the memories of 1956—nor to disguise the fact that the country was heading toward an *ersatz* capitalist economy. Poland seemed of marginal interest, though some Spanish leftists kept a sympathetic eye on Gomulka's attempts to handle the situation (and, limited by ideology, were later unable to understand Solidarnosc).[5] The wave of adulation for Fidel Castro and Ernesto (Che) Guevara came and went; the rhetoric of the unaligned Third World faded away; and Algeria, Vietnam, China were all, in the end, a rosary of disappointments. Yet little was learned from observing these changes, and dreams continued to prevail for twenty more years. When reality began to intrude, however, and political decisions with real consequences had to be made regarding foreign investment or geopolitical alliances, the post-Franco generation demonstrated remarkable adaptive ability—though it still harbored caveats and reservations that paid tribute to their past persuasions.

Other institutional and cultural routines and proclivities also helped to reduce people's ability to develop and refine a realistic approach to public business. For example, Spain lacked strong institutions which would have accustomed the public to be on the alert, to seek precise information and proof, and thus to see to it that specific responsibilities were established. It was important to develop such habits, but in the 1980s and early 1990s neither the judiciary nor the press worked in a way that could foster them. The justice system moved very slowly; the press had been too timid with regard to political power for too long, and then was either too partisan or too lax about verifying information. As a result, facts were easily submerged beneath rumors, suspicions, accusations, denials, silences, and omissions, leaving the public confused.

A bewildered public was therefore inclined to accept magical thinking, in the form of conspiracy theories and the aforementioned tribalism. In general, this sort of thinking makes it easier for the administration to present complex situations in a simplified way, and to make the public believe it can understand them. In Spain, the use of magical thinking was frequent and its success considerable. For people who never understood the working of extensive and open structures such as markets and many other forms of spontaneous coordination (in social, political, and cultural life), it was natural to believe that they function by means of agreements among the powerful. These agreements can be overt or secret. The conspiratorial view systematically misinterprets the importance of these agreements (which, of course, do exist). The tribal interpretation brings the focus of attention on the tribe and its interests, and urges everyone to give his full loyalty and support to it. This reasoning becomes a call to uphold the solidarity of one's own tribe against the others.

To be sure, the use of these and other forms of magical thinking does not prevent each individual from following his or her particular political or economic interest, and to do so with determination and cunning. No amount of flowery digressions will win a particular election or arrange a specific business deal or help attain a promotion. What we can say of the public sphere is that it was dominated by the language of hyper-realism—like a painting in which the atmosphere is misty, but the details are sharp. As in the works of this school of painting (by Antonio López and others; works which, by the way, were much admired in Madrid's artistic circles at that time), precise pieces of reality float in a diffusion of unnecessary and disconnected words. But if the political language lacked precision, the practical targets were not missed.

We may conjecture that this hyper-realism corresponds to a static reading of reality and a perception of time passing very slowly. Perhaps this has to do with the experience of time of a generation that did not act decisively to oust the dictator, but waited long and patiently until he died in bed before carrying out the longed-for change in the political regime. Perhaps it relates to some events in the collective memory of Spaniards in more ancient times. What is certain is that the political generation of 1956–1968 tended to take decisions rather late, as if it lacked the sense of the moment in which to seize the opportunity. Its procrastination over most policy problems was well known (in labor and market policies, public spending, audiovisual technology and telecommunications, the regions, health, and others). It acted as if time did not count, just when Spain's integration into the international economy and society accelerated the pace of developments.

People inclined to magical thinking also tend to understand power not as a tool to resolve problems, but as a position (which nobody else can occupy) from which they can display the symbols of its importance. For this reason, they believe that laws and promises are important even when they are not intended to be carried out. For these people (and for their followers), laws and promises are neither formal conditions that outline human activities, nor instruments to solve collective problems. Rather, they are displays of power and expressions of the desire to be respected.

The Making of a Generation

When we examine the generation that entered social and political life in the period between 1956 and 1968 in terms of its original project, its formative experience, and the results of its exertions in the 1980s, that context will allow us better to understand the choices it made, the nature of the social and political world it created, and the kind of moral character that it developed as a result of these choices.[6] If it is true that by the time people are forty years old they are responsible for their faces, that would be doubly true with regard to their character. And this generation was just turning forty by the late 1970s. They were the ones who played a major role in the democratic transition and were to dominate the period of Socialist rule—as suggested by the age of the members of Congress in 1977. Then, 32.1% of the members of UCD parliamentary group and 56.7% of the Socialist one were 39 years old or less;

while another 43.0% of the centrists and 22.9% of the Socialists were between 40 and 49 years old.[7]

A generation is a group of people close in age whose dispositions (and some background assumptions) have been shaped by the characteristics of the world they inherit and react to, and by the crucial events occurring at the time they enter the historical stage—say by the time they are around twenty years old. The university student generation of 1956–1968 was educated during the 1950s and 1960s and began its professional, social, and political activities by then. The crucial events of its time were the student demonstrations in February 1956, which were the starting point for the student movement. At that time, a group of students of the Faculty of Law at the University of Madrid challenged the official student organization and the police, inside and outside the university campus. From the turmoil that followed, the students gained concessions to create their own independent union and to hold free elections to choose their representatives *(consejeros)*. These representatives came together in a body called Syndical Chamber (Cámara Sindical) to elect the executive officers of the local union *(delegado* and *subdelegado)*, who were in turn accountable for their activities to the Cámara. Elections were held every year, and debates within the Cámara were free.[8] A period of intense activity followed, with open, generalized discussions and multiple initiatives. These student initiatives took on ever more marked political overtones until the end of Francoism, and from among these activists emerged the new political class of democratic Spain.

The movement started not long before the 1959 economic stabilization plan and other related developments (see Chapter 1) that began to integrate the country into the Western world. Between the mid-1950s and the late 1960s, the church took a liberal turn while the economy underwent significant change, moving from its traditional agrarian base toward greater industrialization. The resulting massive internal migration had an important impact on the development of peripheral nationalist movements. And while the year 1968 was not a particularly key year for Spaniards, the date served as a reference to a European (even a worldwide) generation with which they felt a deep affinity, and whose demands and general expectations they shared.

The generation of 1956–1968 has been at the center of Spanish life for the last twenty years. It is difficult to do justice to a group of people that made the transition to democracy and consolidated it, and who have occupied many positions of power since then; and more difficult still to do it justice without hurting its feelings and challenging its self-image of part-hero, part-victim.

On the one hand, members of that generation see themselves as heroic and charismatic, as the prime movers of Spain's democratic transition and consolidation, even of its modernization. But even if history chose them for such a high position, their task was unclear, and its accomplishment was largely a matter of chance. Had Franco lived another ten or fifteen years (until the late 1980s or early 1990s), they would have been a "bridge" generation. Indeed, many observers thought it was just that—as the solidity of the Franco regime seemed assured; as political dissent was reduced to a few groups of students, workers, and intellectuals; and as dissenters despaired that the middle class, the peasants, and the bulk of the population would ever join in their opposition to Franco's rule. As a student myself, I still remember the pithy phrase (and a sentiment of dubious pity) of a *maître à penser* and a remarkable teacher and moral philosopher, José Luis Aranguren, a figure of the previous generation, in the early 1960s[9]: "we have been able to do nothing in this country; but you, the next generation, would find things even more difficult. I pity you." Aranguren was a keen observer and even admirer of the young, partly as an indirect way of expressing his antipathy towards his own generation, but he was not without reservations or ambivalence. Perhaps he distrusted the reciprocal feelings of young people, or wanted to sober up the youngsters' spirits. The fact is that he confronted us with a sort of sour affection. Yet it so happened that, against all predictions, the sails of youth filled with propitious winds, the gods were on their side, and their guardian angels were in their most good-natured mood. The young people had room to experiment and to do many things in the last fifteen to twenty years of Francoism. After its collapse, they tended to reconstruct its avatar, somewhat fancifully, as a tale of struggle and conquest of freedom.

At the same time, the young felt a little victimized. They had been forced to engage in rather absurd and exhausting conflicts in an unsophisticated and provincial environment, against authoritarian families, colleges, organizations, churches, and state structures. They had suppressed their desires for too long, as they used to say. And then, after such a period of subjection and prolonged adolescence, they emerged to find themselves with responsibilities to shoulder on all fronts, including taking care of the older generation. No doubt the 1956–1968 generation deserves a sympathetic hearing. But perhaps it is best for us to take some distance from it and try to explain the formation of its moral character, from its origins through its formative experience to its present predicament. Two points of a general nature may be useful in this endeavor.

The first is that this generation has lived with two conflicting impulses: one, to erect a social order based on freedom; and the other, to try to control it (so that freedom would not turn into license). This contradiction was rooted in the formative and crucial experience of the 1950s and 1960s, and in the moral character built out of this experience.

On the one hand, they wanted freedom from all their authority figures. For this reason, they experimented systematically with life styles that were different from or opposed to those of the previous generation, in matters of sex, love, religion, trade union affiliation, politics, and professions.[10] On the other hand, they internalized the authoritarian conduct of the previous generation against which they had fought, although they gave a new content to their own brand of authoritarianism. They were not liberal. For example, they marked the passing of the Generation of 1898 (José Ortega y Gasset and Pío Baroja both died in the early 1950s) with respect, but with distance. To them these were people from another era: too bland, in contrast to the tough new generation (as they thought of themselves). The priests around them (curiously, this liberated generation was full of semi-liberated priests) and their mentors taught them the art of doctrinal insult against the so-called reactionary tribes of the time, as well as respect for, and dialogue with, the robust authoritarian-totalitarian tradition of Marxism. When they did enter politics, they joined parties or political factions that were rebellious/revolutionary/quasi-revolutionary in one way or another; for this reason many generation members tended to interpret their commitment to justice and freedom in rather harsh and militant terms (and understandably so, given the possibility of landing in jail, and keeping the Civil War in mind).

In these pages I do not seek to reconstruct the very complex moral experience of this generation, and even less to follow its later evolution. It is enough to point out that this experience, and the moral education that went with it, taught people certain things about how to conduct themselves as members of a party or faction. These included intolerance of others, respect for discipline, a preference for authoritarian leadership over cumbersome democratic muddling through, and, in general, skills typical of the art of war, among them unscrupulous use of the media. No wonder that twenty years later, in the 1980s, this generation created an order combining freedom and manipulation, cultivated a discretionary use of authority, developed client networks, and used tribal and simplifying (and misleading) types of argument. It is also natural that this generation experienced difficulties in articulating its moral sentiments in the later phase of its maturity. For one thing, its self-confidence seemed to make it unaware of its proclivity to despotism. Then, when it was confronted with an array of political scandals in the 1990s (see Chapter 4), it was astonished and hurt for being condemned instead of being offered gratitude and recognition for what it believed was an altruistic use of power. Uncertain and tense, it refused to recognize its mistakes for too long—and then it could never bring the situation to its proper conclusion. Stuck in the first stages of shock, denial, and anger, it was unable to reach the stage of wise acceptance.

My second point is that I believe that this generation had (and has) a "moral weakness," in the sense in which José Ortega y Gasset referred to people lacking a "moral structure"—by which he meant not moral principles and rules, but the strength and will to stick to those precepts. That is, moral weakness is the incapacity to understand and commit to the principles and rules that apply to specific tasks under specific circumstances. In this regard, two factors or influences of this generation's formative period are important.

First, the morality of success that permeated the middle-class background of most the university members of that generation gave them a start in a trajectory of moral opportunism. For the parents whose moral goal was a career for their children, the key to success in the narrow world of the mid-1940s and 1950s was either a bureaucratic post (for the lower middle class) or a circle of friends and social contacts (for the upper middle class). The god Success was the family deity, and it presided over the hearts of middle-class families of this time. The moral character of the children was thus shaped in a lax moral climate (despite the religious air of some schools) compatible with the *idée fixe* of succeeding in life as it was lived in those years. The middle classes of that period had been demoralized by the Civil War; their moral laxity was in contrast to the (somewhat artificial) official morality of the early 1940s, which in turn was a pale imitation of the heroic morality of the combatants of the 1930s, who fought a fratricidal war for the triumph of moral virtue (whether on the side of the nationalists, the social revolutionaries, or the Republicans). Furthermore, the influence of home was bolstered by the educational system, which tended to lessen personal moral responsibility in schools and later in peer groups. (In these, the traditional Catholic culture, which put emphasis on original sin, confession, and communion, had its counterpart in Marxist or pseudo-Marxist culture, which placed the emphasis on structural determination, collective action, and class identity.)

A further influence on the moral life of this generation came later, as experience in professional life gave some of its key members a training in moral manipulation. While some of the university graduates went into politics, others became economists and civil servants and helped draw up and implement the socioeconomic policies introduced after democracy arrived. They rose from the ranks of government economists and the financial community of the 1960s. Their principal formative experiences were learning to manage the tangle of regulations in Spain's export and financial sectors, and handling the banking crises. They had cultivated relations and friendships with their seniors in the administration and the economic establishment of the Franco regime, and sought their protection. At the same time, they maintained contacts with the International Monetary Fund, the World Bank, and the OECD, learned the language of these organizations, and got familiar with the values of a relatively open economy and a moderately liberalized one. This was their window to the "real world" of worldwide capitalist economy. Their economic liberalism blended well with the anti-Franco position adopted by most of the university generation to which they belonged.

In a state of mildly divided consciousness, they recited a liberal creed in professional circles, daily practiced the discretionary use of public authority in the Franco administration, and, well into the night, listened to the moving Republican songs from the Civil War. This practical experience of mediating between Spain and the outside world, between the elites of the Franco regime and the political opposition, enabled them to carry out useful tasks during the transition and in later years. It also ensured a fair amount of continuity in economic policy, from the late Francoist years to the centrist and Socialist governments.

Their pragmatism and ideological detachment perfectly suited the ambiguity of a transition period which required Francoists to pretend they had never been Francoists, and left-wing compromisers to pretend they were still committed to leftist principles. Such maneuvering helped to de-ideologize the political activism of this generation, but the ambiguity may have contributed to its demoralization or weak commitment to principles and rules. The result was the formation of a fairly cohesive group of pragmatic manipulators.

Taken together, the morality of success and the training in pragmatism help to explain how the objective circumstances of the 1980s, which supplied significant opportunities for personal enrichment (and office-holding), met (on the demand side, so to speak) a generation eagerly ready to take advantage of them.

The elite entered the 1980s with a definite project to make good and to live a different life. Spain's system of social stratification had acquired over the years a diamond shape, with a central mass of around 60% of the population, which was perceived as middle class. Below it lay another considerable stratum, the lower class (with the working class of the past somewhere in between), which had its sights set on breaking into the middle class. Under these was a marginalized underclass, with no political voice. But the elite wanted to distance itself from the ordinary middle class, though of course not in its rhetoric (kept within the politically correct boundaries of universal solidarity), only in the reality of daily life. Hence "living a different life" meant deliberately cultivating a social distance. Members of the elite lived on the green-belt outskirts of the city and drove to work in official cars. They carefully planned the futures of their children, who went to elite schools where they befriended boys and girls of their class, and learned languages so they could get scholarships to study abroad. Their parents enjoyed the leisure and pleasures of ocean cruises or alpine skiing; and at home they obtained all sorts of small favors (from opera tickets to bullfight tickets) outside the normal channels.

In other words, they managed to create a world of their own, a social order which was the opposite of their rhetoric. Keeping their distance from the rest, they operated within a web of influences woven between the state apparatus and the socioeconomic elite. It was a social world of insiders as opposed to outsiders; a political life split between those who had power and information, and those who did not; the fast lane for car traffic, and the slow lane for the rest.

In this way, the generation of 1956–1968 (or rather the bulk of its university graduates) managed to fulfill the dream of their parents. They applied the (provincial) morals of success prevailing in the 1950s, the years of their early upbringing, to the (cosmopolitan) circumstances of the 1980s, the years of their maturity. In retrospect we may say that far from being rebellious children, they managed to make of their lives a monument to filial piety.[11]

One last observation: their difficulty in making moral commitments may have been related in one sense to the difficulty of identifying the proper social referents of such commitments. This was somehow para-doxical, since they had a collectivistic outlook and used a moral lan-guage that favored a commitment to communities over a commitment to rules. The problem, however, was how to identify the groups that deserved their moral commitment. Their interest in social classes—not to speak of the working class or the proletariat or the lower class, once the focus of the moral sentiments of their youthful period of dissent—had faded away gradually (and tacitly), in tandem with their accumu-lated experience of the complexities of contemporary life and of their own social climbing. It was equally difficult for them to offer their loyalty to the Spanish national community. Their sentiments were in-hibited, once again, by their formative experiences: by their negative reaction to the Francoist brand of Spanish nationalism; by their attrac-tion to Europe; and by their perplexity in the face of the problem of defining a national identity for Spain which could be compatible with the various peripheral nationalist movements. Yes, they were as devoted as everyone else to Spanish patriotism and nationalism when it came to sports or bullfighting or songs or untimely emotional outbursts, but they were quite uncertain about how else to express it and what to do with it. And this was how they came back full circle to their origins and to the primary groups of their infancy and adolescence, namely, their families and their personal networks.

At this point, a provisional balance sheet drawn for this generation in the 1990s would show notable achievements and clear merits, but also a certain lightweight quality that resulted in negligence or incapacity to complete its tasks, and a rather disingenuous way to avoid them and to avoid the responsibility for them. After years of exercising social and political power, the kind of civil society they built may be characterized as an unstable structure in a chronic state of "low-intensity disorder": a society apparently without radical conflicts, but upset by noisy outbursts and confusing disturbances which lasted through the 1980s and the early 1990s. It was a democratic state with large vested interests; it had a top-heavy state apparatus; an economy integrated into the European Union but full of tricks and collusions to the detriment of the public interest. It made grossly inadequate use of the country's human capital, with a large level of unemployment and a substantial underground economy; fortunately, it had the counterbalance of the stability of the family and the flowering of many bland and interesting forms of sociability. Because its half-developed public sphere included considerable elements of confusion and tribalism, there were remarkable difficulties in articulating and communicating a sense of Spain as a unified community.

By 1992 the country was enjoying a fleeting moment of glory with the Olympic Games and the World Fair (plus the fifth centennial of the discovery of America)—but that did not last. Almost literally "the morning after," in the very middle of that year, the country plunged into an economic recession and a show of political scandals, against the backdrop of European uncertainties following the Danes' referendum against Maastricht.

When we look back to the 1980s from the vantage point of that eerie moment in mid-1992, as the country passed from the euphoria of games and fairy tales to confront a less pleasant reality, we may be too harsh in judging the 1980s. First, it should be remembered that for all its limitations, the decade ended with the key elements of the institutional framework for a free society still basically intact (liberal democracy, market economy, a plural society, and a tolerant culture). These institutions carried incentives and biases in favor of freedom, internal competition, volunteer solidarity, and diminishing authoritarianism. The 1980s also opened up new horizons, stimulated debate, and experimented with different solutions for political problems. Although these things are not enough, they are the preconditions and essential prerequisites for a civil society.

Second, whatever the weaknesses of the 1956–1968 generation in handling the country's problems, they were the ones who linked the nation to the outside world. Now, external forces tend to lift up a country in the long run. Everything that happens is permeated, penetrated, overwhelmingly invaded by the outside world. Spain's economy is simply a part of the European and international economies. Membership in the European Economic Community in 1986 intensified a marked process of integration that had begun more than thirty years ago. Imports of agricultural and industrial products arrived along with massive inflows of capital and the entry of foreign companies in many sectors, particularly cars, chemicals, cement, building materials, food, electronics, and computers. Between 1983 and 1992, foreign ownership of shares issued by nonfinancial companies increased from 14% to 40% of the total, and from 5% to 22% of financial companies (Banco de España 1993). And the trend was set for an increasing interpenetration between the Spanish and international economies: between 1989 and 1993 foreign investment in Spain (particularly from the EEC) fluctuated between Pta 1.2 trillion and Pta 2.3 trillion a year, while Spanish investments abroad (mostly in Europe, especially in Portugal, but also in Morocco, Latin America, and tax havens such as the Virgin and Cayman Islands) were between Pta 200 billion and Pta 600 billion a year.

Opportunities to communicate with the outside world multiplied everywhere within society, politics, and culture. A yearly average of 52 million foreigners visited Spain between 1986 and 1993 (some 48 million Europeans out of a total EU population of about 300 million), and 20 million Spaniards (out of a total population of about 40 million) went abroad. Between 1980 and 1992, the number of international telephone calls rose fourfold (from close to 50 million to nearly 200 million). The spread of media and telecommunications strengthened the stream of communication beyond the place of residency and the conventional channels. The number of personal computers exploded; and the number of cellular telephones increased 30 times, from 29,000 in 1989 to 1,000,000 in 1995. The state's refusal to regulate cable TV was countered by building an extensive network operating in a semi-underground economy (estimated at about 1 million homes wired in 1993).

The explosion of communications brings a constant expansion of horizontal communications in the domestic sphere, and the country's frame of reference expands internationally. Engaging in scientific activities means being linked to international scientific communities; setting up companies means exporting or being able to compete with foreign firms in the domestic market; reestablishing trade unionism means doing it in harmony with the internationalization of economic life and learning from what is being done in other countries; conducting Spanish politics increasingly means understanding how to promote Spanish interests in Europe and at the same time carry out European policies; and doing all of this means being linked to what happens in the world through the international media.

But it is necessary also to qualify the accomplishments of the decade of the 1980s. They produced no guarantee that the disorder of those years would not get worse. The institutions and external connections may facilitate the development of a civil society, but they are not sufficient guarantees for it. The construction of a civil society (or a liberal democracy) is a normative task, which the Spaniards themselves must carry out. They may or may not succeed in it.

Remember our symbol from Chapter 2: Ishmael, who followed his heart's desire. We left him on a path that could not be more benign: he went off to the sea, understood as a civil(ized) society. But it is time to remind ourselves of what happened in Melville's novel. While still on land, Ishmael listens to a preacher telling the story of Jonah, praising the man who speaks the truth however ill-received and stands firm (in his inescapable identity) against all. He suggests to Ishmael that perhaps the man who takes this stance will, like Jonah, have the opportunity, if swept to the bowels of the sea, to be brought back to the light by the sea itself. A curious sermon. Nevertheless, Ishmael embarks on a ship captained by an obsessive and vengeful man, surrounded by weak and indifferent officers and an erratic crew that gets infected by the captain's madness. And he finds himself sailing the seas in search of an intelligent and malignant monster, with all reasonable restraints loosened and acting against the very rules of his profession. Then, after days of fever and fierce struggle, the monster destroys them. The ship and the captain and the crew vanish into an immense whirlpool—all but Ishmael, who lives to tell the story.

An interesting end. Will we end up as Captain Ahab and his crew? Or Ishmael-Jonah? What will the sea of civil society look like? The ongoing story suggests that soon after the events described here, the Spanish ship started making its first circles around the abyss—though we also get glimpses of the ways she found to escape the force of the whirlwind.

CHAPTER FOUR

Public Drama and the Rule of Law

THE SCRIPT WRITTEN in the 1980s became a somber drama played on the Spanish public stage in the years between 1993 and 1996. Above all, a seemingly endless string of political scandals put into question the rule of law and the principle of political accountability. The second issue—the fact that about one fifth of the labor force had been out of work on average for more than ten years—threatened the social fabric as well as the viability of the market economy and the legitimacy of the political regime.

As Victor Turner suggests (Turner 1986: 39ff), a social drama of sorts takes place when political leaders break the rules they are supposed to uphold, revealing hidden clashes of character, interest, and ambition. This infraction leads to a crisis in the group's unity and continuity, unless the tear is sealed off by redressive public action, which is often ritualized and may be undertaken in the name of the law. If the social drama runs its full course, the outcome should be the restoration of peace and normalcy—or else permanent division. It may also happen that redressive action fails, division is averted, and yet society remains in a state of chronic or endemic disorder for a time. Redressive rituals, including those performed by the legal authorities and other masters of social ceremonies (for instance, cultural or media elites), include an inquiry into the causes of the crisis as well as curative measures (punishing the law-breakers, healing the wounds of the victims, and voicing the complaints and softening the feelings of the community). These are usually life-heightening experiences or liminal states: that is, they are crucial for the formation of the character of the group and, eventually, of the whole society.

The intensity of the Spanish drama of the 1990s fell short of the extreme pathological form it took in the 1930s, which ended in civil war (Linz 1978). By contrast, this more recent drama met with a redressive ritual that did somehow, though not without lengthy detours and some indirection, restore a degree of normalcy in due time. Yet it had its dangerous and ominous aspects. In the bureaucratic and authoritarian regime of the past, General Franco had declared himself accountable to God and History, not to his fellow citizens. After his death, the people chose a political system based on the principle of the rule of law applied equally to rulers and citizens, and on the principle of the political accountability of government. The political scandals went to the heart of these principles—and they were not mere political embarrassments, as the government and its friends tried to portray them. They represented the "moment of truth" in the public arena. Only if those principles were upheld could the democratic transition be deemed to be finally successful; if they were not, a critical step would have been taken toward a grave distortion of a civil society, leading eventually to some form of authoritarianism.

On the other hand, and on a less dramatic note, the country was required to put its economy in good order by the application of the Maastricht Treaty and the timetable of Europe's monetary and economic unification. At this time, however, about one out of five Spanish workers was unemployed—indeed, had been for more than a decade. The choice for Spain was either to be left out of the core membership of the European Union, or to apply the strict conditions of monetary and budgetary policy that would presumably mean more unemployment, at least in the short run.

The public was mostly aware of the seriousness of these problems. When the Spaniards were asked which news they had paid more attention to during 1995, their overwhelming answer was "the political scandals"; when asked about the issue they considered the most important one, their answer was "unemployment" (81% put unemployment first; the next item got only 23%).[1] At the same time, their apprehensions regarding the European Union became more noticeable: the difference in percentage points between those who thought that belonging to the European Union "was [is] a good thing" for Spain and those who did not narrowed from (about) 50% in 1991 to (about) 10% in 1995 (CIS 1995). The events of the 1990s were thus a crucial test for the institutions as well as for the dispositions of Spanish citizens, and they posed some complex choices.

The country's economic status and its foreign relations have multiple aspects and long roots and deserve to be examined at length. In fact they used to be the focus of most political debates. But there was one incident that needs to be noted—a half-forgotten, apparently minor piece of *Realpolitik* to which nobody paid much attention at the time. In 1983, a salesman by the name of Segundo Marey, who lived in Hendaye, France, near the border with Spain, was mistakenly identified as member of a Basque terrorist organization. He was kidnapped by mercenaries paid by Spanish police officers, brought to Spain, detained and kept under the supervision of those officers, and then released. This marked the beginning of a number of illegal antiterrorist government-sanctioned activities that lasted until 1987—and included more than twenty assassinations.

Stories like this surfaced in the early 1990s. And from then on, the Socialist government and Prime Minister Felipe González had to spend most of their energy trying to exorcise those ghosts from the past, while attempting to go about public business as if nothing happened and to keep the public focused on the ordinary matters of governance, including economic policy. It was an impossible task, particularly as lugubrious stories of torture and death were displayed alongside near-daily revelations of economic corruption and impropriety.

Disclosures of political and financial scandals were compounded by learning of the judges' difficulties in enforcing the law and bringing those responsible for illegal activities to stand trial (and eventually go to prison). Some of the main public officials became prime suspects in breaking the law and obstructing justice. This came as a shock to much of the public and created considerable confusion. The scandals were many; the plots, intricate; the legal procedures, arcane; and the interpretations, highly partisan. The public felt its way through that maze of facts and imputations with difficulty and in some trepidation. The drama tested the public's intelligence, *sang-froid*, endurance, and civic virtue.

The Scandals

On March 25, 1993, Prime Minister Felipe González went to a meeting with students at the Autonomous University of Madrid. He expected a friendly audience. The president of the University and convener of the meeting, a well-known physicist, was a Socialist sympathizer. Most students, it was assumed, leaned toward the left. Besides, the government was proud of its educational policies that had increased the numbers of the students and provided many of them with financial aid and fellowships. But much to Mr. González's surprise, he was not at all well-received. It turned out that the students were much more concerned than he had expected about the current political and financial scandals—disclosures which, at this time, focused more on economic corruption (the Mariano Rubio and the Juan Guerra affairs, and especially the FILESA affair) than on the state's antiterrorist tactics. The Prime Minister seemed to be taken aback by the intensity of feelings of indignation the students harbored. As one of them told him bluntly, either he knew about the matters, and then he was an accomplice to the felonies, or he was not aware of what was going on, and then he was an incompetent leader. Either way, he should be ousted from office.

The scene was astonishing from the viewpoint of somebody who used to think of himself as a modernizer-hero.[2] González knew he could not pass into history as the maker of the democratic transition, because that honor belonged to Suárez and the King. Yet he hoped to be remembered as the man responsible for the definitive integration of Spain into Europe. Now, far from praising him for this accomplishment, the students were holding him responsible for the corruption of Spain's political and economic life. The youth being the embodiment of the future, they were giving him a sour anticipation of history's judgment. The scene was also a bad omen for the next election, due to be held fairly soon.

Soon after the student debacle, I met Prime Minister González for the first and only time. The conversations lasted for about eight hours; they took place within a small circle of people, most of whom were his friends and sympathizers, plus a few entrepreneurs and journalists. When I was invited to join them, I was told that González was upset by that dramatic university scene; that he was looking for advice and was in dire need of hearing from people of an independent cast of mind. To stress the last point, my host added, with regret, that González had not been seeing people of this sort of late.

The Prime Minister referred to the scene at the University, but he did not look deeply touched by it. Rather, he behaved as if he had seen a sign of danger to which he must react quickly and effectively. He conceded that the student who said he must choose between being corrupt or being incompetent had a point, and he appreciated the logic of his argument—but, of course, politics was not logical. The young people's feelings of indignation were perhaps understandable. He started by saying: "Once upon a time I was young too, and my career started by booing at a Francoist leader visiting the University of Seville." But this charming touch of nostalgia for the good old days was not meant seriously.

Whatever his personal sentiments may have been, I did not have the impression that the remarkable professional politician I saw before me could be easily hurt. He simply seemed to be looking for practical ways to handle the issue. In fact, I was surprised by how little disconcerted he was, and how little he listened. People argued, trying to score points, eagerly and at times with some trepidation. They were obviously concerned about him. And there he was, courteous and distracted, barely taking stock of what was said to him. His mind was already made up.

He did become animated when he talked, as if he were mainly interested in exploring the effect his arguments had on his audience. Maybe, I thought, he was just rehearsing: testing a line of reasoning to be applied to a larger audience later on. His basic point was to beware the danger from the right: the right-wing extremists threatened the modernization of the country, which it was his historical task to carry out. Yes, he and his government had made mistakes, had not been alert enough to corruption. But that was a peripheral issue anyway. The real issue was the choice the country had to make between them and the reactionary, incompetent right; between the modern hero and the shadow of the past. Thus corruption was, for him, a nuisance and a misunderstanding. In retrospect, his attitude seemed to be that talking would clear it up; all that was needed was an expression of concern.

To my mind corruption was a serious matter; furthermore, I was skeptical about his portrayal of his political fortunes as the saga of a modernizer-hero, and of the country as being on the verge of a takeover by an evil empire. Spain was, I suggested, a relatively modern and mature country already. In short I took the possibility of defeat of Prime Minister González and his party in the next election as neither a tragedy nor a national setback, but as quite a normal event from which neither the country nor the party nor even himself would suffer too much in the long run; all might even benefit from it. And I told him so, quietly and with some sympathy for his predicament, but in those very words. No wonder that my advice (apparently unexpected) to change his diagnosis and take a more philosophical view of the situation was not taken.

On April 12, González announced national elections for June 6. The Prime Minister himself and his entourage took charge of the campaign; the PSOE apparatus played a subordinate role in it. There were two memorable public debates between González and José María Aznar, the leader of the Popular Party, with even results (the first debate was supposed to be "won" by Aznar, the second, by González). During the campaign, González made vague appeals to "the danger of the right" and, more specifically, to the right's supposed threats to the welfare state. Then, in a surprise move, he brought in Baltasar Garzón, a judge known for his prosecution of GAL-related[3] and drugs-related crimes, and a symbol of the fight against corruption. He was on the slate as the number two candidate of PSOE for Madrid, González being number one (the then Foreign Minister and later General Secretary of NATO, Javier Solana, was number three).

The election results gave a fairly narrow victory to González. The PSOE got 39% of the votes; the PP, 35% (up from 26% in the previous elections). Since the PSOE did not have a majority, the party was in need of political alliances. González chose CiU, the coalition of Catalan nationalists led by Jordi Pujol, as a partner. Together, Socialists and Catalanists gained a majority in Congress (by just one vote). González's and Pujol's interests obviously coincided in holding onto their positions of public authority. What brought them together were economic and regional policies (particularly devolution of power and transfers of public money to the regional authorities).

Once González got the arithmetic of parliamentary power right, he seemingly lost interest in the fight against corruption, which he had made one of the rallying points of his electoral campaign. Now that there was no electoral campaign in sight and no further need for a symbol, Garzón lost his political standing and was shunted off to a position with no real power. He stayed there for about one year and resigned on May 6, 1994, making clear and public his feeling of having being used, misled, and lied to concerning the Prime Minister's commitment to fight corruption. Upon his resignation he was immediately portrayed by González's partisans as an ambitious, unreliable, naive fellow-traveller, unable to put together a course of action and to understand party politics.

By the fall of 1993, it appeared that González was once again in control of the situation, and the problem of corruption was solved without having to be dealt with. He was back to the best of all possible worlds: a clean image with no catharsis. And yet . . . and yet the appearances of control and political stability were misleading, as events were to prove, much to the disappointment of both González and Pujol. The ghosts of political and politically related scandals of corruption did not go away. They became more and more visible; so much so that the two leaders were forced into a reactive and defensive strategy. In the end, Pujol lost his majority in the Catalan Parliament in 1995, and González was forced to call for national elections on March 3, 1996, a contest in which the PSOE was defeated by the PP.

The political scandals that destroyed confidence in the government were of two kinds: corruption (with money, or money-and-politics) and criminal violence. At the beginning, the problem was a pervasive atmosphere of public (and private) corruption. In a sense, this was a worldwide phenomenon that prevailed in several countries. What happened was a combination of economic and political circumstances that provided politicians and public servants with greater opportunities for improper and illegal gains, at a time when higher standards of ethical conduct in public life were applied to them.

On the one hand, the globalization of the economy in the 1980s facilitated huge gains in fast and hard-to-trace financial deals. On the other, higher standards were applied to the political and business elites, partly as an indirect result of the demise of the totalitarian and authoritarian regimes. For one thing, the resurgence of liberal democracies everywhere in the world brought with it the rediscovery of the role of citizens and public opinion; judges and journalists thus gained a golden opportunity to redefine their roles as guarantors of the rule of law and public watchdogs. Also, the proper functioning of the world market required more exacting ethical standards, and public regulatory agencies to oversee them, in order to make economic life on a global scale more predictable.

The new higher standards caught the previous generation of old political hands off guard; party politicians and civil servants (and businessmen) were used to the free-wheeling ways of the past. The Spanish case is not unique but is just one among many—Italian, French, German, Japanese, and other recent political-financial scandals (della Porta, Mény 1995). Its specific interest lies in its peculiar mix, compounded of irony, a particularly elaborate condensation of corrupt practices, and a surprise effect.

The irony is that the Spanish Socialists came to power with the slogan "one hundred years of honesty" and preached incessant sermons on political ethics. They were certainly not a party of professionals known for their survival tricks, for compiling embarrassing dossiers with which to silence their opponents, or using their municipal power to fill the war chest of the party (as some people thought their French and maybe their Italian counterparts did). They rather looked like a party of young idealists eager to change the world and to clean those practices out of it.

As latecomers both to the world of advanced capitalism and to parliamentary democracy, the Socialists got into an accelerated course of illegal or improper deals, both many and diverse. But their subsequent discovery and transformation into public scandals were also remarkably speedy. Thus, in a very short period of time, Spain lived, in a condensed form, through experiences that other democracies dealt with over longer periods—a time lag that may have given those democracies more time either to perfect their institutions or to get used to corrupt practices.

As neither the Spanish institutions nor the public were prepared to deal with these facts, they were slow in reacting to them. This gave an initial advantage to the transgressors and left them, for a time, with a feeling of impunity. But this very surprise effect could be construed as a hopeful indication that the public did not see the institutions as corrupt, nor had (yet) reached that particular state of so-called maturity (that people in older democracies may have developed) that brings an understanding and lax disposition regarding the corruption of their public figures.

The various political scandals had something in common. They all involved public officials breaking the law of the land which they were sworn to upheld. Their wrongdoings ranged from assassinations (in the form of state counterterrorist activities) to spying on private citizens, to private embezzlement of public funds or illegal financing of political parties; and they usually implied subsequent coverups, lying to the public, and putting obstacles in the course of justice.

Our story may well start in the very first year of Socialist rule. That year, 1983, began with the RUMASA affair. The government decided early in the year to take over the company's holdings to avoid its bankruptcy. The expropriation proceedings were dubious in the first place, and were followed by an even more dubious reprivatization of the many companies that had been part of the holdings: a matter on which there never was a parliamentary inquiry (some of the many judiciary proceedings are still pending). But almost nobody paid much attention to the matter. The financial community thought of the original owner as an outsider and, eager to make peace with the new political masters, bowed to the *fait accompli*. Chalked up as a piece of extravaganza in the political landscape of the early 1980s, the RUMASA incident seemed soon forgotten. At the very same time, a hidden drama of much greater consequences was just unfolding. Somewhere at the top echelons a strategic decision was taken in 1983 to start counterterrorist activities in French territory; these were later known as the tactics of GAL (Grupos Antiterroristas de Liberación), and they continued through 1987.

Before proceeding with the discussion of the GAL affair and the other scandals—the use of reserved funds, the Roldán affair, other incidents of private enrichment out of public funds, and the FILESA affair—I want to mention my sources. In reporting the facts, I have made use mostly (but not exclusively) of *autos de instrucción* (the formal document of indictment by a judge before trial) and also of the actual sentences by the higher courts. These sentences have been delivered at a later stage (see Chapter 6).

The GAL affair may be read as an extraordinary story of lawbreaking. But it should also be understood as a personal and political tragedy for many of those who became involved in it. In a sense their drama was part and parcel of the larger Basque drama. Like Carl Jung's "shadow" accompanying the human soul,[4] this drama has followed the Spanish democracy from the beginning, and its ramifications have loomed large in Spain's fortunes. And no matter how hard the Spanish politicians and the Spanish public have tried to marginalize it or to forget about it, its tragic consequences have caught up with them again and again—most notably in the form of the military coup in 1981, and of the GAL and its activities a few years later.

After the democratic transition, the ETA (Euskadi Ta Askartasuna; the Basque separatist organization) stepped up its terrorist activities. The number of assassinations went as high as 80 people (mostly military and civil guards) a year in 1978–1980. Other than political considerations, one of the reasons why prosecution of these activities proved unsuccessful was the French sanctuary. France was a safe haven for the terrorists, since the French administration apparently refused to collaborate with the Spanish police to control the terrorists living in French territory (an attitude that changed after Jacques Chirac became Prime Minister in 1986). In view of these circumstances, the GAL came into existence (in 1983) for the purpose of conducting counterterrorist activities in France. Between 1983 and 1986 this organization murdered 26 people on the grounds that they were, or were believed to be, connected with ETA.

During those years, neither the politicians nor the media showed great interest in investigating these deaths or finding out by whose orders they were perpetrated.[5] But as a result of judicial inquiries in France, the Audiencia Nacional (the Spanish court in charge of terrorist crimes) took the case in 1988 and imprisoned two Spanish police officers, José Amedo and Michel Domínguez, presumably involved in the activities of GAL. Three years later, both policemen were tried, found guilty of conspiracy to commit murder and falsification of public documents, and sentenced to more than one hundred years in prison. The police officers remained silent about their superiors' involvement, and Judge Baltasar Garzón could not prove the complicity of higher state officials in the GAL operations. The suspicion that the crimes committed by GAL mercenaries were paid for with state funds led him to demand that the Ministry of Interior provide information on the use of the reserved funds. Minister José Barrionuevo refused to do so, alleging the secrecy of these funds.

The condemned policemen did obtain government support. According to their subsequent testimony, Rafael Vera, once director of State Security and by this time secretary of state in the Ministry of Interior, promised them a government pardon through his assistant, Juan de

Justo. Amedo also declared that he received a similar message a few years later, in April 1993, when, accompanied by Julián Sancristóbal (former provincial governor of Vizcaya and later Vera's replacement as director of State Security), he met Attorney General Eligio Hernández.[6] In addition to the promise of a pardon, Amedo and Domínguez got financial support from the Ministry of Interior. As the *auto de instrucción* of Judge Garzón stated later,[7] starting in 1988, they received monthly payments of between 450,000 and 600,000 pesetas. In 1989 they received 200 million pesetas; the sum was taken to Switzerland and deposited in a Swiss bank by Juan de Justo and two officials of the Ministry of Interior. The money came from the reserved funds of that ministry.

As the promise of a pardon failed to materialize, Amedo and Domínguez began to insinuate in public declarations that high state officials had participated in the GAL activities. Then, at the beginning of 1994, Juan Alberto Belloch became Minister of Justice and Interior. He opposed the pardon and stopped the monthly payments.

In the summer of 1994, Baltasar Garzón left his parliamentary seat in protest against González's lukewarm approach to the fight against corruption, and returned to his position as judge of the Audiencia Nacional. He then found that the dossier of the kidnapping of Segundo Marey, the first criminal activity of the GAL (back in 1983), had been reopened (thanks to the initiative of a group of civic-minded lawyers, academics, and other citizens). Garzón decided to press the case, and called for Amedo and Domínguez to testify. By this time they were ready to talk. In their testimony they implicated high officials of the Ministry of Interior, including Julián Sancristóbal (former director of State Security and former provincial governor of Vizcaya); the former chief of police in charge of coordinating antiterrorist activities, Francisco Álvarez; another highly placed police officer, Miguel Planchuelo; and the former secretary general of the PSOE in Vizcaya, Ricardo García Damborenea; as well as former Secretary of State Rafael Vera. By the end of December 1994, the judge ordered preventive detention against Sancristóbal, Álvarez, Planchuelo, and some other policy officials, and put them in prison; a few months later he also sent García Damborenea and Vera to jail.

Though the indicted officials initially denied all charges, in the end all of them, except only for Vera, changed their testimony and incriminated themselves. By July 1995, according to the *auto de instrucción* of Judge Baltasar Garzón, mostly confirmed by a later *auto* by Judge Eduardo Móner (who took the case up to the Supreme Court[8]), the picture looked as follows.

The GAL activities resulted from top strategic decisions to initiate actions against the ETA in France. They involved the top officials of the Socialist party and the Ministry of Interior, up to Secretary of State Vera and Minister of the Interior Barrionuevo (according to several testimonies), and possibly up as high as the head of the government, Felipe González (according to one direct testimony). A document of the secret services (CESID, or Centro Superior de Información para la Defensa [Higher Center of Information for Defense]) outlined the strategy in the summer of 1983. (The document was leaked to the press;[9] the judge required it officially, in order to be able to use it as a presumptive proof. The government refused to give it to the judge; and a court for jurisdictional conflicts, headed by the president of the Council of the Judiciary Power, sided with the government.) Implementing that strategy required a complicated and extensive network of covert operations and use of public (reserved) funds for a period of several years.

Garzón thought the recent testimonies of Sancristóbal, Álvarez, Amedo, Domínguez, de Justo, Planchuelo, and García Damborenea were plausible. They were in a position to know; their testimonies were consistent with each other; they incriminated themselves. Despite denials by Vera and Barrionuevo, the judge found no facts that persuasively contradicted the testimony of Sancristóbal, Álvarez, and the others. Consequently, Judge Garzón concluded that he had enough evidence to incriminate Barrionuevo and González (as well as Vice-president Narcís Serra, as supervisor of the secret services, and the former secretary general of PSOE in Guipúzcoa, "Txiqui" Benegas). Since these people were top state officials and members of Parliament who enjoy certain legal privileges, Garzón had to leave the case and to transfer the proceedings to the Supreme Court (Tribunal Supremo). Then it was up to the Tribunal Supremo to demand from Parliament the special permission (*suplicatorio*) to examine Barrionuevo, González, Serra, and Benegas, whether as witnesses or as accused. The Tribunal Supremo did ask for the *suplicatorio* of Barrionuevo, and Parliament conceded it in November 1995, with 122 votes against it, presumably of Socialist deputies (the total number of Socialist deputies was 159). The majority in the PSOE reacted by organizing a gala in honor of Barrionuevo, and the party put him in its lists for the next national elections (though some Socialists were dismayed by this show of support).

The court proceedings are still continuing. In this chapter I intend to follow the events from the time they were brought to the attention of the public to the time they led to the Socialists' defeat in the 1996 elections. (I leave for Chapter 6 the unfolding of those proceedings.) This is why my focus is on the very first steps of the GAL, the kidnapping of Segundo Marey: this case just ended on July 29, 1998, when the Supreme Court condemned the former minister and his secretary of state to ten years in jail. But we must keep in mind the whole picture, which probably includes 26 assassinations. By 1995, another eight *sumarios* (proceedings) had been opened, all of them concerning actual killings—for instance, José Antonio Lasa and José Ignacio Zabala, who had been presumably kidnapped in France, brought to Spain, and killed.

During all this time, the Socialist government (with its party's support) kept denying any responsibility in the GAL activities. Its responses varied, but we may distinguish four general lines: (1) that it was innocent; (2) that the people involved in disclosing the facts were guilty of various charges; (3) that it was hypocritical to pretend to be scandalized by the GAL; and (4) that whether or not the government was innocent of wrongdoing earlier, it was now engaged in uncovering the facts and should be judged exclusively by its present activities. Clearly, it did not matter that these allegations contradicted each other.

The first and foremost response of the government was one of outright denial of its involvement, as it tried to contain the scope of the affair while making occasional avowals of poor judgment. Only two police officers, José Amedo and Michel Domínguez, were involved, and they were made to pay for it. Though the Ministry of Interior paid them salaries while in jail, this was because of a misguided *esprit de corps* and poor judgment. If Sancristóbal, Álvarez, and Planchuelo (three of the top officials in the antiterrorist strategy), along with García Damborenea, have confessed to their participation in the kidnapping of Segundo Marey, that was regrettable, but it implicated them only as individuals.

The second line of response was that of questioning the motives and

the intentions of people and institutions involved in the task of determining the facts. The public was encouraged to suspect the motivations
of the witnesses who provided testimony and incriminated themselves
(Amedo and Domínguez first, and all the rest later, particularly García
Damborenea), and to question the motives of the judges who searched
for the facts (notably Garzón, and later Gómez de Liaño): they tried to
take revenge against González for a variety of reasons. García Damborenea, for example, had good reasons as an ambitious politician who
was expelled from his party position and later from the party; Garzón
wanted to be famous and was disappointed by not having been made
minister in González's government. At a second remove, the individuals
who credited and repeated these allegations were also suspect, particularly the media people and members of the opposition parties. The
Socialists were particularly incensed by the position of Izquierda Unida
and its leader Julio Anguita, whose zeal in the prosecution of GAL
activities made it impossible for the defenders of the government to
portray the case as an ideological struggle of left and right.

The third line of argument emphasized that there was much tacit
public support for activities of this kind. Besides, it was insinuated that
those activities dated back to previous democratic governments (a point
that called forth some strong denials). Moreover, the use of covert
(illegal) operations was the proper way to deal with terrorists in any
civilized country (this proposition was bolstered by examples, such as
the way the French authorities dealt with the OAS, the German authorities with the Baader-Meinhoff band, and the United Kingdom
authorities with some Irish terrorists in Gibraltar).

The inconsistency of these arguments was not important. One assumption was that no state policy on the matter existed; another simul-
taneous assumption was that state policy (which, by implication, did
exist) should be given tacit support. Taken separately, they might appear
more or less founded; taken together, the point was to confuse the issue
utterly.

Finally, the fourth line of response stressed the efforts undertaken by
the government to clarify the facts once they were brought to light by
the press and once the judges had reached a certain point in their
investigations. Here we may remember that at the beginning of 1995,
González said that he had known about the GAL activities through the
press; the implication was that as he had no knowledge of that problem

before then, he could not have done anything about it. This response—
of doing the right thing now rather than dwelling on past misdeeds—
was the one apparently followed by the Minister of Justice and Interior
since 1994, Juan Alberto Belloch. He refused to keep paying the salaries
of police officers Amedo and Domínguez while they were in prison (and
did not agree to grant them a pardon), and he replaced a notoriously
partisan Attorney General, Eligio Hernández, by a more professional,
even-handed one, Carlos Granados (who, in contrast to his predecessor,
did not support the idea of pardon for Amedo and Domínguez).

The GAL affair revealed the lax rules of the Ministry of Interior in
the use of the reserved funds. It turned out that the funds had been
routinely used for a variety of illegal or improper activities, including
the payment of additional salaries to top officials in the ministry (Sancristóbal admitted he received an extra salary while he was governor of
Vizcaya, an amount which was increased when he was designated director of State Security in 1986; Roldán too hinted in a letter to González,
leaked to the press, that he and some other high officials of the Ministry
of Interior got monthly compensations of ten million pesetas). Some of
the money went to purchase jewelry and personal gifts that former
Minister José Luis Corcuera offered to the wives of his closest subordinates.[10]

These funds found their way into the pocket of one of the most
conspicuous officials of the ministry: Luis Roldán, the first civilian to
head the Civil Guard since the creation of this institution in the middle
of the nineteenth century. He was director from 1987 to 1993 (at one
time González seriously considered him for Minister of the Interior).
The Civil Guard was in charge of fighting terrorism and was also the
prime target of terrorist attacks (both the guards and their families,
including their children).

Toward the end of 1993, the press began to interest itself about
Roldán's rapid enrichment since he became director of the Civil Guard.
Minister José Luis Corcuera declared that he had no doubts about the
sources of Roldán's wealth. But the official's credibility decreased when
the press found out that he pretended to have a university degree he
had not earned.[11] All the parties represented in Parliament, except
PSOE, demanded a parliamentary commission to investigate the rumors; this was finally set up at the beginning of 1994. In the course of
the investigation, it was discovered that Roldán had taken some 5 bil-

lion pesetas abroad, to be put in his personal accounts. In due time, Judge Ana Ferrer traced the origins of most of these funds to a variety of sources: bonuses out of the reserved funds; illegal commissions for public works, mainly for the construction of the barracks of the Civil Guard; payments by businessmen threatened by ETA in exchange for protection; tax fraud in the amount of Pta 1 billion.[12] The case fascinated public opinion, particularly when Roldán fled from Spain and disappeared before the parliamentary committee could conclude its investigation. The new Minister of the Interior (after José Luis Corcuera), Antoni Asunción, resigned. Contradictory reports on Roldán's whereabouts circulated for ten months. Finally, in February 1995, he was arrested in Laos, after an exciting police operation; back in Spain, he has been prosecuted on several charges and sentenced to jail.

The government and the Socialist party tried to isolate the Roldán case and present it as an individual episode. The man had simply taken advantage of their good faith, and they were not prepared to deal with such people. Roldán was a villain who had deceived his superiors. The only problem with this portrayal was that new cases kept turning up, and old cases were also being resurrected. They did not look like isolated episodes. The pattern looked, rather, like an epidemic of corruption.

There was the case of Juan Guerra, brother of Alfonso Guerra, Vice-president since 1982, who was forced to resign in 1991 precisely because of the embarrassment produced by his brother's involvement in dubious real estate dealings and alleged misuse of political influences.[13] Corrupt practices of this sort came up everywhere, south or north. The Manuel Ollero case, in Andalusia, involved illegal commissions received by the director of public works of the Socialist regional government. In Navarre, even more grave accusations implicated PSOE's Gabriel Urralburu, president of the regional government.[14] The press also brought to the fore many instances of misuses of power resulting in huge increases in personal wealth of the officeholders, mostly (though not always) Socialists. As a final note and a picturesque illustration of someone taking advantage of her office for private enrichment and to indulge personal fantasies, let us take the case of Carmen Salanueva. This former director of the *Boletín Oficial del Estado* (the bulletin of official texts of laws and government decrees) was indicted (and later sentenced) for overcharging the government for newsprint and pocketing the difference. Caught in another scheme, she was also sentenced to four years in prison for impersonating none less than the Queen of Spain (and also the Prime Minister's wife) in a swindle to acquire paintings and works of art for her private collection.

Such an epidemic of crimes of embezzlement for private gain is clearly regrettable, and it says something about the moral character of the people who failed in the top responsibilities they had held in the Socialist party or the government or both. It says something too about the poor judgment of the leaders who selected them in the first place, and should have monitored their performance afterwards. The accumulation of misdemeanors suggests a climate of neglect regarding devious and dubious behavior. But this is not the end of it. Until now, we have considered individual misbehavior; we must still consider what the Socialist party itself did in the course of financing its own activities.

Let us set aside possible improprieties in the first years of the transition; such improprieties were most likely shared by all the parties, one way or another. The point is that once the PSOE took power, it enacted two laws (*Ley Orgánica del Régimen Electoral*, in 1985; and *Ley de Financiación de Partidos Políticos*, in 1987), in order to regulate the financing of the political parties. Immediately afterwards, the PSOE went heavily into debt, chiefly because of its participation in the pro-NATO referendum of 1986: the PSOE's outstanding debt went from Pta 3.5 billion in 1985 to Pta 6.5 billion in 1986, and then up to Pta 11 billion in 1991. This was more than the party could afford to finance on the basis of the state's contribution (not to speak of the meager contribution of its affiliates). Breaking its own laws, the party set up a network of illegal financing in imitation of the French Socialist party (as illustrated in the Urba affair: Díaz Herrera and Durán 1997, 227ff.). They established intermediary societies which, under cover of producing technical reports to business companies, channeled illegal funds to the party.

In the spring of 1991, the former bookkeeper of three consulting firms, FILESA, MALESA, and Time Export, revealed some practices that involved the PSOE in a plot of illegal financing of its own activities. After a three-year instruction, Judge Marino Barbero (who persistently complained about harassments and obstructions of justice by members of the PSOE) established the existence of a financial plot centered on these three companies, which had been in operation between 1986–87 and 1991. Between 1989 and 1991, some big banks and big companies—private, public, and multinational—had paid to FILESA and the other shadow companies Pta 1 billion in exchange for nonexisting studies or reports (or reports that were Xerox copies of pieces of legislation). Or was it in exchange for favors? In turn, FILESA and the other companies paid for services of marketing and advertising related to political campaigns which were provided to the PSOE by its usual suppliers. As a result of this investigation, at least two Socialist members of Parliament, Carlos Navarro and José María Sala, stood trial. Marino Barbero left the case before its conclusion, apparently disheartened by the vicious attacks of some Socialist leaders (the president of the regional government of Extremadura, Juan Carlos Rodríguez Ibarra, likened his activities to those of ETA) and the poor protection he got from the Council of Judiciary Power.[15] In the end, once again, the Supreme Court sentenced both politicians to time in prison.

The accumulation of scandals finally led the Catalan CiU (the PSOE's coalition partner) to withdraw its support from the minority government of González in the fall of 1995. This decision was taken after the press revealed that the military secret services (CESID) habitually spied on private and public citizens, including the King and the King's friends. As a consequence, Minister of Defense Julián García Vargas and Vice-president Narcís Serra resigned.

Testing the Rule of Law

The key difference between a civil society kind of polity, such as a liberal democracy, and an authoritarian regime is this: in a civil society, the public authority is subject to the law and is accountable (or responsible) for its actions (this includes its *illegal* actions) before its fellow citizens. But the principle of political accountability remains an empty word unless there are institutions that guarantee its application, stand up to the abuses of the public authority, and keep it within the bounds of the law. In today's Spain, these institutions have been tested by the political scandals; some of them have been found lacking, while others have risen to the occasion.

To begin with, the executive did little to police itself. Thus the government kept Eligio Hernández as Attorney General, a docile instrument to its wishes, during the two critical years of 1991–1993, just until two weeks before the Supreme Court ruled that his appointment to the job had been illegal in the first place. The only police investigation into the GAL affair (according to the testimony of police officer Jesús Martínez Torres before Judge Garzón on November 18, 1988) took place in 1986, and consisted of putting together a dossier of press clippings.[16] Furthermore, the Tribunal de Cuentas, an administrative agency of financial control, at first complied with the wishes of the government and exonerated the Socialist party of any responsibility in the FILESA affair, moving only later to a more even-handed position.

The Socialist party showed little disposition to investigate how its officials had handled the party's finances. In general, the Socialists' policy was to veto, whenever possible, any investigation or parliamentary committee on the matter. Their veto worked as long as they had a majority, that is, until 1993. Afterwards, they had to appeal for support to the CiU and PNV (Partido Nacionalista Vasco), which they got occasionally (but not in the case of Roldán, and a few others).

But the Socialists were not alone in showing such reluctance. The PNV and CiU had their own problems (usually in connection with party financing) which they tried to keep out of the public eye; and they used their political clout in their regional parliaments to do so. The People's Party also had a few localized affairs of its own, but having understood the importance of corruption in the public perception, moved swiftly to impose sanctions on the latest scandals that might affect its image.

In sum, the Socialist party and, to some extent, the political class as a whole tended to shun controls for a long period of time. However, between 1993 and 1996, the Parliament set up more research and study commissions than in any parliamentary period before then, even though these bodies seldom brought new evidence and never pushed so far as to provoke a single political resignation or dismissal. The Parliament also passed three "anticorruption" laws in the spring of 1995: the law of state contracts, the law of reserved funds (which established a parliamentary commission to control the use of these funds), and the law of incompatibilities (which called for fuller disclosure of the financial activities of high officials and members of Parliament).[17] Moreover, the new criminal code of November 1995 added or reinforced criminal sanctions for a variety of corrupt practices by public officials (including insider trading).

Though the judiciary institutions used to be careful and respectful vis-à-vis the executive, particularly during the ten years when the Socialists ruled with little opposition, afterwards they became more assertive. In an important ruling (TC 90/1985 of July 22), for example, the Constitutional Court stated that there were limits to a discretionary decision of Congress concerning whether or not a deputy could be brought to trial before a tribunal: a parliamentary decision that the Court could revoke if necessary.[18] Later on, the Court did rule that some articles of the *Ley de Protección de la Seguridad Ciudadana* (Law for Internal Security or "Corcuera's law," named for the Minister of Interior who promoted it) was unconstitutional, and obliged the government to remove the provisions that granted the police the right to enter the legal domicile of suspected delinquents without a judge's warrant.

In its original conception, the composition of the Council of Judiciary Power was designed to reflect the main currents of opinion both in the judiciary and in Parliament. After the Socialists' victory, the government decided to take full control of the Council and have Parliament appoint all its members. The Constitutional Court, consulted about the matter, did not rule out the measure as unconstitutional, but did advise against it. Since 1993, as the composition of Parliament changed, so did the Council, which became a more balanced body. Even so, the president of the Council managed to put together a court for jurisdictional conflicts that departed from the legal doctrine of the Supreme Court when it blocked Garzón's search for some documents which he believed would be evidence for a government connection with the GAL. (These documents had appeared in the press, but they had to be officially submitted to be allowed as a proof in a trial.)[19]

In the last analysis, judiciary controls were effective because individual judges and prosecutors dared to take their jobs seriously, to stick to their inquiries, and to stay firm despite the initial reluctance of some state officials to cooperate and even despite being harassed. Criticism of Baltasar Garzón and Javier Gómez de Liaño was unusually harsh. Moreover, the state-controlled public television allowed Julián Sancristóbal, who had been sentenced to a prison term by Garzón, to launch a personal attack against the judge (in prime time, from jail itself). He accused the judge of acting out of personal and political motives, and of participating in a conspiracy against the present government. Sancristóbal promised to produce proof for his assertions. This never materialized. Indeed, quite to the contrary, some weeks later he changed his testimony and incriminated himself in the GAL affair.

When he became Minister of Justice and Interior, Juan Alberto Belloch steered a course which avoided an open confrontation with individual judges; thereupon, the new Attorney General and the state attorneys played by the rules. The judges were encouraged by the support they generally got from the legal profession (and a variety of legal professional associations) and from the general public. But crucial support for their task came from outside sources, namely, from the international bodies. For the alterations in the international climate we may go back as far as the Lockheed scandal in the 1970s, concerning corrupt practices of American businessmen dealing with foreign officials; changes were also fostered by the general climate of international competition, the spread of democracy, and the fight against drug traffic in the 1980s. Closer to home, the Swiss authorities implemented a series of specific measures in the early 1990s that required banks to give the names of the holders of formerly secret bank accounts, and this was followed by bank regulations that facilitated control of criminal activities of foreign depositors (or domestic fiduciaries) (Robert 1996). Swiss judges seemed eager to make sure that Switzerland and its banking system were open to judiciary investigation of delinquents all over the world—and these measures yielded results in the 1990s for France, Italy, and Spain.[20]

The other basic institutional control had been that exercised by the media, and particularly by the press. But we had to wait until the late 1980s to see coverage of the Juan Guerra affair and a brief mention of the GAL affair. It was not until the early 1990s that investigative reporting escalated to expose most of the corruption stories: the FILESA affair (in 1991 by *El Periódico* of Barcelona and *El Mundo*); the Rubio affair (in 1992 by *El Mundo*); the Roldán affair (in 1994 by *Diario 16*); the GAL affair (in its final stage, in 1994 by *El Mundo*), and all the rest.

Why these matters were kept for so long out of the public eye is an interesting question. Part of the answer lies in the cozy relationship established between the journalists and the politicians back in the transition period. All the citizens were presumably engaged in the common task of building a liberal democracy—as yet a frail structure, to be strengthened by a generally benevolent journalistic treatment of politicians. After the Socialists won in 1982, 1986, and 1989 with majorities in Parliament, the press adjusted to the realities of power to some extent. The most read newspaper nationwide, *El País*, had probably bet on the new government from the very beginning, and so it maintained an editorial line supportive of González and of the main lines of his policies, though it did have occasional reservations about the party or specific issues. The situation became more complicated in the fall of 1989, with the appearance of the daily *El Mundo*, which decided the quick road to success was to adopt a critical attitude toward the government. Its criticism was based less on ideological or party-political considerations than on the exposure of corrupted practices and illegalities. At the same time, a new wave of "muckraking" journalism was beginning to develop. In the late 1980s it found its opportunities in the competition between the established media, and also in the first signs of trouble within the Socialist party (after the general strike of 1988).[21]

More specifically, why was the matter of the GAL (or state counterterrorist activities in general) not fully scrutinized by the press (with some remarkable exceptions: see Miralles and Arqués 1989)? True, there was stonewalling by the government, but also, there was some sort of tacit understanding about the "realities of dirty wars." This shared attitude resulted in the assurance of mutual discretion between politicians and journalists.

What contributed to it was a confluence of sentiments: moral indignation against ETA terrorists, who had already killed about three hundred people by 1982; a sense of frustration in the face of France's refusal to control its borders; and an understanding of the political class's reluctance to propose the death penalty or life imprisonment for terrorists guilty of assassinations (possibly assuming that these punishments would be considered either "cruel and unusual" or unconstitutional or both). At any rate the media was unwilling to discuss (and therefore appeared to sanction) a *de facto* policy of state counterterrorism.[22]

A psychological aspect may also have contributed to the conspiracy of silence. Many of these journalists, with their radical pasts and in sympathy with the government's predicament, were people of progressive minds and hearts. Their political sentiments perhaps resonated to Jean Paul Sartre's *Les mains sales*—something of a eulogy for immoral (not to say illegal) practices done for a so-called higher political end. The opportunity to shake the dirty hands of politicians—men who carried the burden of the responsibility for the illegal killings of terrorists—may have been part of the excitement of getting close to the realities of political life and of sharing vicariously in them. This is how literati could turn into instant statesmen for one day.

But leaving these dubious but powerful emotions aside, a noticeable cognitive misperception was at work here. The media's sympathetic position reflects a distorted understanding of Max Weber's distinction between the ethics of ultimate ends or principled convictions, and the ethics of responsibility (Weber 1958 [1919]). The ethics of responsibility is characteristic of a "vocational" or professional politician, with two important provisos. First, the true or authentic politician (that is, one who is faithful to his calling) is expected to try his best to reconcile both sets of ethical aims, so that dismissing ethical principles cannot be viewed as an accomplishment but as a failure. Weber does not profess a trivial glorification of *raison d'état* over private morality. And second, to the very extent that the professional politician subscribes to the ethics of responsibility, the ultimate test of his professional calling is, precisely, to accept responsibility for the consequences of his acts. But this solemn and lugubrious talk about the politicians' need "to defend the state in the sewers"[23] (that is, by means impossible to disclose in public because they included illegal activities), and along with it the appeal to a superior ethics of responsibility, were just posturing—because no one was ever willing to accept any responsibility for the consequences.

In any event, the situation changed in the late 1980s. The Guerra affair had exploded, and the newspapers (whose circulation had been declining for a while) grabbed this opportunity; it also gave the journalists a taste for aggressive reporting. Soon more and more affairs came to the surface, most notably the Rubio affair (highlighted by *El Mundo*) and the Roldán affair (by *Diario 16*). Finally, in the last months of 1994, the GAL affair bounced back with a vengeance. It became not just one among the many, but the most dramatic one. Suddenly (and rather mysteriously, in "deep throat" fashion) dossiers and reports started to land on the journalists' desks, and a sort of media competition developed in which *El Mundo* tended to have an edge over its competitors.

The journalistic importance of the GAL affair was considerable. According to a survey carried out by the CIS, by the late 1994 and early 1995 it commanded the attention of the public: 49% ranked it first, in terms of giving more attention to it than to any other news (39% mentioned the BANESTO affair); and 32% took the GAL affair to be the most disquieting news they had heard (next came 19% who said "none"; and 9% who said "corruption in general").[24] During the three years from 1993 to 1995, rarely one day passed without some political scandal commanding the front page of most newspapers. As a result, distrust of government politicians paralleled increasing trust in the press. In fact, the Crown and journalism (radio and press) were the institutions in which the Spanish people claimed to have the most confidence (de Miguel 1995).

The deeper cumulative effect has been to change the rules of the media game. Gone or almost gone are the good old days of mutual discretion between journalists and politicians. In the early 1990s a journalist could still boast about how some highly placed political personage told him that of course "they" (that is, the government) were involved in the dirty war. But by the mid-1990s such loose talk seemed just impossible, and tacit complicity with the dirty war was no longer acceptable. The secrets of the political power were not to be leaked in the intimacy of long talks into the night among journalists and politicians. The risk was that they would find their way into the newspaper and the people's houses the next morning.

Testing the Rules of the Public Space

Laws and rules become mere rhetorical statements without institutional sanctions, and institutional sanctions will not be applied in any consistent and predictable way unless there is a steady public sentiment behind them. Knowing this, both sides in the ongoing argument over the political scandals sought to persuade the public with utmost zeal. They fought for the heart of public opinion: the soul of the country. The Socialist government ultimately lost the fight, by a narrow margin, as proved by its defeat in the elections of March 1996.

The writing had been on the wall, though the text was not as clear as most had thought. For quite a while the opinion polls had been forecasting the PSOE's defeat. In a poll of May 1, 1994, the public perceived the corruption of the current government to be much higher (7.8 on a scale of 0 to 10) than the corruption of the democratic governments of UCD (4.5), higher even than the corruption of the Francoist governments of the past (5.5).[25] In a CIS survey (carried out in May 7–9),[26] 63% of the public considered that González carried some responsibility for the scandals of political corruption; and also by then, 70% of the public had little or no trust in González.[27] By November 1994, 66% disbelieved González when he said that he had not enriched himself, and 72% did not believe him when he said that he had done no favors for his friends.[28]

By January 1995, 69% of the public stated its belief that the government had been involved in the GAL, and 44% thought that González had known and authorized GAL activities. Concurrently, 65% said they rejected these activities, while 22% were in favor of them.[29] After a TV interview with González on this question (on January 9, 1995), 52% thought that González had lied when he said that the government was not responsible for GAL activities, and only 27% believed his assurance that he had never authorized or tolerated them.[30] By mid-July 1995, 65% of the Spaniards stated their belief that González had been *au courant* concerning GAL activities.[31]

The public's growing certainty that González both knew about and was responsible for the activities of the GAL did not result from any direct testimony to that effect. Rather, the hypothesis gained plausibility in view of the convergent testimonies of those indicted by Judge Garzón; and in view of González's own actions in the face of the situation.

It was already a serious charge to hold against a Prime Minister that he presided over irregular party financing and illegal behavior by subordinates he should not have appointed in the first place, and having appointed them, that he should have monitored them more carefully. But the most serious charge laid against González was his failure to react appropriately and forcefully once the affair became known, and the scandal developed. Indeed, González did not immediately launch an internal investigation; nor did he appear to support the judiciary process wholeheartedly. To the contrary, he seemed to create a climate of suspicion and confusion about the motivations of the press and of the judges involved in bringing the affair into the open. Thus he failed to measure up to his role of political and civic educator of the country and do what had to be done: to explain the problems honestly and candidly; to take responsibility for his actions; to place the country first and his electoral fortunes second. He did the opposite, and to the Spanish public this was a sign of moral weakness.

It was also disquieting to see how the Socialist party, following its leader's cue, was nervously overreacting to the scandals. The party allowed itself to be led by its tribal instincts in sorting out friends and enemies, supporting its party leaders, attacking the judges and journalists, and attributing their motivations to its political rivals.

By the end of this period, the public came close to the conclusion that the government should answer for GAL activities and for general misuse of its powers; and this was, indeed, important. But in observing the evolution of the public sentiment in Spain during these years, and in testing the terms of the public debate, the *most* important thing to note is the learning process involved in reaching this conclusion. This would mean that the public had acquired, at least to some extent, a trained capacity for public debate, to be applied later to new issues and new circumstances.

The debate was messy. Arguments, replies, and counterreplies were exchanged in great disorder. Contradictory allegations, passionate indictments, all sorts of accusations got mixed up. It is hard to see how *any* learning could take place in these circumstances. However, there is a thread to follow in the confusion: learning to recognize the crucial condition for a reasoned appraisal of the central issue under consideration, namely, the political accountability of the public authority.

In general terms, three conditions have to be met before the political accountability of the public authority can be properly debated. First, the issue has to be placed in its proper setting, at center stage. Second, the visibility of the issue has to be sharpened against all sorts of diversionary tactics. Third, the public has to gather its moral and emotional resources for the civic courage it takes to dare to take the public authority to account. This applies to the inquiry into the GAL affair and other scandals, the original strategy of denial and indirection by the authorities, and the ensuing confusion of the debate. It seems likely that the Spanish public, or at least a majority, gradually intuited these conditions, and developed the frame of mind needed to draw the logical conclusions and to put them in practice—as manifest both in a moral assessment of the situation and in the electoral shift.[32]

The Proper Setting

An inquiry into the political responsibility of a public authority may be treated as a dramatic performance that should command the public's attention. But the public may be, and in the Spanish case has been, systematically confused and distracted, beginning with the attempt to rewrite the script—to change the scene in which the public authority renders an account for its activities into a scene of a tribal confrontation in which friends and enemies of the public authority fight against each other.

In the scene of "the public authority renders an account of its acts" the spotlight is on the officialdom standing in front of the concerned citizenry. The public authority's acts are to be weighed and judged. The audience is invited to examine the evidence, to consider principles and rules, and to pass judgment.

Not so in the scene of "tribal confrontation between friends and enemies of the public authority." The focus changes. The lights are not concentrated on one spot but scattered throughout the stage. Two sets of actors confront each other. The audience is invited to leave its seats and join one of the two groups that confront each other, while the public authority is right in the middle of one of them, surrounded and protected by its followers.

Meanwhile the script has been rewritten, and the issue of political responsibility has practically disappeared. People do not debate the public authority's responsibility for specific acts, but rather its character, tribal identity, or charisma. Of course, since the plot has unraveled, the public authority cannot be accused with any degree of precision and thus manages to avoid sanctions.

The crucial move is to get the public audience divided along tribal lines. To accomplish this, the public authority and its friends have to simplify the issues and frame the debate in terms of a confrontation between "the good party" and "the bad party"; between the friends of the good state/political regime and the enemies of the good state/political regime; or even simpler, between people of good moral sentiments and people of bad moral sentiments.

When the scandals became public, some government officials and members of the Socialist party tried to follow this strategy by systematically questioning the motives of the judges and journalists involved in exposing the facts of, and prosecuting the crimes presumably connected with, these misuses of power. The question of specific political responsibility for specific acts had to be restated as (a) a problem of partisan politics between a Socialist party which constituted the legitimate gov-

ernment (by a popular mandate in the elections), and politically motivated groups acting in complicity with the opposition parties, which
intended to rob the Socialists of their legitimate power; or (b) a problem of good democrats confronted by undemocratic forces, which
"conspired in the dark" to reduce the political legitimacy of the regime
(or even to provoke the King's abdication, as a first step toward a change
in political regime); or (c) a problem of good people being harassed and
threatened by individuals and organizations of low or bad moral sentiments (for instance, Garzón was presented as a man moved by the spirit
of revenge; and *El Mundo* as a scandal sheet).

But the extremes can touch in a curious way. At times, the cause of
the Socialists and their defenders was strengthened by their adversaries
when they adopted the mirror-image of the same strategy—that is,
proceeding to stigmatize the Socialists and portray them as power-hun-
gry, blinded by interests and partisan emotions, indifferent to democratic freedoms and democratic principles, even willing to promote an
authoritarian polity and a corrupt regime if they felt that was their last
recourse. Once again, the lack of plausibility of these claims could only
confuse the specific issues that needed specific clarification, and investigation of specific people who could answer for them.

Masks and Diversionary Tactics

Another evasive maneuver in the general strategy is to reduce the visibility of the issue of political responsibility. This effect is produced by
means of various cognitive mechanisms. I will deal with only four of
them here: replacing a limited responsibility by an unlimited one; replacing an individual responsibility by a systemic one; blurring the line
between the office and the office-holder; and blurring the line between
linguistic statements and the extralinguistic referents of these statements.

First, the matter of responsibility can be handled only if we make it
specific and clearly defined. We are responsible only to the extent that
we could have acted otherwise; and only to the extent of the consequences attributable to our acting or not acting (Enzensberger, 1993).
Thus we have to set limits to the actions or failures to act which are to
be accounted for. They have to be determined with some degree of
precision and connected to specific consequences, which, in turn, must

be weighed and measured. Only in this way is it possible to arrive at a careful, fair, and discriminating judgment.

In the Spanish case, to come down to specifics meant the following: definite actions or failures to act that implied breaking the law; likewise, negligence in the oversight of top officials who broke the law through a pattern of illegal activities of massive proportions ("massive" in terms of the number of killings, the amount of money embezzled, the number of people and institutions involved in carrying out these activities, and the number of years those activities lasted, as well as the quality and the number of lies to the public, acts of obstruction of justice, and acts of conspiracy performed to keep the pattern going and to cover up for it).

By engaging in a sort of *fuite en avant*, the government's supporters attempted to shift the issue of responsibility into the realm of the un-manageable. They tried to make believe that the responsibility in question referred not to specific acts but to the whole set of tasks associated with the policy of antiterrorism, or with the general governance of the country, or the general functioning of the political system, thus turning a specific demand into a general attack. The hope was that the people who demanded political responsibility would fall into the trap of the tribal confrontation, discredit themselves, and become subject to easy ridicule. In fact, however, being responsible for everything was too much, and, in practical terms, became the equivalent of being responsi-ble for nothing.

Second, responsibility is an individual thing. Yet the responsible par-ties and their supporters attempted to transform individual responsibil-ity into a systemic one, in which there was no specific responsible agent for any misdeed. Thus there was talk of putting the illegal or improper actions "into a context." References were made to "the usual practices of the Ministry of the Interior" (presumably common under pre-Social-ist governments), and to "the usual practices in civilized societies" (thus diverting attention to other countries); there were claims of "the tacit support of the public" and "the general understanding that the state is to be defended in the underworld with underworld tactics." This was another way of avoiding the issue of the individual responsibility of the individual agents.

It is true that some societies have developed traditions of moral laxity that minimize individual responsibility. In such a climate of opinion people tend to find extenuating circumstances for individual misdeeds in what they call structural conditions or systemic factors, which are held to be ultimately responsible for the individuals' actions. In the Spanish moral climate of the 1960s, when most of the political leaders grew up, these traditions were alive and well both in their Catholic and Marxist variants; it may well be, therefore, that this formative experience of the 1960s influenced their conduct later on. But since the current outlook seemed rather to incline to moral rigor, the attempt to substitute structural for individual responsibility was not successful. The fact is that while the Spanish people have become increasingly tolerant with regard to the morals of private life, they have proved much less tolerant with regard to public morality—as if, in an ironic historical reversal of a centuries-old controversy, they now leaned toward Jansenism (or moral rigor) in public life and Jesuitism (or casuistry verging on moral laxity) in private life.

Another cognitive mechanism used to diffuse the responsibility issue was the attempt to blur the line between the office and the person who occupies the office, as if the responsibility resided not with the office holder but in the office itself. The implication was that those who demanded that the office holder account for his/her acts had no respect for (and indeed were attacking) the office. This is a patrimonialistic view of public office, as if the office belonged to the office holder—a premodern view of the state, which might look plausible to people who actually experienced the client-oriented practices of the office holders.

The linguistic cognitive mechanism was employed as well, to blur the line between what the public authorities said and what their statements referred to. Sometimes the political leaders acted as if merely saying "I (we) assume responsibility" was enough. This suggests an inclination toward prelogical and magical thinking, in which words and gestures are equivalent to reality. But more than that, by accepting responsibility in words only, the public authorities were leaving the matter to the public in a peculiar way. Instead of submitting to a reasoned judgment and, eventually, to proportional political sanctions, they rather seemed to be asking for a new political mandate. Avoiding scrutiny, the leaders were making an appeal to the voters (presumably a silent majority) to give them support in recognition of their charismatic qualities: that support would presumably absolve them from any specific responsibility regarding any specific action.

Emotional and Moral Resources

In pursuing the status of political responsibility, a civil society must deploy moral and emotional resources of inner self-confidence. Only by rallying these resources can the public get to the level of self-assertiveness needed to challenge the public authorities and make them answer for breaches of the law. Accumulating a fund of those inner resources requires habits of (and training in) responsible behavior, as well as the experience of challenging the authorities to account for their acts.

Now, it may be that to reach this stage a society needs to be law-abiding and follow the rules under normal, ordinary conditions. So the question arises, whether people used to everyday cheating in financial dealings, public appointments, tax statements, unemployment subsidies, underground economic activities, and so on, do keep an image of themselves that is consistent with their asking their public authorities to behave properly and within the law. Those everyday experiences would seem to provide a "structure of plausibility," so that abuses of power by the public authorities look normal and are commonly expected.

In Spain, however, although the public authorities and their friends hinted that the general public should not be too strict in demanding the application of high standards, given that the public did not apply these standards to itself, this logic had little effect. Possibly this illustrates the *sui generis* Jansenism in public morals in this country.

In fact the public *did apply* this double standard to the public authorities and to themselves. First, people seemed to think that the public authorities act on the basis of a special relationship of public trust, and that betraying this trust should be considered particularly unacceptable behavior. Second, people seemed to make an implicit distinction between corrupt practices by the elites, which are predatory strategies that should be checked and counteracted, and corrupt practices by ordinary persons, which might be understood as survival tactics in a disorderly and complicated world (such as cheating about unemployment benefits, or engaging in underground economic activities, or simulating disabilities to get public pensions).

At the same time, it may well be that the public would develop a certain propensity to shun responsibility for political events of a larger character, and even for public policies, particularly if this implies facing painful memories or painful decisions. Thus in Spain the conception of the Civil War as a tragedy played a role in preparing the public for the complexities and ambiguities of the transition; and, by definition, this conception implied a reduction, in retrospect, of the responsibility of both sides for the war. Likewise, the diffusion of responsibility was useful in the consensus policy of the first years of democracy (and possibly in Spain's emotionally charged drive to join the European Community as soon and as thoroughly as possible). We will see in the next chapter a few more instances of this inclination to avoid responsibility for public policy, particularly in connection with unemployment. However, there were built-in limits to stop these inclinations from going too far, and the character of Spanish democratic politics was such that competing leaders were compelled to take credit for the consequences of their actions or at least to try to put the blame for them on their rivals.

Finally, we may speculate about an additional source of moral and emotional inhibition: the public has simply become accustomed to being lied to by its political leaders.

There is a fascinating passage in Aristotle's *Rhetoric* (book II), in which he suggests that those who refuse to acknowledge the obvious, and thus lie in the face of people, engage in shameless behavior that implies contempt for the people, "since we feel no shame [for an otherwise shameful behavior] before those whom we hold in contempt." To be lied to is to be humiliated, an experience which only slaves or small children may be forced to get used to. Free people have an understandable reluctance to be treated like slaves since they know that slaves live in fear and that they may be bought (and sold)—these two features are the main roots of the lack of esteem and self-esteem of the slave condition, and they humiliate the slave in the face of an outright lie.

Thus free people, once they know or suspect that their leaders lie to them, have a choice: to submit and be humiliated, or to fight back and keep their self-esteem. If they submit, they can still avoid being humiliated by identifying with their leader. They may develop an admiration for his *sang froid*, his cunning, and his willpower and share his contempt for the ignorant public. Conversely, if they identify themselves as people who have been lied to, they may feel unworthy enough to be insulted with impunity. Later, feeling powerless, they may lose interest and concentrate on other things. Either way, they will develop an attitude of cynicism and distrust of what politicians say. But they can also fight back.

In the Spanish case, the polls suggested that by 1996 many people had reached the conclusion that González was lying to them—or, to put it another way, not telling the truth. Yet instead of paralyzing them, that perception seemed to galvanize a significant number of people, getting them to ask for his resignation and to demand early national elections. Already in December 1994, even before Judge Garzón ordered the imprisonment of some of the top officials involved in the GAL activities, 36% of Spaniards thought that González should dissolve the Parliament and call for elections.[33] By June 1995, 47% considered that the Prime Minister should resign, and 43% thought that he should call for early elections.[34] This suggests that, at least for those people, the feeling that they had been lied to was not followed by a feeling of humility or subservience, nor did it develop into cynical expectations of politicians' regular behavior.

In short, the debate about the responsibility of the public authority was disturbed in three ways: first, by maneuvers aimed at making the conflict between parties (politics) overshadow the accounting for actions (policies); second, by tactics aimed at obscuring the topic; and third, by the difficulties the public experienced in summoning the emotional and moral energies to demand responsibility from the political class. Nonetheless, by the end of this period, the distracting maneuvers and tactics had largely failed, and the difficulties had apparently been overcome.

Unemployment

WHILE PUBLIC DEBATE focused on the drama of the GAL and other scandals, other matters of governance needed urgent attention. The Spanish economy went into a serious recession, and the unemployment situation, already very bad, got worse. At the same time, the administration had made commitments to structural adjustments in fighting inflation as well as in debt reduction and interest-rate policies, as a result of Spain's signing the Maastricht treaties and in view of its willingness to be among the founders of the European Monetary Union.

In addition to the difficulties created by these divergent domestic and foreign policy concerns, the game of governance had radically altered after 1993—not only because of the scandals and upheavals, but also because the PSOE had lost its parliamentary majority. This meant the end of the Socialist hegemony and the beginning of a period of coalition politics. To keep things running smoothly required working out some understanding between the Socialists and CiU and this, in turn, brought to the fore the complicated relationship between the central government and the peripheral nationalist movements.

To the outside observer, Felipe González's government between 1993 and 1996 was either an exercise in survival politics or a prolonged political agony. The Socialists had used diversionary and dilatory tactics to confuse the issue of political accountability and to postpone bringing to light the truth about the GAL affair (and the FILESA affair). During these years they also had to cope with the other problems of governance—in the end, as we will see, with only partial success.

One of the most extraordinary circumstances of the two decades of Spanish democracy, from the transition in the late 1970s to the late 1990s, has been the country's apparent ability to live with unusually high rates of unemployment without suffering social and political upheavals. Furthermore, the public had dutifully elected and reelected, time and time again, the party responsible for the labor market institutions and the socioeconomic policies that led to such extensive unemployment.

At the time of the 1982 elections, 16% of the Spanish labor force was unemployed, which amounted to 2.2 million jobless workers. González and the Socialist party declared this figure was unbearable. In their view, the high rate of unemployment demonstrated incompetence and class bias on the part of the UCD government, and the Socialists were committed to change the situation. Their electoral slogan, "for change," implied both a radical change in policy and a push for full employment. In a spurt of self-confidence, the Socialists specifically promised to create 800,000 new jobs. Yet three years later, in 1985, the number of unemployed had instead gone up to 2.9 million (hence 700,000 jobs had been eliminated), and the rate of unemployment rose to 21.5%. In the decade of 1985–1995, unemployment figures oscillated between 2.5 and 3.5 million unemployed, and the rate of unemployment between 16 and 24% of the labor force (Alcaide 1995). (See Table 2 on Spain's long-term economic statistics.)

This was roughly twice the average rate in Western Europe. By 1993, Spain had about 3.4 million people out of work in a population of about 40 million people. By then, the United Kingdom had 3 million unemployed; Italy, 2.6 million; and France, 2.6 million (all of them with populations of about 60 million people). Germany had 2.8 million unemployed, and a population of about 80 million (after the reunification). The United Kingdom, France, and Italy had unemployment rates of 10–11%; Germany, of 7.2% (OCDE 1994). Double the European average rate of unemployment seemed to have become an accepted fact of life in Spain: in 1985 the Spanish rate was 21.1% and the European one, 10.7%; in 1990, the rates were 16.1% and 8.3%; and in 1994, they were 23.8% and 11.2%. For comparison purposes, unemployment

Table 2. Long-term trends: GDP, external sector, public spending, and employment in Spain, 1964-1997

	GDP in trillions of 1986 Spanish pesetas	External sector as a % of GDP	Public spending as a percentage of GDP	Employment in millions of people	Unemployment rate
1964	14.2	16.9	—	12.0	2.8
1975	26.5	26.8	27	12.7	4.5
1985	31.3	36.0	40	10.8	20.8
1988	35.9	41.9	41	11.7	18.8
1991	39.9	48.0	45	12.6	15.7
1994	40.5	57.8	48	11.7	22.4
1997	44.0	70.7	44	12.7	20.8

Sources: Fuentes Quintana, 1995; *Estadísticas básicas de España 1971-1980.* (Madrid: Fundación FIES); García Pereda and Gómez, 1994; Instituto Nacional de Estadística, 1992; Instituto Nacional de Estadística, 1998; Ministerio de Economía y Hacienda, *Síntesis Mensual de Indicadores Económicos* (Various issues).

rates in the United States were between two-thirds and one half of the European average: 7.1% in 1985, 5.4% in 1990, and 6% in 1994 (Feito 1995).

There is little doubt regarding the magnitude of Spanish unemployment. Data are obtained through methods similar to those used in the rest of Europe, and these methods have been under scrutiny for some time. Some people argue about the figures, pointing to the underground economy (and other factors). Some specialists think that the real rate of unemployment should be around three points less than the official statistics (but most of their arguments apply also to other European countries) (Alcaide 1995, 1998).[1] Moreover, the huge number of unemployed in Spain should be seen in a context that makes the picture look even darker and the prospects more ominous, if we consider long-term unemployment in general and that of household heads, youngsters, and women in particular. In 1995, 58% of the jobless workers were long-term unemployed: 33% had been without a job for two or more years, and 25% for one to two years (Ministerio de Trabajo y Seguridad Social 1995). Their chances of getting back to the labor market were very low, especially for the older workers. During the

1980s, the number of unemployed household heads was relatively low, but it increased steadily through the years. Between 1991 and 1995, the number of unemployed in this category grew from half a million to about one million people.

A disproportionately large proportion of the unemployed consisted of young people. In 1995, 44% of those under 24 years old were unemployed. Once again, this was twice the average European rate (22% in 1994, when the Spanish rate was 45%). At the same time, the young people who did work could expect fixed-term contracts no longer than three years (about 80% of all contracts signed from 1985 to 1995), and a very high turnover rate on the jobs. By 1994, a survey showed that the only work experience of 65% of all male workers 18 to 29 years old, and 72% of female workers of that age, was that of fixed-term contracts (CIRES 1994). The possibilities of promotion and on-the-job training associated with these conditions were usually very limited. The drama of the situation, then, was not confined to the present but extended into the future—the cumulative effect that an ongoing experience over a long period might have on the training capacities and the aspirations of the new generations. These youngsters also had to face the prospect of more women entering the labor market. Though the unemployment figures for women were bigger than those for men, the rate of activity of women was on the rise, and was expected to stay on the rise in the following years. That would tend to keep the general rate of unemployment high, and would make competition for jobs, particularly in the service sector, ever more intense.

Labor Practices and Policies over Time

Experts have debated the reasons for this extraordinarily bad performance of the Spanish labor markets for many years, with little academic consensus. However, the *combined effect* of three sets of factors may offer a plausible explanation: specific labor practices and policies (such as high severance payments, rise in real wages greater than gains in productivity, and generous unemployment subsidies); socioeconomic policies that reinforced each other (in particular anti-inflation and social spending policies); and sociocultural accommodations which have compensated for the social consequences of unemployment.

But first, a brief explanation of why I give only a moderate weight to other factors, whether demographic or economic. The comparison with Portugal (with an unemployment rate of 6.8% in 1994 compared to Spain's 24.2%) suggests that we should not put too much emphasis on the return of emigrants from Europe (in fact Portugal had to integrate both its emigrants from Europe and repatriates from Africa), or on the volume of underemployment in the agrarian sector. Also, the effect of the baby-boom of the 1960s was offset by the lower rate of activity of the Spanish population as compared to that of other European countries.[2] At the same time, though some people still think that openness to the world markets and technological change increase unemployment, the facts do not support them. Germany's unemployment rate has tended to be lower than France's, although the German economy is more open than the French; the same applies to the comparison between Portugal and Spain. Nor does the incorporation of technological change appear to aggravate employment problems: Spain is technologically far less advanced than Germany, France, Italy, and the United Kingdom (or the United States for that matter), yet its unemployment rate is far higher than theirs.

Thus the Spanish unemployment rate cannot be attributed to an excess of demographic pressures on the labor market but to the inability of the Spanish economy to generate enough employment to meet the (rather moderate) increase in the labor force. Between 1970 and 1992, the United States was able to increase the ratio between the number of jobs and the working-age population by 8.7 percentage points; France, by 1 point; while in Spain it decreased by minus 11.1 points. Yet the Spanish rate of economic growth for this period was higher (3%) than that of the United States (2.6%) or France (2.5%) (Feito 1995). In other words (and in absolute figures): in 1975 there were 12.6 million employed people in Spain; that figure went down to 10.8 million in 1985; then up to 12.6 million again in 1991, and down to 12.0 in 1995. Even taking into account the cycles of economic activity (1975 and 1991 were good years in relative terms), this is a dismal record. In a twenty-year period the Spanish economy was able to "generate" *minus* 0.6 million jobs. This very poor employment performance of the Spanish economy is rooted in the labor market institutions and policies that were set up in the second half of the 1970s during the political transition—practices that were only partly reformed during the years that followed.

The new democratic governments retained the traditional Francoist labor practices of fairly high severance payments for dismissals, allowed for generous increases in real wages, and gradually augmented unemployment subsidies. Taken in isolation, these measures might have had minor (and some may argue even beneficial) effects on the economy. Taken together (and at critical times) they had quite harmful consequences on employment.

Severance payments were among the highest in Europe: 45 days per year worked, up to two years in salaries (even though redundancy payments for fixed-term workers have been, at least since 1984, much lower: 20 days of salary per year worked). Some of the reforms implemented in 1994 may have reduced severance payments for workers with indefinite contracts, but not significantly; the courts that rule on the conflicts on these issues seem to go on applying the best terms for the worker. Severance payments are considerably higher in the public sector, often twice as much as those given by the private firms (on average, in 1994, Pta 10 million per worker in the public firms; Ministerio de Hacienda 1995). High severance payments costs (and high transaction costs, in the form of cumbersome administrative proceedings for collective layoffs) accompanied high unemployment subsidies (a combination alien to Portugal) and a substantial increase in real wages in the late 1970s and early 1980s (again, in contrast with the Portuguese experience) (Blanchard, Jimeno 1995). Taken together, these measures left the business firms little room to adjust (through manipulating prices or work force) to the oil crisis and anti-inflation policies of the late 1970s, which helped to reduce even further the rate of return of capital; hence they resorted to a labor-substitution strategy. As a result, the productive economy and in particular the industrial sector shrank, and the unemployment rate shot up from 4.5% in 1976 to 21.6% in 1985.

In the main, these labor practices continued through the 1980s, except for a reform passed in 1984 that offered cheap fixed-term contracts for the new entrants. This created a dual labor market with a protected core and a semi-protected periphery. The high severance payments, high unemployment subsidies, and increases in real wages for the protected core went on as before, now in a context of increasing global competition and increasing public debt (which kept interest rates high and therefore pushed up the financial costs of the firms). The consequence was that the Spanish economy was launched upon a course of economic growth with very small increases in employment opportunities in the long run.

Economic Policy

The "perverse" effects of labor practices on employment were worsened by the perverse effects of a policy of public deficits and high interest rates. In turn, these budget and monetary policies derived from the political choices of the Socialist governments in the 1980s and early 1990s. When they took power in the early 1980s, the Spanish Socialists thought they had learned from the experience of the British Labour party and the French Socialists not to antagonize the capital markets. But they had their own mistakes to make; and what they really learned was how to make mistakes without paying a political price for them.

The Socialists kept the labor market policies they inherited from the UCD governments (which had inherited them from Francoism, with the substantial addition of free unionism, which Franco had never tolerated). From 1984 on, they engaged in political trading with the unions: in exchange for not touching the status quo of those who were already employed, the unions, more or less reluctantly, accepted changes regarding the new entrants into the labor market. As a result, many new (fixed-term) jobs were created, and, in the good economic climate of the second half of the 1980s, this lowered the unemployment rates, though not below 16%.

But since the unions refused to see the connection between increases in real wages (linked as they were to employment protection of the core of the labor force) and the rate of unemployment, they felt free to voice denunciations and complaints. In fact, they thought that the situation called for them to demand higher increases in wages. Union leaders were also unhappy with the fiscal and monetary policies of the government, which they regarded as too conservative. So the peculiar political trade-off between the government and the unions did not prevent a growing difference in political sentiment and increasing mutual distrust. This had a bearing on the tense campaign about the referendum on NATO in 1986, which pitted the government against an ill-assorted leftist opposition, including the unions. The government nevertheless won the referendum and was duly reelected immediately afterwards.

By the late 1980s, the relations between the government and the unions were strained even more, partly because of a disagreement concerning some measures to reduce the unemployment rate. The government was trying to figure out new ways to enlarge the field of term contracts; the unions were adamantly against this move and pressing strongly for increases in social spending. According to the unions, the government had broken the promises embodied in the tripartite agreement of 1984, the Acuerdo Económico y Social or AES. (This is why, from the unions' viewpoint, the government had incurred a "social debt" to them.) In December 14, 1988, the unions called a general strike. Much to the government's surprise, the strike was quite successful. Possibly the unions succeeded in responding to a vague malaise in the population, and they were aided by a general perception of economic prosperity, since the economy was in the upswing of the economic cycle that was to last up to 1991.

The political response of the government to the general strike was a sort of Machiavellian tour de force. Eventually, it gave in to most of the unions' demands, thereby increasing social spending and enacting lax budgetary policies; at the same time, it tried to block further concessions in the long run by sticking to orthodox monetary policies which were tied up to keeping the peseta in the European Monetary System. It hoped it could play it both ways, provided the general trend of economic growth persisted.

Having decided not to confront the unions openly, the government maintained the status quo of the labor market and engaged in substantial social spending, as well as in public spending as a whole. Social spending increased because of greater unemployment subsidies and social security expenses. Health spending grew within limits; but pensions grew so much that, by 1995, the deficit of the system of public pensions could be estimated at 2.16% of the GDP (Pta 1.5 trillion), and was forecast to be 3.46% of the GDP by the year 2025 (on the fairly optimistic assumption of a rate of employment growth of 1% per year) (Herce, Pérez-Díaz 1995). At the same time, the number of public sector employees kept on growing, from 1.5 million in 1982 to a peak of 2.1 million in 1992. By 1995, employees in the public sector made up 23.2% of the total salaried population (15% in 1976; 19.9% in 1982) (Labor Force Survey data from Ministerio de Economía y Hacienda 1993; MTSS 1996). Public spending in the late 1980s and early 1990s also included some infrastructural and ceremonial expenses for the

1992 celebrations of the World Fair in Seville and the Olympics in Barcelona, both seen as useful political investments by the central and the respective regional governments.

Other systemic leaks in public spending helped push up the public debt. The central government overspent beyond the limits of the budget as a rule. In the period 1985–1993, annual average overspending was of 33% over the budget limit (Edo et al. 1994).[3] This reflected not only the growth in social spending and salaries to public personnel, but also the loose practices of the regional governments and of the public firms. Several regional governments (in particular Catalonia and Andalusia) had a clear tendency to run into debt; and more generally, regional and local governments' debt managed to grow tenfold, from Pta 649 billion in 1982 to Pta 6,960 billion in 1995 (Valle 1996: 15).

The financial losses of many public enterprises must also be taken into account. For instance, in 1993 alone, the state-owned railway company, RENFE, incurred losses of Pta 314 billion; total losses of the firms integrated in the public holding INI amounted to Pta 275 billion (and carried over a total debt of Pta 2.5 trillion); and RTVE, the national public broadcasting company, lost Pta 127 billion. Firms owned by regional governments did not fare better. No wonder, then, that the government ran heavily into debt. Public debt stood at about 40–45% of the GDP in the period 1985–1991. In 1992, public debt reached 48.4% of the GDP, and jumped to 60.4% in 1993 and 63.0% in 1994 (Álvarez Blanco 1995).

In contrast to its lax budgetary policies, the government, following the lead of the Bank of Spain, decided to keep a lid on the inflationary effects of the wage increases and the public deficit by aligning the currency within the European Monetary System (EMS), at the then current rate of 1 deutsche Mark to 63 pesetas, and to stick to a policy of high interest rates in order to maintain the exchange rate. Thus the Spanish monetary authorities bound themselves, and the Spanish economy, to the European system. By pursuing a lax budget policy on the one hand and a strict monetary policy tied to that of other countries on the other hand, the government tried to avoid confrontation with the Spanish unions, while the difficulties which might result from its monetary policy could be attributed to reasons of state of the European Union.

In pursuing this course, the government counted on the climate of economic euphoria of the late 1980s: jobs were created at a rapid pace (and the rate of unemployment went down from 24% to 16%) and foreign investment poured into the country, to a large extent attracted by the high interest rates. In the short run the policy seemed to be successful, and the government could harvest the results of those moves almost immediately: it won the elections of 1989, and enjoyed world-wide admiration in 1992. But in fact economic troubles were to hit just a couple of years later (possibly aggravated by the collapse of the Soviet bloc, the German reunification, and the German policy afterwards). Almost unnoticed in late 1990 through 1991, signs of the coming recession were beginning to show up; and they became fully visible just around the middle of 1992.

By that time, the inertia of the policy choices of the past made a timely adjustment impossible, unless the government accepted to pay a political price it was never ready to pay before. It is worth noticing, however, that a limited and late attempt to reform some of the labor market policies and institutions was made in 1994. It had minimal results, since the judges generally rejected broad interpretation of the new rules stating when it was legitimate for business to lay off personnel. An effort too was made to clarify the public budget and to put it in order, even though control of public spending was insufficient (the debts of the regional governments continued to increase, as did current expenses of the civil administration). The question of social security reform was barely touched, but unemployment benefits were curtailed in 1994, and a meritorious attempt was made to reach a consensus of sorts on future reforms (the so called Pactos de Toledo, or Toledo Pacts, which were signed by most political parties in 1996). Contributing to the deteriorating situation were the cumulative effects of many years of absence of active labor market (and human resources) policies such as vocational training policies, and of the lack of incentives to devise more flexible and productivity-oriented forms of collective bargaining (traditionally focused on wages, working time, and employment protection of the core force). Under these circumstances, a policy of well-meant and cautious tinkering (as the one attempted after the 1993 elections) was not enough, and as the economy plunged in the wake of a Europe-wide recession, unemployment rose to new heights: 18.4% in 1991;

22.7% in 1992; and 24.2% in 1994. Thus everything seemed to conspire to make the bold gamble of the Socialist government—to have it both ways, that is—end in a fiasco when the economic cycle turned sour, capital markets contracted, and recession hit the Spanish economy worse than at any time in the previous thirty years (with the GDP growing 0.7% in 1992 and *minus* 1.2% in 1993). (See Table 3.)

The Socialist administrations appeared motivated to act partly by the inertia of past policies and external events, partly by the eagerness to consolidate or expand the domestic base of their power. Confident of a rosy long-term projection that would continue the trends of 1986–1991 (of foreign investment, job creation, and social spending), they developed a curious mentality of "never pay the price; always postpone paying the price" (a sort of free-lunch outlook) that put a premium on short-term political catering to the electorate while shifting the responsibility for long-term consequences to the European system.

For a long time, the government was a study in interesting contrasts, between its showmanship of political cunning and the timidity of its policy and between its open assertiveness and its inner pessimism. Despite all its excitement about modernization and Europeanization, the government seemed to be in the grip of deep uncertainty. On one front, it appeared to doubt its own capacity to lead the country and solve its

Table 3. Spain in the 1990s: Basic economic indicators

	1986-1991 (average)	1992	1993	1994	1995	1996	1997
GDP annual growth rate	4.3	0.7	−1.2	2.2	2.7	2.3	3.4
State Spending							
Expenditure (as % of GDP)	42.6	46.4	49.7	48	47.8	45.8	44.2
Deficit (as % of GDP)	−4	−4.1	−7.5	−6.9	−7.3	−4.4	−2.6
Interest rate: Three-month interbank rate (%)	–	13.3	12.2	7.9	9.2	7.6	5.4
Consumer price index (%)	5.9	5.9	4.6	4.7	4.7	3.6	2

Sources: Cuadernos de Información Económica, 1998; Instituto Nacional de Estadística, *Boletín Mensual de Estadística* (several issues); Ministerio de Economía y Hacienda, *Síntesis mensual de indicadores económicos* (several issues); *Papeles de Economía Española,* 1996.

problems; hence the tendency to displace its political responsibility onto Europe. Furthermore, there was a sense of equally deep pessimism regarding the capacity of the country to cope, of the unions to change their views, and of the public to understand the basics of the economic situation; hence it was necessary to link the country to the world markets, and, in a certain sense, let the foreigners (the Bundesbank, the multinational investors, the European Commission, etc.) take over. This general timidity of the government is evident not only in the way it handled public spending, but more generally, in the way it avoided strategic decisions. This affected a wide range of issues: the soft side of employment policies (education and training), health and pensions systems, water policies, and telecommunications (left until very late and initiated, with great reluctance, in the wake of the European Commission's policies).

This contrast between bold assertiveness in the short run and timidity and reluctance to engage in matters of strategic importance reinforced the government's frequent indulgence in magical thinking and talking. In this sort of thinking, words equal reality, so that ideas (and the "abstract will" of Hegelian parlance) are treated as if they had real power and consequences. It is the belief, for instance, that to say "we are European; we are becoming European; we want to/we will be part of the core members of the European community; we will catch up with the core members" will make these things happen. More: it is as if these words, repeated the right number of times and in the right pitch, could persuade the Spaniards and even the non-Spaniards that these things have happened already (or are about to happen)—especially when friendly media echo the words *ad nauseam*. (And especially if the media could get their faithful readers to read "several copies of the morning paper to assure [themselves] that what it said was true"—thus putting Ludwig Wittgenstein's sly phrase into profitable application.)

In fact, a significant gap separated perception and reality. The data show that, in the long run, the democratic governments since the transition have not been successful in getting the Spanish economy closer to the position it held relative to the European average *before* the transition. Contrary to myth, Spain's per capita income (a shorthand index of the economic standing of a country) was closer to the European average in 1975 (79.3% of the European average) than estimated for 1995 (75.4%) (Fuentes Quintana 1995). It is true, of course, that during those twenty years substantial changes were implemented to accommo-date Spanish institutions to the European ones; in the *very* long run, they may prove quite beneficial to bring Spain up to the level of the rest of Western Europe.

The Welfare System and Sociocultural Accommodation

The extraordinarily high unemployment rate met an equally remark-able muted social and political response to it. This calls for an explana-tion. For one thing, the protected core of the labor market gave its support to the policies (and institutions) that caused the high unem-ployment. This large bloc of employees, eager to protect their jobs and their wage increases, gave a tacit mandate to the unions to fight for the maintenance of the status quo. Another factor is the passive acquies-cence of the (semi-excluded) peripheral social segments of the labor market: older people, younger people, and women.

The policy choices at the moment of the democratic transition, in the 1970s and early 1980s, put in place rigid wage and bargaining pat-terns, high compensation costs, *plus* generous welfare provisions and unemployment benefits, at the same time as they established a tradition of anti-inflationary policies that still allowed for regular increases in the real wages of those who kept their jobs. These policies resulted in unemployment, as thousands of firms disappeared (mostly the small and medium-sized), and many of the entrepreneurs who survived the first shock of high energy and labor costs adjusted to these situation by increasingly substituting capital for labor. The situation created the conditions for the development of a dual labor market.

The unions decided to focus on employment protection and in-creases in real wages for those at work, paying only lip service to issues such as vocational training or productivity. Union membership was low: around 11% of salaried workers by 1990 (OCDE 1994). Yet the two main unions, UGT and CCOO, were able to muster about 70–80% of the votes in works councils elections, which have been held regularly every three to four years since the mid-1970s.[4] Moreover, the unions were able to gather support from sizable numbers of workers during the few big confrontations they have had with the government. Thus the unions acted as tacit representatives of the "insiders"—job-holders who wanted them to block any reform of the employment protection provisions while guaranteeing increases in their real wages—at the expense of the employment chances of the old, the young, and the female "outsiders."

Turning to labor's traditional antagonists, the unions found an entrepreneurial class that was disposed (or resigned) to accommodate them, and a government that was unable or unwilling to confront them. The resulting agreements found their expression in legal provisions (such as the Estatuto de los Trabajadores [Statute of Workers]) and social pacts (from the Moncloa Pacts of 1977 to the Acuerdo Económico y Social of 1984).

The rationale of Spanish labor policy (like the policies of many other European countries) can be reconstructed as the result of an implicit social contract (interclass, intergeneration, and intergender) whose brokers were the union leaders, the leaders of the business associations (even though they had significant mental reservations), and the democratic governments (first centrist then Socialist) (Pérez-Díaz 1993). Eventually, these brokers gave legal form to this contract and guaranteed the implementation of such social pacts or corporatist arrangements. Moreover, these state actors and their social partners engaged in the task of persuading the public that the labor market institutions should be considered social conquests and essential elements of the welfare state; that the unions represented the bulk of the labor force; and that the labor legislation and the social pacts of the late 1970s and first half of the 1980s articulated a general sociopolitical consensus. But how did the other social segments do—the older workers, the young people, and women workers, those who were brushed aside to the margins of the protected core? A combination of welfare state provisions and of sociocultural practices and accommodations made up for the lack of employment opportunities of these social groupings.

As regards older people, several provisions eased their exit from the labor market. The first step was facilitated by the generous severance payments and early retirement benefits the Socialists enacted as part of their industrial restructuring of the early 1980s. Crucial aid came after the mid-1980s in the form of substantial increases in average pensions. To this we may add the soothing effect of complementary social provisions such as noncontributive pensions, disability pensions (with minimal control of the disability requirements until a reform was enacted in 1985), and minimal income measures taken at several administrative levels. The living conditions of older people were improved by the fact (left over from an old state policy dating from the 1940s and 1950s) that most owned their dwellings and had open access to health facilities. Besides, Spanish family patterns are such that old people frequently live with their relatives, or next or close to them, or are somehow taken care by their kin. As city and regional studies indicate, very few old people are left out in the cold.

In a comparison of statistics from New York, Paris, and Madrid, we find that the rate of unipersonal families in Madrid (16 per thousand) is near half of those of New York and Paris (33 and 34 per thousand, respectively); and that the number of homeless people in Madrid has been estimated between 2,000 and 5,000, or twenty to fifty times fewer than in Paris (between 20,000 and 30,000) or in New York (70,000 to 90,000) (in percentage terms, 0.06–0.08% in Madrid; 0.2–0.3 in Paris; 1.0–1.2 in New York). Beyond the big cities, in a regional study conducted in Aragón (Laparra, Gaviria, Aguilar 1995) in 1993, the authors found that only 3.3% of the families (most of them with some old members) found themselves in a situation of "social exclusion." Even so, 56% of those families had at least one member engaged in economic activities, mostly in the underground economy (getting about two thirds of the minimum wage, for a working week of about 25 hours); about 16% got some form of pension or social income; all had access to social security; the children had access to the school system; and 44% owned the houses they inhabited.

For those younger than 25 years of age, some welfare state provisions plus some spontaneous sociocultural accommodations worked to keep them permanently, yet peacefully, on the margins (or out) of the legal labor market. Their situation, however, was the result of several socio-economic policies. For example, the secondary labor market was created by the reforms of 1984 (and from 1992 on, by the employers' loose interpretation of term contracts), which confined the young people to a segment of the market which offered substantially lower wages and no job security. In compensation, the young workers enjoyed relatively high unemployment benefits in addition to the opportunities to be found in a fairly important underground economy. In the 1980s and early 1990s, unemployment benefits could be roughly estimated as about 50–60% of the real wage, and they could be obtained after a first job lasting at least 1 year. At the same time, the underground economy represented probably as much as 25% of the GDP.[5] Many in the state and in society tolerated the underground economy, and nobody paid much attention to this subject. The analysts (with a few exceptions), the media, the unions, the local and regional authorities, the inspectors from the Ministry of Labor, and Social Security bureaucrats all ignored it, as if everybody had agreed to leave the underground economy in the twilight zone: neither in the shadow nor in the public eye. A third mechanism that helped to keep these young people out of the labor market was their longer enrollment in the school system: the numbers of 16 to 24-year-olds staying in school increased remarkably through the years (the schooling rate of the 16–17-year-olds climbed from 56% in 1985 to 77% in 1993; from 33% to 53% for the 18–20-year-olds; and from 17% to 26% for the 21–24-year-olds, according to official statistics [Ministerio de Educación y Ciencia 1995]).

But even more important than these devices was the gradual evolution of a new life style that provided the youth with a universe of meaning for its daily existence, in a way that made it highly unlikely that they might ever challenge the status quo. Their peaceful acceptance of reality was rooted in the family and in cultural tradition. In other words, they accommodated to family life and submitted to key values held by the older generation.

Several surveys on youth document the coziness of Spanish family life. Having been brought up in nonauthoritarian families (this is how children were brought up in the 1960s), the youngsters envisioned staying at home after they finished school or dropped out. In fact, 90% of the 16 to 24-year-olds lived with their parents in 1994 (same as in 1989). Some were employed or looking for a job (30% employed; 19% jobless but searching for a job); many were in the school system (43%); but one way or another most lived off family help, in part or wholly (69%). Living at home and being dependent on family did not, however, lead to resentment or alienation. There was a remarkable normative consensus between generations, which appeared to be growing: 48% agreed with their parents on religious matters (in 1994; up from 38% in 1981); 49% on political issues (up from 26%); even on sexual mores their positions have got somehow closer (24%; up from 11% in 1981). The youngsters were also getting closer to the center of the ideological spectrum: in 1984, on a scale of 1 to 10, left to right, the 15 to 24-year-olds scored 4.24; they scored 4.61 by 1993.

True, the normative consensus between generations was limited. But the point is not so much that there was consensus, but rather that dissent was not acute and that toleration of diversity was the norm. We find only 14% of the youngsters in a state of radical disagreement on sexual mores and 21% on entertainment, and barely any on religion (6%), on family values (6%), and on work issues (4%). No wonder that 89% agreed with the statement: "the family provides the kind of stability you cannot find elsewhere" (all above data from Elzo et al. [1994]). Staying at home implied delaying life projects like marriage and babies, and also often meant putting off commitment to serious work projects and accepting work of a rather vague nature. This accompanied an emphasis on the values of expressive culture, a coolness toward formal organizations (unions, parties), and a fondness for networks of friends. Young people were becoming soft-spoken, low-key pragmatists with low expectations.

In other words, these youngsters found a sort of ecological niche around the family and friends, and this habitat stimulated the development of corresponding cultural dispositions. Chief among these was a disposition toward peaceful coexistence with those whom the younger generation appreciated as its providers of home, food, and a warm social climate. The strength of this feeling precluded the likelihood of any intergenerational conflict becoming too acute. This disposition toward accommodation (rooted in everyday family experience) was reinforced by the powerful and all-pervasive stereotypes that the young generation got through the media (mainly TV), the school system, and the political discourse of educators, journalists, clerics, and politicians whose formative experience had taken place in the 1960s and 1970s. They made moving and loud references to the gravity of the unemployment problem and the urgency of its solution, looking for clues everywhere. But in the end, the main point was to diffuse the responsibility of the protected core and its representatives (both in the unions and in the parties) for the youth's poor employment opportunities. It could therefore be said that the middle-aged generation succeeded in both tasks: reducing the employment opportunities of the youngsters, and avoiding taking responsibility for doing so.

Consequently, young people were left with the predicament of their own employment, a problem for which no political or civic language was readily available. The language of intergenerational conflict was inapplicable: they lived happily with and off their parents. A phrase that came more naturally to their lips was that of their "right to be employed": a right that the left tried to transform into a ("rightful") claim against the state or the business class. But in trying to use this rhetoric, the youngsters ran into some difficulties.

They might indeed make business responsible for their lack of jobs, whether because employers do not create jobs on purpose, so to speak (and should therefore be punished), or because the entrepreneurs cannot help themselves, being powerless against the system that pushed them to do so, in which case the system is to blame and ought to be changed. But when they reached this conclusion, most youngsters found that they lacked the necessary aggressiveness and conviction to punish the employers or to change the system or both; particularly since they were dimly aware they did not belong together with those unionists, politicians, or in general the 25–55-year-olds who suggested changing the system. Moreover, nobody around seemed to know what to put in place of it.

Hence, after a little bit of confused talk, most young people usually settled for a sort of suspension of judgment. Thereby they gained a welcome margin to show some understanding and sympathy for magical hyper-realism, in which they might occasionally indulge themselves, such as the rituals of repeating the mantra of "what is lacking is the political will to fight unemployment" (possibly at some ill-defined European level), and denouncing the politicians and the state (and tomorrow, presumably, some supranational authority) for lacking the necessary will. These recitations might be accompanied by street manifestations and other dramatic performances of the sort French students love to put on every ten years or so.

Ultimately, the key to the sociocultural arrangements which cushioned and counterbalanced the worst effects of the unemployment situation lay in the family. It was the institution that was able to protect the unprotected periphery of the labor market. Bound to bounce between the alternatives of subsidized unemployment, work in the underground economy, part-time or permanent job, being out of work, or parked in the school system, the youngsters built a niche for themselves in and around the family system. The family system also helped the old people to survive; it filled the life of women with more strain and additional experience. This may (or may not) help them in the long run to adjust to current changes in the division of labor, power, and responsibility between genders.[6]

It is an unexamined commonplace that if the family is the cornerstone of the welfare system of the Spanish society, women are the cornerstone of the family system. Over the years, women have been entering the labor market and competing for jobs with men, particularly in the service sector. Concurrently, they have been keeping the different strands of the family together: the youngsters, the middle-aged, and the old. This they have done not only through the (traditional) management of both the family sentiments and its domestic expenses, but also through managing the social services provided to the family members by state or private agencies—a most demanding job these days. Without going into this subject at length, suffice it to say that women are doing an extremely complicated balancing act between several roles, and must continue to do so if the social equilibrium is to be maintained.[7] Many girls in the younger generation seem to grow into the skills their mothers have acquired, along with the capacities they develop in school (where they are beginning to excel over the boys). In fact their social and cultural capacities are admired by their male peers (as indicated in recent surveys: Elzo et al. 1994).

By the early and mid-1990s, despite the success of these patterns of accommodation between the social coalition of the insiders and the habits of acquiescence of the outsiders, the young and women workers were moving away from the unions,[8] and the general public was getting uneasy about the very high rates of unemployment and the policies that led to it. In the last couple of years, and particularly in view of the performance of the economy in the early 1990s, when unemployment reached new peaks, the balance of interests may have begun to shift. The public is more inclined to make the government responsible for the situation and may be getting ready for a change in the policy pattern of the last twenty years.

CHAPTER SIX

A Political Shift
from Left to Right

FOR A GROWING SECTOR of the Spanish electorate in the first half of the 1990s, the pressing question was how to translate its dissatisfaction with the government's performance (the scandals and the economic crisis) into political action, in a period between national elections. For González's government, the question was how to divert attention from the issues of its breaking the law and unemployment, focus on other issues, and get credit for the governance of the country. These contrasting views were translated into an ongoing electoral contest to win over the central bulk of the electorate. It was fought by the two main parties, the PSOE in government and the PP in the opposition—with another party located further to the left, Izquierda Unida, playing a secondary role. The withdrawal of public support from the PSOE was eventually expressed in the general elections of 1996, and it left its mark on a number of local, regional, and European elections.

From a larger perspective, the workings of governance and politics from 1993 to 1996 appear to be just a stage in a complex pattern of political shifts from right to left and back to right, starting in the mid-1970s and going on for the rest of the century. These swings were relatively dramatic and accompanied noticeable generational changes in leadership. Underlying these shifts, however, was a remarkable continuity of institutional commitments (to the basic tenets of liberal democracy and a market economy), as well as of regional policy, orientation toward Europe, and moderation in public discourse. There was even significant continuity in economic policy, though some key changes are worth noticing. UCD stuck to a policy of neocorporative arrangements which the PSOE reduced to a minimum by the mid-1980s. The Socialist governments embarked on a course of lax fiscal policy and public spending, with tight monetary policy. By the mid-1990s, the PP decided on a policy of budgetary restraint and supply-side measures (privatization, liberalization), which the last PSOE government (after 1993) had already tried to initiate. Therefore, the political shifts could be equally portrayed as circling around the center, or simply going from center-right (UCD) to center-left (PSOE) and back to center-right (PP).

In the course of these changes, various sectors of the political class were gradually coming of age. The learning process of these different brands of politicians was tinged with irony: the old reformed Francoists (of UCD) became associated with the democratic transition; the former radical Socialists (of PSOE) became associated with NATO and the capitalist economy; and the heirs to the traditions of Spanish nationalism (of PP) had to learn, in due time, to compromise with the Catalan and the Basque nationalists as best they could.

One of the key mechanisms in this process of shifting and learning was the practice of coalition politics, which the electoral results of 1993 and 1996 made all but unavoidable. In the absence of a grand coalition between Socialists and PP, each of the two main parties had to obtain the support of the nationalists to gain a majority. A first try at coalition politics by the Socialists could not overcome the tensions created by the political scandals. This, more than anything else, opened the way for the coalition between the center-right and CiU, which was to be the key for stable government in the late 1990s.

Thus, in the last analysis, it was not so much the differences between the main parties about Europe, the economy, and regional politics that proved to be the key for the political shift from left to right, since on most of these issues, ironically, both left and right had been moving steadily to the center. Rather, it was the issue of the rule of law that made the Socialists lose heart, pushed the PP ahead, and altered the perception of the public at large and especially that of the nationalists, who hold the parliamentary balance of power.

A First Try at Coalition Politics

After the 1993 election, González's strategy was to convey the impression of an effective government despite the scandals and the high unemployment figures. The key to it was a political alliance with Jordi Pujol's Catalan party, Convergència i Unió. On the economic front the results were meager. The GDP grew by a mere 2.2% in 1994 and 2.7% in 1995. Public deficits were still high in 1994 and 1995 (6.3 and 6.6% of the GDP, respectively, almost the same as in 1993: 6.8%) (OCDE 1998: 219). In 1994 the government introduced only minor adjustments in the existing labor market institutions and policies. The unemployment rate remained around 22–24% of the labor force. Important decisions concerning the reform of the pension system, of health care, and of water policy were announced and postponed.[1] The government acted with its usual caution, as if it all it could do was to live with the poor performance of the Spanish economy in 1993–94 and wait for things to improve along with the European economies in the second half of 1994 and 1995. For a government and its Catalanist allies eager to prove their worth in the economic field, the outcome was rather disappointing.

The government tried to portray itself in a more favorable light in the field of regional politics. At the beginning, the need of an alliance with the Catalanists gave González an opportunity to demonstrate his ability to raise a peripheral nationalist party up to the task of governing the whole of Spain, either through a coalition government or a stable pact in Parliament. The effect of that move would be reinforced by the long experience of a coalition government in the Basque country between the main moderate Basque nationalist party (the PNV) and the Socialists. If this political maneuver succeeded, González could portray himself as the man who ensured the political stability of the system in the long term.

However, this historic opportunity for a coalition government between Socialists and Catalanists failed to materialize. González never offered a serious dialogue for a coalition government (which would have included agreement on a government platform). Pujol preferred to administer his political support to González in small doses, limited to a few critical issues (economic reform, regional issues, and presumably European politics), and in short spurts of time (to end by late 1995).

What came out of it was a feeling of suspense and an impression of short-term tactical agreements dependent on constant bargaining (which the public found hard to follow and mistrusted): in short, the alliance gave signs of chronic instability rather than of political stability. The Catalanists' support looked as if it could be withdrawn any time; the partners gave every indication that they did not trust each other.

Furthermore, the Socialists' attempt to capitalize on their agreements with the Catalanists, by pretending the PSOE was their natural partner and the only party that could have reached such an accord, ran against the elusive character of their alliance and against the real circumstances when seen from a wider perspective. The Catalanist policy of limited support could be seen as an experiment in accommodation with the Spanish central government whatever its political leanings. In fact, Catalan nationalists had cooperated before with the center-right government in Madrid during the transition. There was no reason, then, not to expect this pattern to continue with a post-PSOE government if need be, particularly since there was so little love lost between Socialists and Catalanists anyway.[2] In other words, the policy of limited support could be repeated later with a PP government, either in the unstable form of Pujol's support to González in the mid-1990s or in a more stable manner.

Meanwhile, politics in the Basque country also became more complicated. After years of political near-normalcy (leaving aside the endemic terrorism), partly as a result of PNV-PSOE coalition governments since 1987, votes for the non-nationalists increased and peace movements developed. Regional and local elections revealed an ever more complex political landscape, which favored coalition experiments. A regional coalition government brought together the PSOE, PNV, and EA (Eusko Alkartasuna, or Basque Solidarity, another nationalist party which had split from the PNV some years earlier), and diverse local experiments took place, including a PNV-PP coalition government in the city of Bilbao. On the other hand, terrorist activities surged in 1994 and 1995. It was not that assassinations were more numerous, but the targets were qualitatively different. The PP leader in San Sebastián, Gregorio Ordóñez, was assassinated; an attempt to kill the leader of PP, José María Aznar, failed by pure chance; even King Juan Carlos was a target. In 1996, Francisco Tomás y Valiente, former president of the Constitutional Court, was assassinated. At the same time, street violence intensified. All these events suggested the potential but also showed the limits of local agreements between the PSOE and the Basque nationalists.

The ups and downs in the relations between the Socialist government and peripheral nationalisms suggested that such understandings would not prosper on the basis of tactical and partisan considerations. In a complex political landscape that required coalition politics for effective government, any combination of one or another of the two main national parties with one of the regional nationalists could be tried and could work. What the Socialists nearly accomplished, other could try with similar or maybe better results. As the future collaboration of CiU and PP in Madrid would show, the range of possible coalitions was wide and open to deep strategic understandings. This is the fruit of the long history of accommodation between the Spanish parties (PP and PSOE) and the nationalist parties that grew out of some basic realities of Catalan politics and Basque politics, which were too deep to be affected by party politics or even by parties. First, strong economic, social, and cultural ties linked most of the population living in Catalonia and the Basque region to the rest of Spain. Second, the people living in Catalonia and the Basque Country had complex identities, interests, and party preferences. They were not homogeneous groups but each was three quasi-communities of natives, immigrants, and mixed; these groups had much in common but also many differences. This situation seemed ready-made to foster internal strife, but instead it led to reciprocal tolerance with very positive consequences for the long-term adjustment between nationalist parties and the state.

The third issue of governance for which the government wanted to win the approval of its fellow citizens (and which Pujol supported) was that of European politics. In the field of the European Union politics, the Spanish government was an enthusiastic player. It so happened, however, that Europe was full of uncertainties following the ratification of the Maastricht treaties (1992 and 1993) and frustration in the face of the wars in the former Yugoslavia. At the same time, the Spanish public had its own uncertainties about the European Union that were just beginning to come to the fore (helped by the domestic and European bad economic situation). The government, however, lacked the time, the will, and most likely the capacity to confront these uncertainties.

The Spanish public was beginning to have second thoughts regarding the advantages of the European Union. The numerical difference between those who thought that belonging to the EU brought benefits and those who thought that it brought disadvantages narrowed significantly between 1991 and 1995 (from about 50% to about 10%; CIS 1995). The public was becoming more realistic in its assessment of the practical advantages of the Union. In the previous years, questions had been raised about Moroccan competition, the fate of Spanish agricultural exports, and the fishery industry. Business associations in the export-oriented sectors denounced the government's weakness in defending what they considered not only their particular interest but also the national interest. Some went so far as to publicly thank other European governments for having defended their interests better than did the Spanish government in the contest that pitted them against the Moroccan state in late 1995.[3]

In the view of the critics, the Spanish government was doing little more than preaching the virtues of nominal convergence of the European economies and repeating the mantra, "we want to be among the core nations of the European Union." Though 49% of Spaniards declared in 1995 that they would like Spain to make an effort to be among the core countries that would meet the Maastricht criteria in time, many thought that this was an impossible task. In a parallel poll of "leaders," most of them thought it unlikely that Spain would meet these criteria (only 36% thought that it would meet the inflation criterion; 16%, that on public deficit; 21%, that on public debt; see del Campo 1995). This looked like a sensible appraisal of the situation, since it coincided with the current estimates of the European Commission itself, according to which the Spanish economy in 1997 (the critical year for the assessments to be made in 1998 for countries which would qualify as core members in 1999) was expected to have an inflation rate of 3.6% (well above the current convergence level of around 2%), a public deficit of 3.6% (above the level of 3%), and a public debt of 65.4% (above the level of 60%).[4]

Meanwhile, the public's perception of the effects of the EU on the Spanish economy became more pessimistic. The difference between those who expected these effects to be good and those who considered them to be bad was of 40 percentage points in 1991, and it went down to 5 points in 1995. The difference between those who considered the effects of the EU on the Spanish job situation to be good and those who thought them to be bad, which was negligible in 1991, went down to *minus* 25 points in 1995 (of course, this had much to do with domestic unemployment). Partly as a result of this perception, through the early 1990s, and certainly by 1995, a large majority of about 80% of Spaniards thought that there should be some protection of Spanish products against the products of other countries of the European Union (CIS 1995).

By the mid-1990s, it was clear that although interest in European affairs and a general vague support for the EU remained high, the Spanish public was ambivalent about the EU. From the beginning of the new democracy in Spain, the public had taken it for granted that Spain should belong to the European Union, with very little disagreement among political parties on that score until very recently. It was slow to realize the practical implications of being part of the European institutions, and subject to European policy. By the time the French held a hotly contested referendum on the matter, in mid-1992, opinion polls showed that the Spaniards were 29% for and 9% against the Maastricht Treaty, with a huge 62% undecided.[5] By 1995, there was a slight majority in favor of an ill-defined concept of the United States of Europe, but when it comes to a choice of where to place the center of gravity of political decision, the national state usually ranked first. It is worth remarking that an interesting evolution of this point has taken place during the last few years. In 1988, about 30% of the Spaniards thought that the last word on important decisions should be made by the European Union: we may call them federalists. By 1995, the percentage of federalists had gone down to about 20%. Also in 1988, about 50% of the population thought that the last word on important decisions should be left to the member states: we may call them confederates. By 1995, the confederates were 60%. Thus between 1988 and 1995, the gap between confederates and federalists doubled, from 20 to 40 percentage points (CIS 1995).

This renewed interest in the national polity as the focus for political decision was consistent with deep-rooted attitudes of the public about both the nature of the European Union as a political association[6] and the general economic crisis. Moreover, the public's feelings regarding national identity have changed. Some opinion polls show that the percentage of those who said they felt themselves to be "only Spaniard" and "more Spaniard than a member of his/her region" went up from

23% in January 1993 to 33% in 1995; while those who declared that they rather felt themselves to be "only members of their region" and "more members of their regions than Spaniards" went down from 24% to 20% (CIRES 1993, 1995).[7] These were soft data and subject to many unpredictable factors in the short run, but they indicate a general direction of the public sentiment and point toward an internal debate on the general direction of policy regarding Europe and Spain's role in Europe, which had been, so far, avoided by the political class.[8]

In sum, the government's effort to divert attention away from the issues of corruption and unemployment was relatively unsuccessful. The government did little more that administer the economic crisis and wait for better times to come, and in fact an economic recovery started to materialize by mid-1994. Regional politics proved to be fairly complicated, and the administration's moves in this area remained inconclusive. In the first half of the 1990s, European politics was still a secondary issue viewed through the lens of Spanish domestic politics, even though there were signs that it would not remain so in the future.

In the end, tactical alliances and political moves did little to help González to undo the consequences of the political scandals and counter the growing fatigue of the economic crisis. A number of electoral contests after the national elections of 1993 showed a very clear trend: in local, regional, and European elections the PSOE consistently lost 8 to 10 percentage points as compared to the previous equivalent contest, while the PP gained about 8 to 10 points. As a result, the Popular Party got first place in each of them.

Local elections were held in May 1995, with the PP beating the PSOE by 35% (up from 25% in 1991) to PSOE's 30% (down from 38%). Elections held on the same day for 13 regional parliaments (out of 17) also produced big losses for PSOE (31% of the votes, with a loss of 9 percentage points from 1991) and huge gains for PP (45% of the votes: 11 percentage points more). The remaining four regions held their elections at different dates between 1993 and 1996. Galicia, which is PP country, opened the way in October 1993, with a landslide victory of PP at 52%; PSOE got just 23% (44 and 32% respectively in 1991). Andalusia is PSOE country, but even there the Socialists' hold on power was seriously weakened. The elections in June 1994 gave PSOE a narrow victory over PP (38% to 34%), in contrast to the more than two to one margin in 1990 (49% to 22%). Basque and Catalan regional elections are peculiar, since both regions are ruled by nationalist parties. Even so, elections in the Basque country (1994) and in Catalonia (1995) also punished the PSOE (though moderately: from 20% to 17% in the former; from 27% to 25% in the latter) and improved significantly the standing of the PP (from 8% to 14% in the Basque country; and from 6% to 13% in Catalonia). The European elections confirmed the general tendency. The PP went from 21% of the vote in 1989 up to 40% in 1994, almost doubling the number of seats in the European Parliament (from 15 to 28). By contrast, the PSOE went from 40% down to 31% and its European deputies from 27 to 20.

The meaning of these election results leaves no room for doubt. But the shift requires further assessment of the dramatic events of those years and the inner tensions within the ruling party, the rise of an opposition party which seemed to offer a plausible political alternative, and the changes in the demographics of the electorate.

The Socialists Drift

Together, the economic crisis and the political scandals dealt a hard blow to the electoral fortunes of González and the Socialist party. On top of having to deal with the problems already discussed above, grave as they were, González had to cope with the consequences of having five out of seventeen ministers of his last cabinet resign because of political scandals in just two years. Vice-president Narcís Serra and Minister of Defense Julián García Vargas had to step down because they allowed electronic surveillance of private citizens by the secret services (the CESID affair). Minister José Luis Corcuera resigned after some provisions of the so-called Corcuera law were declared unconstitutional (see Chapter 4), and Minister Antoni Asunción did so because of a climate of distrust toward the Ministry of Interior in the wake of the Roldán scandal, after the latter fled the country. Finally, Minister of Agriculture Vicente Albero had to submit his resignation because of tax fraud committed years earlier but discovered in the context of the Rubio affair. Meanwhile, in the background, the government and the party were seen to be drifting and surviving from one day to the next. The internal problems and contradictions of the Socialist party's political project, which came particularly into light in the early 1990s, reflected a general loss of direction.

Three of these contradictions come to mind upon reviewing PSOE's ideological and strategic orientation. First, there was the obvious division between a populist left wing and a social-liberal right wing (leaving aside a more leftist-oriented formulation, which was of a testimonial character), both of which called themselves social democrats (to the confusion of the observer). The populist wing, under Alfonso Guerra's leadership, was eager to organize a social coalition of protected workers, pensioners, public sector employees, and rural dwellers, plus some ideologically minded youth, and it was ready to use the welfare state as a basis for clientelistic practices. The social-liberal wing aimed at influencing government policies and favored integration into the world markets and NATO. The undisputed leadership of González, the common language of the welfare state, and the common goal of staying in power forced the two groups into coexistence. This gave rise to some calculated rhetorical ambiguity and a division of labor: electoral campaigning and the party belonged mainly to the populist wing; government action and control of some critical areas of the public administration went to the social liberals. Since the coexistence of such sectors and the corresponding ambiguity have been second nature to Socialist and social-democratic parties from the very beginning, this could have gone on forever, with only the minor cost of periodic disappointments of sensitive souls lost in the dark waters of politics.

But this conflict, endemic to socialist parties, was compounded by a second internal contradiction that was leading the Spanish Socialist party far away from its original conceptions. The Socialists started out as true believers in the virtues of an active, interventionist, developmental state that had a mission to fulfill. They aspired to an independent foreign policy and desired to keep a distance from both sides in the Cold War. But eventually, by dint of its very activity of governing, the PSOE ended as the unconscious and reluctant bearer of a completely different kind of state (and policy): it ended up bringing the country into the regulatory fields of the European Union, of the world markets, and of the Western alliance. In this way the Socialists enacted their final reconciliation with the tenets of capitalism (domestic and worldwide) and brought their foreign policy in line with the strategy of the Atlantic Alliance.

The course the PSOE governments followed was without ideological guidance. They acted mostly by pragmatically adjusting to the circumstances of the day, because they knew that to stay in power they had to win over the center of the electorate, since an alliance with the real left (that is, the Communists, who by the mid-1980s decided to play the role of hosts to several minor parties in a new political formation, Izquierda Unida) could only be a futile exercise in testimonial politics. But even so, the loss of the last vestiges of a belief in the virtues of an active, interventionist, developmental state in favor of a merely regulatory one was hard to accept.

But now came a third contradiction. What happened is that in real life, some of the very same people who embraced the role of rule-bearers or rule-keepers showed themselves to be rule-breakers. They developed a pattern of breaking the rules and eventually of breaking the law, even their own laws (the law of party financing or the criminal law). It is not easy to understand why these Socialists got in the habit of breaking their own rules. Maybe some of them slipped into it unawares, merely by letting things happen. It may well be that it all goes back to their original identity as social transformers (in the wake of a class struggle leading to a new socialist society), later changed to that of modernizers. As social transformers, they were brought up to denounce the laws of the Francoist state and the rules of the market economy, seen as the expression of the interests of the predatory entrepreneurial class characteristic of capitalism or of worldwide imperialism. By the late 1970s, they saw themselves as the architects of a developmental state.[9] But the point is that whether as transformers or modernizers, they did not feel bound by the rules. They had little appreciation for the niceties of the division of powers, and they thought that the legitimacy of their rule depended less on the institutions than on the ten million votes that backed them.

To the Socialist party members the ideology may have come full circle much too fast, changing them from transformative heroes to modernizers and state activists. Then they were hesitant to take the next step to being mere office-holders in a regulatory state. And when they reluctantly started to move in this direction (as some of them did), they and the public discovered that they shared the party with fellow Socialists who had broken their own rules—the rules of party financing, the criminal code, the civil or the commercial code (as suggested by the importance of inside trading)—and lacked basic respect for the rule of law. For many, it was a disheartening and sad realization. In the long run, this development may prove to be a useful, though hard, educational experience for the party. But in the short run, and from the viewpoint of their constituency (at least the younger, more urban, more educated, and more economically active members), this proved to be a different kind of learning experience. They learned to put a distance between themselves and the Socialist party.

When the scandals began to explode, Felipe González was of little help to the party, for he identified his personal career with its fate. He decided to deny and stonewall the charges and hoped to get away with it by increasing his control, and by trying to persuade his followers that specific allegations against specific acts of misconduct were in reality an all-out operation to destroy the party. Thus he claimed that he and his party were victims of a vast conspiracy, depicted his adversaries as public enemies of his grandiose modernization of Spain, and portrayed himself as the last bastion of the country's freedom and the rule of law—the leader braced to fight to the bitter end.

To be sure, this strategy may be partly understood as a sober calculation of interest. An apocalyptic tone might have helped him to rally his supporters and intimidate his adversaries for the purpose of defending his political record and his legal position, at least in the short run. But he also displayed a curious emotional readiness to take great risks in the long run, possibly at the expense of his own record in history, by allowing his party's predicament to worsen and putting in jeopardy the country's very institutions. This behavior seems to contradict his statesman image, and requires additional explanation.

By the time these events took place, González had been the top figure of his party for about twenty years, and Prime Minister for more than ten years. There was no doubt that he had remarkable political gifts. He had adopted several political and ideological outlooks and outlived them all. He was elected secretary general at the PSOE Congress of Suresnes, in 1974, on an orthodox leftist platform;[10] by 1979, he had persuaded his party to leave Marxism behind. By 1981–82 he hinted he was in favor of getting Spain out of NATO, and by 1986 he persuaded his countrymen to stay in. He got the Socialist union's firm support for years, but when the main union leader, Nicolás Redondo, challenged him, González was able to erode the power basis of his adversary and have him replaced by a friendly figure. His success could have given him the feeling that he was a master of political infighting, and that he had outsmarted both enemies and friends, including his long-time political companion, Alfonso Guerra. Many acclaimed him as a charismatic leader in his relations with the masses, since he was elected with a majority in three consecutive occasions in seven years (1982 through 1989), and even managed to win a last time in 1993. In a comparison with his historical rival, Adolfo Suárez, González comes out well. Suárez had been the man of the democratic transition, but he did poorly in Parliament and was unable to survive the conditions of political life in the 1980s. Ultimately, González thought he belonged in the big league of contemporary European socialist statesmen, on a par with Willy Brandt, Olaf Palme, Bettino Craxi, Andreas Papandreou, and François Mitterrand: a heterogeneous mix of idealism, statesmanship, political craft, survival instincts, and lack of scruples. In the Spanish leader's case, the weight of his undoubted political exploits grew heavier with the adulation that comes with power, and the effect was compounded by the long period of time he had to be insulated from criticism, to feed his hubris, and to develop illusions about the true character of his historical accomplishments.

Henry Kissinger made an interesting observation that a statesman only passes "the crucial test of leadership by moving his society from the familiar into a world it has never known" (Kissinger 1994: 704). We might call it the Moses criterion: the leader helps his people to adjust to uncertainty and to the mixed reactions of discovering a new land. What González did, other than survive and hold power, was to ease the way for Spaniards to stay in the already familiar territory of a liberal democracy, a market economy, and the Western alliance. It was not a minor accomplishment, but it fell short of the Moses criterion.

So the way González reacted to the situation may have included an element of rational calculation, but it also demonstrated a great deal of recklessness and anger. This less rational response may be attributed to a cognitive and emotional dissonance between his exalted self-image and the rather depressing, down-to-earth allegations of improper, if not criminal, conduct of his close collaborators, for which he had to answer and which threatened to destroy the heroic figure he sought to project in the Spanish imagination, and in his own.

The Long March of the PP and a New Electorate

Time is of the essence in politics. Sometimes the politician's sense of timing is critical for making an immediate, urgent, and determined move. Sometimes what is needed is just the time for a problem to fade away, for a misdeed to be forgotten, or for a new generation to mature and come to the fore. To a point, this last is what happened with PP, the center-right party that was finally able to challenge the Socialist hegemony only in the 1990s. Before that, we witnessed an aimless search, several failed attempts, and experiments with an assortment of tactics, images, and leaders; afterwards, we observe a group eager to take prompt advantage of the circumstances and win the contest.

The starting point was a conservative group of people who were displaced to the periphery at the time of the democratic transition (as were also the Communists). Their party, Alianza Popular, was founded by Manuel Fraga, an ex-minister under General Franco and also one of the framers of the democratic Constitution of 1978. It tried to represent a constituency of moderate ex-Francoists and conservative democrats but went nowhere so long as UCD was alive and well. By 1981–82, however, UCD was in disarray, and some of its sectors were plotting to join AP and create what they imagined would be a large center-right party. This, however, proved to be much harder than expected. The fact is that when UCD nearly disappeared in the 1982 elections, AP got only about 26.5% of the electoral vote.

Setting aside the public's infatuation with the Socialists at the time, the AP's meager results had much to do with popular distaste for Francoist ways and symbols, which it appeared to have inherited from its Francoist past and was unable to shed. Nor did it help that the AP leaders failed the very first serious test of statesmanship they had to face, namely, the issue of the referendum on NATO that dominated public debate in 1985–86. At this critical juncture, the AP leaders decided to treat a crucial matter of foreign policy on a par with ordinary party maneuvering and posturing in domestic politics. They saw an opportunity to make the PSOE pay a political price by losing the referendum, and in December 1985 they decided to recommend abstention. As the prospects of a negative result were high, the international community put some pressure on the AP leaders to change their minds—to no avail. A vote against Spain's membership in NATO would be a defeat for the Socialists, and the AP even suggested that if that happened, they would hope to win the next election and then be in a position to reverse the NATO referendum. This revealed both deviousness and foolishness, for this attitude seemed to take too lightly the democratic process itself.

But after some agony and a touch of comedy (since they bore the main responsibility for the mess in the first place),[11] the Socialists got the results they wanted, in the wake of which they convoked elections in 1986 and won handsomely, while AP got only 25.9% of the votes— about the same as in 1982. For the next three years the conservative party functioned in a sort of no man's land. Fraga was out, and there was a turnover of leaders or would-be-leaders trying their hand, losing, and leaving the scene.

This went on until 1989, with the accompanying tactical confusion, personal infighting, electoral tests, and unremitting outside pressure. When the experiments ran their course and the dust settled, it turned out that a learning process of sorts had taken place. What was needed was a new strategy, a new image, and a new organization. The strategy was to capture the center; the image would be that of a renewed party at a clear distance from the Francoist past; and the organization would produce a united party in which crucial claims for leadership had been settled once and for all, and external pressures could be contained (particularly those of business organizations). In August 1989, a group of young leaders in their late thirties, sharing the basics of this diagnosis of the situation, went to visit Manuel Fraga (in his half-retirement in Perbes, Galicia) and persuaded him to come back to head the party, just long enough to apply these measures, including the election of a young like-minded leader. Thus a new party was formed, the Partido Popular or PP, and a new leader was chosen, José María Aznar, first as the PP candidate in the 1989 elections, and then, in 1990, as president of the party.

From then on, the PP aimed at reaching out to the center of the electorate, establishing an image of moderation, and keeping a rein on its internal divisions. To accomplish this the new party carved out a viable economic and social policy that searched for a more liberal approach than the one advanced by the Socialists but made sure to keep the basics of the welfare state. Its leaders emphasized the Socialists' uncertainties and contradictions on the matter, particularly once the government decided to respond to the general strike of 1988 by increasing public spending and by allowing a huge increase of the national debt. They searched for a rapprochement with the peripheral nationalist movements, with poor results for the time being but trying to pave the way for some understanding in the future. When attacked as heirs to Francoism, they claimed (with some disingenuousness) continuity with UCD, whose legacy they embraced (and some of whose leaders had joined their ranks). Besides, if they were heirs, it was only by birth, so to speak, as they could have almost no personal recollection of Franco's times other than memories of kindergarten and primary schools. The fact is that the main Socialist leaders were in their early forties when they came to power in 1982; now, almost fifteen years later, they were confronted by a new generation of PP leaders who had come of age during the democratic transition.

From the restructuring in 1989 to 1996, the steady increase in numbers of PP affiliates and voters suggests that this new strategy of new identity, organization, and leadership worked. PP had about 262,000 affiliates in 1989, 375,000 in 1993, and 504,000 in 1996. It got around 5 million votes in the elections of 1989–1991; about 7.5 to 8 million in those of 1993–1995; and 9.6 million in the general elections of 1996.

In the period under consideration, not only did circumstances alter and the two contending parties change, but so did the public's character. In a large sociodemographic shift, a significant sector of the more urbanized, but also the more educated, younger, and more professionally active people moved away from the PSOE, and, from 1989 on, embraced the PP. On the rural-urban divide, while in 1989 the PSOE had more votes than PP in 28 provincial capitals (out of 50), in 1993 PP had more votes than PSOE in 39 capitals (Wert, Toharia, and López Pintor 1993). That same year the PP won in 12 cities with 200,000 inhabitants or more (out of 20; including Madrid, where the PP obtained 47.7% of the vote against the PSOE's 32%); the PSOE gained in 6 cities; while CiU came first in Barcelona and PNV came first in Bilbao.[12]

A case can be made that the rural vote corresponds to a less civic-minded population which is less demanding of political leaders. There is some evidence that the rural vote that supported the PSOE is to some extent a deferential vote. The provinces with larger agricultural population and fewer means of communication (as measured by the number of kilometers of national roads) tended to vote for the centrist party (UCD) when it ruled; the same provinces switched their vote to the Socialist party while the Socialists were safely in power, that is, during the 1980s. This suggests the existence of an instrumental or deferential vote for the party-in-government whatever it may be, with little or no particular loyalty to the party program, the party leadership, or the party identity (Cruz 1994). Also, the PSOE vote was particularly high in the rural districts which received special subsidies (for instance, the PER, in Andalusia and Extremadura).

In any case, the urban-rural divide aside, over the years the shift of the younger, professionally active and educated people away from PSOE and toward the PP was unmistakable. In 1982, 42% of the Socialist voters were less than 34 years old; in 1989, only 32% were less than 34 years old (28% of PP voters); and by 1996, just 29% (33% of PP voters). In 1982, 44% of the Socialist voters were employed and 4% were students. These percentages were almost the same in 1989 (42% and 3% respectively) and quite similar to those of PP: 42% and 5%. By 1996, however, 34% of the Socialist voters were employed (4% students), the percentages for the PP voters being 40% and 8%.

On the distribution of the population with various educational degrees between PSOE and PP, the data tell a similar story. By 1989, 33% of those voters with "second degree" studies and 16% of those with "third degree" (or higher) studies voted Socialist; the percentages of those who voted PP were 15% and 20%. By 1996, 29% of voters with second-degree studies and 19% of those with third-degree studies voted Socialist, while those who voted PP were 29% and 37%, respectively.

The trend can be explained by the hypothesis that the more urban, younger, more professionally active, and more educated members of society tend to have a higher level of civic demands, to pass judgment on their rulers, and to take them to task for their political activities. If we accept the assumption, then it turns out that in view of the circumstances of these last years, this is exactly what a significant sector did regarding the Socialist government.

This hypothesis brings us back to the main line of the argument sketched in Chapter 4. Against it, it may be argued that in most democracies, the public lacks information and has a simplistic and probably distorted interpretative frame for processing information, so that politicians have ample room for persuasion and manipulation. Still, the scope for manipulation varies according to the institutional and cultural resources the public may have at its disposal. The point is that in those years these institutional resources existed in Spain, expanded, and were put to use (both good and bad). The level of information increased thanks to the freedom of the press and other media, and more particularly to the competition among the different media. The educational level of society rose gradually as a result of a long-term trend that accelerated in the 1960s, 1970s, and 1980s (and the spread of education, incidentally, probably worked against having the public give much credit to the conspiracy theories). The public grew relatively detached vis-à-vis the political parties. Various ways to monitor the political class became institutionalized (not only by the media, but also by the very competition among the parties, and by the judiciary). There were ways for the public to express its approval or disapproval of politicians, such as opinion polls, which indicated the level of public trust, and, most importantly, frequent elections. Besides, manipulation by the parties was limited by the sheer complexity of the issues. If they tried too hard to manipulate public opinion, they might expose the politicians' amateurism and their dependence on experts in economic and social as well as legal matters. But after all this has been said, a few facts are still perplexing. To explore them may help to explain why, despite the extraordinary scandals of the early 1990s and the high rate of unemployment, the PSOE was able to keep the support of a big minority of Spaniards, and capitalize on the fact that its political adversaries found it difficult to gain the support of the majority of the citizenry.

The persistent support for the PSOE has several explanations. Some people did not feel much concern about the government breaking the rules in a fight against terrorism, and regarded the ensuing judicial proceedings with indifference. Public discussion of these issues was tainted by party politics, and friends of the Socialist government were often successful in blurring the issue of political responsibility and in stimulating emotional tribal reactions (the rhetorical excesses of the adversaries of the government may have contributed to this outcome). These sentiments were reinforced by practical considerations. As shown, unemployment affected a fifth of the labor force, but not directly the remaining four fifths. Youth under short-term contracts was just one third of the salaried population. The effects of unemployment were softened by the protection provided by the family and the welfare state (especially in regions such as Extremadura and Andalusia). They were played down by the center-left and center-right alike, in their cautious and conservative discourse on socioeconomic matters. In this context of general uneasiness, the protected wage earners, beneficiaries of the welfare state, worried about uncertainties that could precipitate labor market and welfare state reforms and saw the Socialists as guarantors of the status quo.

At the same time, certain sectors of the population did not trust the

PP for historical reasons. Most Spaniards had lived under the Franco regime, and many of them had come from regions where people held bitter memories of the Civil War and remembered the years that followed as times of repression. They felt uneasy about the PP and felt that its origins, despite the notable change in its image, its discourse, and its leadership in the last ten years, were still polluted by the links of its founders with the Francoist regime.

The electoral campaign and the results of the election on March 3, 1996, confirmed the primary relevance of the factors that pointed toward defeat of the Socialist party and the secondary (but not insignificant) importance of the factors that continued to support it. The *populares* (from the Popular Party) began the race as clear winners. Their leader, content to rely on the prognosis provided by the polls, chose to carry on a soft and respectful campaign, imagining their adversary defeated from the outset. The Socialists, on the contrary, fighting for sheer survival, contended ardently in an aggressive (some times uncivil) campaign which explicitly linked the PP with the Francoist dictatorship. The PSOE also claimed that the right (a term rejected by the PP, which portrayed itself as a center-right party) harbored the hidden project of dismantling the welfare state, especially the public pension system. Disoriented, and thinking that the Socialists' tactics were dictated by desperation, the PP reacted blandly. The Socialists' attacks gained momentum; by the end of the campaign, González repeatedly invoked the motto *"no pasarán"* ("they will not pass") that rang out against the Franco forces during the Civil War in republican Madrid (in fact, the motto originated in the French defense against German troops in Verdun, during the First World War). The Socialists' use of this phrase, with all its associations, in an electoral contest that was taking place in a peaceful, democratic polity showed them willing to forsake, for an electoral advantage, the whole edifice of prudent discourse elaborated during the transition to democracy. In that early campaign, the protagonists deliberately softened their speech and were most careful with the use of symbols, in order to initiate a period of mutual respect and toleration between the parties and gain reconciliation between the antagonists in the Civil War. To this provocation the leaders of the PP reacted with moderate indignation, confident they would gain victory by a wide margin.

In the end, the PP won the elections by a slight margin. Clearly, the expectation of a secure victory had been counterproductive, while the excesses of the Socialist leaders had been successful. The People's Party got 156 deputies (141 in 1993), the PSOE got 141 (159 in 1993). The PP was far from a majority (176 deputies), which forced it to enter into difficult negotiations to get stable parliamentary support for a PP-led government. The PP had widened its electoral base (4 percentage points more than in 1993) and had won in most of the provincial capitals (except for the ones in Catalonia, and Bilbao, Seville, and Huelva), but its margin, with just 38.8% of the vote, was too short. The PSOE got 37.4%, just a slight decrease from its 38.7% in 1993. Going back to the beginning, the PP went from 21.8% in 1989 to 38.8% in 1996, but the PSOE seemed to keep a relatively high ceiling (39.3% in 1989, 37.4% in 1996). Yes, the PP had won, but its victory was not complete.

Coalition Politics after the 1996 Election

The electoral results of March 1996 reflected the complex motivations of the voters. The problems of unlawful behavior, political responsibility, and unemployment affected a crucial segment of the population, contributing to the decisive increase in the vote for the PP and its victory over the Socialists. But for different groups of voters, concerns about the future of the welfare state, feelings of party loyalty, and attachment to the symbols and traditions of nationalist groups were strong enough to counteract the effect of scandals and unemployment. Errors of judgment too influenced the election results. The Socialists, no doubt convinced by pre-electoral opinion polls that the PP was close to obtaining an absolute majority, decided to mount an aggressive campaign. The PP offered only a mild response (in retrospect, this was probably a mistake). Conversely, part of the electorate tried to limit the extent of the PP's triumph, which everybody had taken for granted.[13]

The PP's failure to achieve the resounding victory which all had anticipated was disconcerting for many, but it sweetened the bitter taste of defeat for the Socialists and their supporters. Even that sweetness was soon to turn sour, however, as the expression of coinciding interests and affinities between the Popular Party and the nationalist parties began to grow, slowly but inexorably. This was an unpleasant surprise to the Socialists, and there were other surprises as well. What had seemed marginal, that is, the question of the peripheral nationalist movements and what role to assign to their representatives, proved fundamental. An agreement between the center-right and the nationalist groups, which had seemed almost inconceivable, soon appeared almost inevitable, as if it were perfectly natural. And at that point, the Socialists' apparently marginal defeat was revealed as outright defeat, pure and simple.

The election results brought to an end more than thirteen years of Socialist rule and presented the Catalan (and, to a lesser extent, the Basque) nationalists with the opportunity of playing a pivotal role in Spanish politics. The victorious PP and its leader, José María Aznar, could not even form a government, let alone govern, without their support. Under the new circumstances, CiU decided to offer it, even though the nationalist spokesman had previously made public his decision not to support the PP. The nationalists were forced to justify this turnaround by explaining that their electoral commitment had been circumstantial and provisional; their main commitment was to maximize their influence in government, which would benefit Catalan interests as a whole.

In Catalan nationalist (or Catalanist) discourse, Spanish and Catalan interests were usually presented as compatible and mutually reinforcing. This was vintage formulation and had been reiterated over the last twenty years at various critical junctures: to justify support for UCD during the transition; for the Partido Reformista, led by Miquel Roca, during the mid-1980s;[14] and for the Socialist government between 1993 and 1996, after the ground had been prepared by earlier agreements between 1989 and 1993. This formulation centered squarely on economic policy and regional policy, even when these were in fact interconnected and led, in turn, to other matters such as European policy and the rule of law. For their part, the Basques, who did not wish to feel responsible for the governance of Spain, had been part of a regional coalition government with the Socialists for almost ten years, and they had continually dealt with problems of economic, regional, and European policy and the issue of respect for the law (in particular as regards the fight against terrorism).

Hence the novelty was not the nationalist discourse as such, but that it was a possible strategic option to collaborate with a center-right government on matters of fundamental importance such as the rule of law, the problems of the economy, and participation in the European

Monetary Union, while getting closer to a solution to the problem of Spain as a pluralistic, multinational society. The situation seemed to provide a rapprochement between Spanish nationalism and the peripheral nationalisms, which had a history of antagonism and had fought each other in the Civil War—and therefore to provide Spain with a golden opportunity to take another significant step forward in its long-delayed and fairly protracted civilizing process.

The Rule of Law and the Maastricht Requirements

For the new government, the two pressing issues were to wrap up the trials and straighten out the economy. This had to be done with an eye to the country's political stability, that is, to the stability of the political alliance with the nationalists, and therefore with proper and careful attention to the politics of identity and to the devolution of power in economic and other fields to the Autonomous Communities (see below). I will discuss briefly how those two fundamental issues have been handled before looking into the problems raised by the nationalist movements. It is not necessary to chronicle the government's performance and every step of the judiciary proceedings during the two years following the elections of 1996; it will suffice to outline the general course of events, for, in a sense, these were rather straightforward—and, if we ignore all the sound and fury, relatively simple to characterize.

To begin with, the application of the rule of law followed the path initiated in the prior period, so that most judiciary proceedings just took one or several steps further down that road. A few cases reached their final stage, and the judges' instructions culminated in trials before the Supreme Court (which issued its final verdict in the cases of FILESA and Segundo Marey), and before the Audiencia Provincial of Madrid (in the case of Roldán). In another case related to the GAL (the kidnapping, torture, and assassination of José Antonio Lasa and José Ignacio Zabala), the preliminary phase by the judge of instruction (Javier Gómez de Liaño) brought a formal indictment of one high-ranking officer and two others from among those accused (in May 27, 1996), while in other cases[15] either the system worked at a slower pace, or the evidence remained inconclusive, or the matters became so entangled as to require additional time, so that (by August 1998) the cases were still pending. The cases of FILESA, Roldán, and Segundo Marey deserve a summary of the actual findings and sentences.

The FILESA case was about illegal financing of the Socialist party. Front companies were set up, allegedly to provide advice and research to business corporations. In fact the funds they obtained were channeled to the PSOE: that much was established by the Supreme Court according to the ruling of October 28, 1997. The Court condemned José María Sala, a Socialist senator and an important figure of the Catalan Socialist party (a branch or associate of the PSOE), to three years in prison; and Carlos Navarro, a former secretary for the finances of the parliamentary group of the Socialist party and himself a Socialist representative in the Spanish Parliament, to eleven years in prison (and five other persons accused received diverse jail sentences).[16] The Socialists reacted with anger and accused the Court of having issued a "political" verdict. They also appealed to the Constitutional Court (which is not a court of appeals for the sentences issued by the Supreme Court, but is there to make sure that there has been no *indefension*, or inability of the defendant to have a proper defense). Last but not least, the Socialists asked for a pardon or *indulto*.

Luis Roldán, former head of the Guardia Civil, was accused of a number of crimes. He was first sentenced in February 27, 1998, when the Audiencia Provincial of Madrid found him guilty on many counts (of misuse of public funds, taking bribes, tax evasion, and others) and sentenced him to 28 years in jail (and also to pay a fine of 1.6 thousand million pesetas, and to pay back taxes up to another 957 million). The sentence starts with an emblematic phrase: "The indicted Luis Roldán, *mayor de edad* [of legal age; not a juvenile] and without a prior criminal record, immediately after being designated the director general of the Guardia Civil on November 4, 1986, and until his resignation on December 7, 1993, engaged in unremitting *(incesante)* criminal activity, under the cover and protection of his public office, in order to enrich himself in an illicit way."[17] And from this general condemnatory statement, the sentence goes on to detail *some* of the criminal activities of Luis Roldán (Roldán's *other* criminal undertakings being the target of several other criminal proceedings). They involved an intricate web of front companies, fiduciaries, and Swiss accounts constructed during the seven years of his full tenure in office (acting under orders from then-ministers José Barrionuevo and José Luis Corcuera). By the time of the sentencing, the Socialists had succeeded in putting some distance between themselves and Roldán; and at least the sentence did not credit Roldán's claim that he funneled part of the missing money into the PSOE's finances. The proceedings did, however, suggest a disturbing connection between the lack of control in the use of public funds, personal enrichment, and the fight against terrorism, as many of Roldán's criminal activities were closely linked to his ability to make discretionary use of the reserved funds (which were supposed to be used for antiterrorist activities), and also to decide about allocations for public works such as building the housing compounds of the *guardias civiles* in the Basque country and in other places (these became favorite targets of the terrorists).

The biggest case so far, the kidnapping of Segundo Marey in France on December 4, 1983, had been dormant for about ten years. It was reopened in July of 1993, and took another five years (and two consecutive *autos de instrucción*, by Judge Baltasar Garzón and by Judge Eduardo Móner) to get to the Supreme Court. In July 28, 1998, the Court delivered its verdict and condemned José Barrionuevo (then Minister of the Interior), Rafael Vera (then Director of State Security and later secretary of state for State Security), and Julián Sancristóbal (former provincial governor of Vizcaya), to ten years in jail for their participation in the kidnapping and for their misuse of public funds. Other former police officers and a former secretary general of PSOE in Vizcaya received prison terms ranging from two to nine years.[18] Barrionuevo and Vera were adamant in denying the charges until the last minute; all the rest admitted to their participation in the crimes. The police officers alleged they had been punished because they had obeyed the state twice; first, by following the orders of their administrative superiors to engage in activities which, they were told, were affairs of state, and later, by telling the truth.

The majority of the Court (the verdict was passed by seven votes to four) considered that the weight of the evidence (presented in the two previous *instrucciones* by Garzón and Móner, and again during the trial) was more than sufficient. It included many sworn testimonies, documentation of proposals and decisions,[19] and proof of the actual implementation of those decisions. Carrying them out involved many officials, who had to coordinate such things as several illegal crossings of the international border and transfers of sizable sums of money. The

Court decided that the overall responsibility rested with Minister of Interior Barrionuevo and his immediate collaborator Vera—among other things, because it was "inconceivable" and "unbelievable" that these activities could have been going on "without the knowledge and the approval of the people in position of maximum responsibility at the Ministry of Interior."[20] Barrionuevo, Vera, and the Socialists in general reacted in anger, and asserted that such a sentence would tear society apart. But the majority of the public did not feel this way, and the social cleavage they referred to seemed unlikely. In fact, repeated surveys in the prior months suggested that about two thirds of the population wanted the judiciary proceedings to be carried out in full, and most of those who responded (assuming one third was still undecided) stated that they believed Barrionuevo and Vera were implicated in the affair (4 to 1 for the whole population) and that González himself was in the know *(estuvo al tanto)* of the affair (2.5 to 1 for the whole population).[21]

These Court rulings ought to be valued for putting the proper end to a judiciary process. They were also part of a complex process of self-regulation and adjustment of the Spanish system of justice. The scandals of the 1990s provoked a general malaise and uncertainty on the part of the public over whether justice would be done when important economic and political figures were involved in criminal proceedings—in other words, would the principle of equality before the law be realized. At the same time, the public was deeply concerned about the ordinary functioning of the system of justice, and increasingly restless about the slow pace at which the justice seemed to work. Very long delays were the norm for just the *beginning* of civil proceedings (eleven months of delay as an average) and more than twice as long for administrative ones (twenty-eight months).[22] Yet on the whole, the trials and the sentences of recent years demonstrated the process of putting the principle of the rule of law in operation. They showed that the system of justice was on the move and tried to meet the concerns of ordinary citizens.

The trials obviously had significant political effects on the Socialists' fortunes, and some of these surprised them. After Felipe González was forced to leave his position of top leadership in the party, one of his trusted ex-ministers, Joaquín Almunia, was chosen for the post. Hoping to strengthen his position, Almunia took a risky decision. He proposed to hold primary elections for the top post, and also for the positions of presidents of Autonomous Communities and mayors of all cities of more than 50,000 inhabitants. The move intended to galvanize the party and to gain the public's favor at a time when the trials monopolized the media's headlines. So Almunia ran against José Borrell, a candidate who tried to distance himself from the trials and claimed he represented the masses while Almunia was the candidate of the party apparatus. Despite González's support, Almunia lost by a wide margin. In April 24, 1998, 55% of PSOE's members voted for Borrell and 44% for Almunia. Borrell won in all but three of the seventeen Spanish Autonomous Communities.[23] The party members appeared to be sending the message that they wanted a change in leadership and wished to leave the past behind.

The end of the trials meant prison terms for some leading Socialists. Moreover, these sentences cast a shadow on Felipe González himself, even though the Court refused to indict him (there was no direct evidence against him) and allowed him to testify on behalf of his subordinates. It was easy to conclude, however, that either he was disingenuous or his judgment and competence should be questioned. After all, everybody knew that while the trial was about a minor incident at the beginning of the activities of the GAL, these activities had continued for about four years and had resulted in more than twenty killings. It could therefore be argued (by applying the same logic at work in the Supreme Court's sentence of July 27, 1998) that it was "inconceivable" and "unbelievable" that all these activities could have been carried out without González's knowledge and his approval. But more than the leader's political fortunes were at stake; so were the identity and self-perception of the Socialist party, which depended on whether the party decided to identify itself (and its future) with its traditional leader (and his past). Either way, it was bound to be a painful and difficult decision for the party.

That Spain passed in the spring of 1998 the "examination" for entry in the European Monetary Union in 1999 is a simple and straightforward story of *fortuna* and *virtú*. The economy benefited from an upswing phase of the economic cycle, and at the same time, the key decisions were made to lower the interest rates and to reduce the public debt. This in turn stimulated the economy and sent the right signals to the European authorities and to the capital markets, which reacted favorably, and thus a virtuous circle was allowed to develop. The European Council's final decision to include Spain in the EMU (beginning January 1, 1999) followed: an outcome that had seemed unlikely at the time of the elections of March 1996 and the advent of a PP government (in May 1996).

Part of the merit for this development rested, therefore, on outside factors, and part on sensible monetary policies by the Bank of Spain (which became independent in the spring of 1994) and also (to a point) on the preliminary efforts by departing Minister of the Economy Pedro Solbes—for the goal of Spain's entry into the EMU was shared by *populares*, socialists, and Catalan and Basque nationalists alike. But it was the government of José María Aznar and his Minister of Economy Rodrigo Rato, which (with the parliamentary support of the Catalan nationalists) bore the main responsibility for the budgets of 1997 and 1998, and for a host of ad hoc and structural measures that paved the way for the remarkable growth of the economy from 1996 on.

The fact is that the differential in long-term interest rates with the German ones fell from 450 basic points in mid 1995 to 50 by late 1997; that inflation fell from 4.5% by late 1995 to less than 2% by late 1997-early 1998; that the public deficit, which was 6.5% of the GDP in 1995, had gone down to 2.9% in 1997. So Spain, which in 1996 fulfilled none of the Maastricht criteria, had met them by late 1997 and the spring of 1998—the only exception being its public debt (68% of the GDP in 1997), a "low mark" it shared with Germany, the Netherlands, Austria, and Portugal (not to speak of Italy, with 123%, and Belgium, with 124.7%) (See Table 4). By late 1997 and early 1998, as the first objective of entering the EMU seemed practically attained, the government started preparing itself for the next move, this time a conflict with Germany, the Netherlands, and others over the cohesion funds and how to finance the Eastern enlargement.

I do not intend to go into the specifics of the economic and social policies in the two years after the 1996 elections, but once more to suggest the general direction they took. Other than the measures needed to meet the Maastricht criteria in the short run, the government followed a general logic of continuing to open the Spanish economy to the European and world economies. In 1997, with the agreement of the unions, it attempted a modest reform of the labor market that helped to reduce severance payments for a segment of the labor force and was meant to stimulate employment—which in fact grew at a remarkable

Table 4. Basic demographic and economic indicators in Spain and other
Western countries, 1995

	Population (in millions)	Employment (in millions)	GDP (in billions of US dollars)	GDP per capita (in thousands of US dollars)
Germany	81.6	35.8	2412	29.5
France	58.1	21.7	1537	26.4
United Kingdom	58.6	25.5	1101	18.7
Italy	57.2	20.0	1087	18.9
Spain	39.2	11.7	559	14.2
Canada	29.6	13.2	560	18.9
Poland	38.5	14.6	118	3.0

Source: OECD 1998b: 234.

pace during 1997 and 1998. By mid-1998, the government had pushed through an ambitious program of privatization of telecommunications and energy, keeping control only over public television, railroads, the post office, and some coal mining. It committed itself to reduce taxes in 1999, and to get the marginal rate of the income tax from 56% down to 48%, and possibly down to 40% a few years later. It did little more than to sketch the rough draft of reforms of health and pensions, real estate and water use—but it seemed likely that the changes would be toward increasing the role of the market mechanisms in all these fields.[24] In effect, the economic cycle combined with economic policy to generate a net increase in employment of 1.1 million jobs between the first quarter of 1996 and the third quarter of 1998 (and a reduction of about 4 percentage points in the unemployment rate).

Whatever the prospects for these policies in the future, their pro-market philosophy seems to be tempered by a keen sense of the need to obtain a social consensus, to work with the unions whenever feasible, and to retain the basics of the welfare state. This way of thinking could be a matter of political principle or common sense realism: the perceived need to adjust to social and political pressures coming from many quarters, from inside and from outside the party, including its nationalist allies. Whether or not this combination of cautious liberal economic policy and a soft approach to social policy will do the job, to what extent, how, and what might be the price to pay in economic efficiency for these sociopolitical adjustments—these and many other questions cannot be answered here. The answers depend on specific measures taken under incalculable circumstances in the future. But my point here is that all this political activity seems to deepen and intensify a long-term transition from a developmental toward a regulatory state—that is, one that depends less on specific interventions and more on setting the general laws and rules for investors, producers, and consumers to make their own decisions and live with the consequences. In short, this is the trend we already noticed during the last stages of Socialist rule, though then it was implemented hesitantly and inconsistently.

CHAPTER SEVEN

The Challenge
of Nationalism

BOTH THE RULE OF LAW and the pro-market economic pol-
icy point to the development of a form of polity characterized by governance by rules (which may in time yield a corresponding style of
politics). Indeed, this may be what it means to belong to the European
Union: being part of a political association that is governed by rules, not
by strong leaders with extraordinary missions to accomplish.[1] The same
characterization applies to what has been going on in the domestic
scene regarding the relationship between the Spanish parties and the
Catalan and Basque nationalist parties. In the end, they are coming full
circle to an understanding based on the need to follow rules, in this
case, the constitutional rules that frame the Autonomous Communities.

The idea of nationalism comprises distinct elements. It includes the
feeling individuals may have of belonging to a sociocultural community,
which normally is associated with a particular territory: a *(socio)cultural
nationalism*. It is often implied that this feeling should lead to some form
of political activity which guarantees respect for the signs of that sociocultural identity, and this *political nationalism* may be, in turn, of a
minimal or of a maximal character (or anything in between). A minimal
nationalism would be defensive in character, limited in its institutional
goals, and respectful of the national feelings of other people who live in
the same area. At the other extreme, nationalism would be an aggressive
movement which brings together individuals who share a particular

national sentiment. They may attempt to control the state and use it as an instrument to impose their beliefs on the rest of the population. Some moderate versions of political nationalism and all the maximizing ones argue for a highly differentiated national public authority or, in the extreme, an independent national state—a *state nationalism*. Finally, it is assumed quite often that this national public authority or state is the bearer of an extraordinary mission. The mission may be formulated in many ways, but it has often been a mission to modernize the nation—even to put the nation on a par with the most advanced nations in the world according to the standards of the time. This type of state nationalism with a modernizing mission (with specific plans for industrialization and education)—a *modernizing state nationalism*—has always captured the imagination of politicians and academics. This was the kind of nationalism on which Ernest Gellner wrote most persuasively (for instance, Gellner 1983).[2] Of course, politically moderate or even state nationalisms may well adopt other missions, such as that of going back to a golden age, or building a society with a mix of futuristic and archaic components. Furthermore, political nationalism (in whatever form) could also have a minimal mission, a libertarian one, in which the public authority or the state would have no other mission than that of making it possible for individuals (and their families) to pursue their own missions, including decisions to develop the feelings of national belonging that suit them best.

Hence various forms of nationalism combine cultural and political elements in different ways. Some forms and combinations lead to aggressive and exclusionary kinds of nationalism—of an uncivil kind. Catalan and Basque as well as Spanish nationalist movements, as they have developed in contemporary history, have been characterized by confusion, by ambivalence and misunderstandings, and by immoderate claims that had put them quite often on a collision course. Yet the record also shows recurrent attempts at working out compromises between them. It may even be argued that if the strands composing the nationalist movements can be separated out, they could be used to form new combinations to make these nationalist expressions relatively harmless and bring them together in peaceful coexistence, even in fruitful cooperation; what used to be an uncivil kind of nationalism may be transformed into one of a more civil nature.

This may happen in a variety of ways. For instance, (1) the sociocultural element is stressed but provision is made for mixed feelings and for mixed identities; (2) room is left for experimenting with diverse varieties of political nationalisms so that the state nationalism is one among many; (3) the mission attached to nationalism, political or sociocultural, is defined in a way that makes it compatible with maintaining and magnifying freedom. In all these hypothetical cases, a political community of several nations may develop.

Such a community would have to ensure that the feelings of belonging to any particular group do not exclude their belonging to the whole; that the design of the state allows the elites and the people of different regions access to political power; and that some version of socioeconomic and cultural modernization (if this is what is intended) is everywhere perceived as common to all. The solutions to the problems of modernization must be coherent with the project of forming a civil or open society and with the definition of a (common) national interest which could reasonably be defended to the outside world—for example, the national interest involved in the integration of Spain into the European Union. The current Spanish experience with Catalan and Basque nationalist movements, and their relationship with the larger nation, could be examined in light of the above, as a case study to test those hypothetical considerations.

Society, Culture, and Economy

Catalonia has some six million inhabitants, and the Basque country a little over two million. Their present populations are, to a large extent, the result of great migratory waves which flooded both regions from the end of the nineteenth century up to the 1970s. According to survey data, 39% of adults in Catalonia at the end of the 1980s were native children of native parents; 23% were native children of immigrants or mixed couples; and 38% were immigrants (Pallarés et al. 1991). In the Basque country in the early 1990s, 40% of adults were native children of native parents; 29% were native children of immigrants or mixed couples; and 31% were immigrants (Ruiz Olabuenga y Blanco, 1994). The majority of Catalans speak both Catalan and Spanish correctly; those who only speak Spanish usually understand Catalan and the transition from one language to another can be made without much difficulty. In contrast, in the Basque country, everyone knows Spanish but only one quarter of the population speaks the Basque language, Euskera.[3] The highest percentages of speakers of Euskera are to be found chiefly, though not exclusively, in five areas in Guipúzcoa and a few others in Vizcaya that have small and medium-sized nuclei of Euskera speakers. To date, the nationalist government has accepted that the policy of expansion of the Basque language will be slow and gradual, though there are indications that point to a recent acceleration of the process.

When Catalans and Basques are asked about their identity, a majority admit to feelings of dual identity. According to recent surveys, only a minority of 14% of Catalans and 20% of Basques claim an exclusively Catalan or Basque identity; only 11% of Catalans and 16% of Basques refer to an exclusively Spanish identity. For all of the rest who replied, that is, for 72% of Catalans and 59% of Basques, the two identities are compatible, although naturally there are degrees and differences between natives and immigrants, and between speakers of Catalan and Euskera and those who only speak Spanish (García Ferrando et al. 1994). Furthermore, it is the children of natives who tend to identify themselves as only Catalans or only Basques in a far higher proportion than the children of mixed or immigrant homes, and than immigrants themselves. In Catalonia, 23% of the natives considered themselves as only Catalans, whereas the percentage drops to 7% for those of mixed origin, 6% for people of immigrant origin, and only 2% for immigrants. Naturally, these percentages are reversed in the case of those who reply "only Spanish": that is, 20% of immigrants, 4% of native children of immigrants, and 2% of both natives and children of mixed origin. The distribution is similar in the case of the Basques (Pallarés et al. 1991).

What is most interesting, however, is the far wider spread for the intermediate group. According to the survey in 1990 (and prior to examining the finer differences between natives and immigrants), a total of 36% of residents in Catalonia said that they considered themselves to be as much Catalan as Spanish, and another 36% stated that they felt an affinity with both identities although not in the same proportion (5%, more Spanish than Catalan, and 31%, more Catalan than Spanish). The point is that, one way or another, 72% place themselves in a wide intermediate zone, and only two small minorities remain in the extreme zones of exclusive (national) identities (García Ferrando et al. 1994). The two zones of exclusive identities appear to be larger in the Basque country than in Catalonia: 16% of residents considered themselves to be only Spanish and 20%, to be only Basque. However, yet again a majority of the population (59%) placed itself within the intermediate zone of dual or shared identity (35% said that they felt as much Basque as Spanish; 3%, more Spanish than Basque; and 21%, more Basque than Spanish). These results were repeated in the Basque country in a more recent survey in October 1998: 64.1% of the respondents admitted to feelings of shared identity.[4] In this respect, Catalonia and the Basque country may be considered as multinational as Spain; that is, they contain groups of people who have different feelings of national belonging, whether to one nation only, or to several simultaneously.

Economic history suggests a similar reciprocity between the Basque, Catalan, and Spanish economies. Catalonia and the Basque country pioneered the industrialization of Spain. Catalan and Basque industrialists cornered the Spanish market for their textile and metallurgical products, among many others. The Basques founded the Spanish banking system and constructed many public works. The industrialists had formed a strange sociopolitical coalition with Andalusian and Castillian farmers, and managed to convince the Spanish government of the virtues of a protectionist policy in the 1890s. Such a policy served their interests for decades, until the gradual change toward a more liberal economic policy in the foreign sector began in the 1960s. In terms of economic growth, the consequence of dominance by these industrial (and agrarian) interests was greater development of Catalonia and the Basque country, which then became the focus of attraction for immigrants from other parts of Spain.

From the economic point of view, Catalans and Basques have led and dominated Spain for quite a considerable time, with the Spanish state protecting them from foreign competition and from the radical social movements of the anarcho-syndicalists (in Catalonia) and the socialists (in the Basque country) between the 1890s and the 1930s. The Francoist state continued this tradition of support for the Catalan and Basque regional economies in its essentials, although it also promoted greater geographic diversification of Spanish industry, converting Madrid and other cities into industrial centers of major importance from the 1950s onwards. Even today, the enterprises located in Catalonia and the Basque country are oriented toward the Spanish capital, product, and labor markets.

In the last twenty-five years, Catalonia has continued to be an economically powerful region. Its per capita income is one-fifth higher than the national average, and its rate of unemployment is considerably lower. In contrast, the Basque country has gone down in ranking: its per capita income is now only slightly higher than the national average, and its unemployment rate is above average. This downturn almost certainly reflects the effects of the economic crisis which affected its basic industries, and the social climate of unrest resulting from many years of terrorism. Nevertheless, the Basque business tradition continues to be important, and it affects Spain as a whole, in the industrial sector as well as in the distribution and service sectors in general.[5]

Politics and Memories

The above demographic, sociocultural, and economic facts have affected the composition of the electorate and its attitude toward the relationship between these regions and the rest of Spain. In this extremely complex interplay, the nationalists play a very important part but do not have local hegemony. Thus in the general election of 1996, all the nationalist parties combined (two coalitions in Catalonia and three Basque parties) obtained less than a third of the votes in Catalonia, and less than half (46%) in the Basque country. The nationalist vote is higher in regional elections, in which the nationalists usually win half the votes in Catalonia and between one half and two thirds in the Basque country (55% in the 1998 elections). Territorial distribution should also be taken into account: in the Basque country, for example, the differences are enormous between Alava, where non-nationalists received more than two thirds of the vote in the 1996 general elections, Vizcaya, where the vote is usually split equally, and Guipúzcoa, where the nationalists predominate.

Nevertheless, a vote for the nationalists does not mean a vote for independence and separatism. In 1990, an overwhelming majority (of between two thirds and three quarters) declared in favor of a federal structure, more or less similar to the one existing at present (García Ferrando et al. 1994). In 1998, in response to a question asking "what would be best for the Basque country, independence or regional autonomy within Spain?" 18.2% favored independence and 67.6% favored autonomy. Moreover, only 29.4% of the voters for nationalist parties (and 21.2% of PNV voters) favored independence, while 63% of nationalist voters (and 70% of PNV) favored autonomy.[6]

Because of this fragmented political landscape, and in the absence of a clearly marked sociocultural division between natives and immigrants (which does not exclude appreciable differences, but is probably less than that between Italians of the northern and southern regions, for example), no violent antagonism has erupted between moderate nationalists and non-nationalists. In Catalonia the CiU has governed through negotiation and compromise with the Socialist party (as the main party in opposition); and in the Basque country, the PNV and the PSOE have governed together from 1987 to 1998 (largely owing to the split in the PNV and the formation of Eusko Alkartasuna, EA). Furthermore, coalitions have been, and still are, common practice in local politics. In the Basque country, local alliances tended to exclude the PP and to include Herri Batasuna (a coalition of radical nationalist groupings) for a time. In the late 1980s HB began to be left on the fringe, probably due to the position adopted at the conference of Ajuria-Enea (in January 1988) in the face of the terrorist phenomenon. The change in the political landscape was also due to the evolution of the PP toward the center since the end of the 1980s (which has led to its presence in municipal governments in the main cities of the region; in Bilbao, for example, in coalition with the PNV for several years after 1991, and for an earlier period in San Sebastián).

Four other factors have fostered these "live and let live" attitudes and practices of compromise evident among the majority of politicians in both Catalonia and the Basque country so far.

First, there has been the day-to-day experience of peaceful coexistence with no confrontations between native, immigrant, and mixed origin groups. They have worked together; they have carried out their transactions and commitments to daily linguistic coexistence without a fuss; they have diversified their votes and political preferences (of all shades); all, or the majority, have displayed a sentimental attachment to a common land, and loyalty to their institutions. In the Basque country, civil coexistence between communities has continued in spite of the counterpoint of terrorist violence (in the shape of major bomb attacks and intermittent violence).

Second, in keeping with this experience, the Basque population prefers political compromises and political coalitions formed between the nationalists and the non-nationalists in the Basque government. In a recent survey, 52.4% of those interviewed favored coalitions of nationalist and non-nationalists, as against 26.3% who favored coalitions of nationalists. Even PNV voters preferred mixed coalitions (48.8% versus 41.7%).[7]

Third, the regional political elites gained the experience of forming part of a wider political class and grew accustomed to the language of a Constitution and statutes which guarantee a pluralist Spain. Together, the regional and national politicians have shared most of the democratic experience (although, to some extent, in opposition) and together, on one memorable occasion, they suffered the consequences of being part of a single democratic political class (during the attempted coup d'état, on 23 February of 1981).

Fourth, the politicians (and later society in general) have gradually become aware of the distinction between political rhetoric and political reality. Possibly the experience of having Socialist governments carry out economic (and foreign) policies that were traditionally attributed to the right accustomed the public to being a little more tolerant of the ambiguities of political life (even though the political class still gave vent to occasional outbursts of rhetoric left over from its ideological adolescence). In turn, this newly acquired capacity to tolerate political ambiguity (though not political deceit of the kind used to cover up criminal activities, which is something else entirely) has brought improvement in the civility of political discussion.

On the other hand, feelings of nationalists are closely tied to what they call the "differential fact" of their group personality, and the historical memory of a long experience of self-government. This personality difference is based on language and, in the Basque case, ethnic composition. Catalan is a Romance language like Spanish, whereas Basque not only is not Romance, it is not even Indo-European. Nevertheless, it had fundamental importance for the development of Spanish.[8] The native Basques themselves are probably a western-Pyrenaic people; they predominate in some parts of their territory but are present in almost all parts of the Basque country and in some neighboring areas (Azaola 1988). All the differentiating factors (which are also applicable to Galicia) are reinforced by a memory of self-government (weaker in Galicia) that dates back to the Middle Ages.

These historic memories are profound and indelible yet cannot be reduced to a single, simple version. The nationalist and academic elites, as well as the local clergy, share a reading of the medieval and modern history of their regions (up to the eighteenth century) that emphasizes the regional autonomy of Catalonia and the local freedoms of the Basques. Indeed, some centuries after the Arab invasion, Catalonia became a regional power under the Crown of Aragón, with an outstanding cultural tradition and flourishing trade in the Mediterranean. For a number of reasons (partly as a result of the hostility of the Holy See, with which they were federated), the kings of Aragón lacked the necessary means for developing a centralized state apparatus which, up to a point, the kings of Castille and León were able to do.

These constitutional distinctions fit the tradition of complex political arrangements typical of Christian Europe in the Middle Ages and the early modern era. At that time, monarchs were obliged to respect the exemptions and immunities of nobility and of local urban oligarchies that controlled municipal governments, all of which were locked in incessant conflicts of interest with the peasants and the lower classes in the towns. This situation continued in Spain during the reign of Ferdinand and Isabella (who, through their marriage, brought about the union of the different kingdoms in Spain) and the reigns of their descendants, the Hapsburgs. An attempt at unification and centralization was made in the middle of the seventeenth century, but it failed. Regional powers disappeared only in the early eighteenth century, when the victorious Bourbon king took the opportunity to suppress the *fueros* (the regional codes of law; some institutions of civil law were respected) and hence all tradition of self-government, as punishment for the support of the Catalans and Valencians for his rival in the Wars of Succession.

The Basques had a more limited tradition of local self-government in the *señoríos* or provinces of Vizcaya, Guipúzcoa, and Alava. At first they came under the protection of the king of Navarre, then of the kings of Castille and Leon and later, of the kings of Spain. Although the two Carlist wars were fought on Basque soil in the nineteenth century, the Basque provinces found formulas by which to maintain a certain degree of self-government, like the *conciertos* or agreements on fiscal matters, whereby the Basque provinces collected most taxes and then paid an agreed amount of money (which was periodically renegotiated) to the central government. This system has been in place since the late nineteenth century (with the exception of the provinces of Vizcaya and Guipúzcoa, during the Francoist period).

Hence both regions have a long tradition of self-government, although it was always within the framework of and subject to a higher sovereign rule. The tradition was interrupted, in the Catalan case, in the early eighteenth century, and maintained (with exceptions and changes) in the Basque case. However, this sense of tradition fragments as it passes through the prism of contemporary experience over the last two centuries, which have been witness to intense internal conflicts. These, logically, have given rise to different memories.

Between 1820 and the 1830s, the attitudes of Catalans and Basques in rural areas tended to be opposite to those of the inhabitants of the cities. Many of the former, under the influence of the Catholic Church, identified themselves as *Carlistas* (that is, supporters of Don Carlos, who disputed the crown with Isabel II), were hostile to the liberal state, and defended the restoration of the Holy Inquisition. Their attitude toward the cities in their regions veered from ambivalence to hostility (in the case of Bilbao, for example). Indeed, the Carlists never managed to control the cities, either militarily or politically. The urban bourgeoisie was liberal and was prepared to play an active, at times a leading, role in the Spanish politics of that period. Thanks to their activism, they were able to limit the scope of some local *fueros*, which would otherwise have prevented the exportation of iron and the unification of the internal market, both of which proved decisive for the momentum of Basque capitalism in the twentieth century.

At the end of the nineteenth century, the situation became more complicated as a result of the effects of industrialization, the creation of an industrial proletariat of mainly immigrant origin, and the corresponding social movements. These were led by anarcho-syndicalists in Catalonia and by socialists in the Basque country. The tensions between the countryside and the cities, the industrialists and the unions, form the background to the emergence of the nationalist movements (for which the original impulse often came from people whose families had supported the Carlists).

Nationalism developed a special affinity with the native industrialist class, but not without problems. On the one hand, the industrialists needed the Spanish market for its products and the cheap, available, immigrant labor that came from the rest of Spain; they also needed the Spanish state to protect them from foreign competition and worker radicalism. On the other hand, their links with the Spanish market implied dependence on a very slow-growing demand; the immigrant workers were a foreign element; and although they used the state, they never came to consider it their own. Never were they able fully to control the Spanish state nor get it to promulgate all the public policies they wanted; and they did not believe that the state was fulfilling the tasks of modernization that the French or Germans appeared capable of achieving. As a result, they, and particularly the Catalan industrialists, sought to achieve at least some degree of regional self-government in which they could play the undisputed role of protagonists. However, this endeavor was balanced by the melancholy reflection that, in the event of violent social confrontations, they would have to appeal to the central state.

It is not surprising that the history of the two regions between the end of the last century and the 1930s left diverse and contradictory memories in the various social milieus. In the memory of immigrants, these were times of economic exploitation and social discrimination. The industrialists and the middle classes felt ambivalent, and the nationalists themselves felt trapped. They were caught up in the confrontation between *las izquierdas* and *las derechas* (interestingly, the terms were used in the plural) which finally led to the outbreak of Civil War in 1936. At the very last moment, after many doubts and almost by accident, the nationalists found themselves on the same side as their old enemies, the anarcho-syndicalists and the socialists.

To some extent, the Civil War and the defeat of the nationalists along with their allies simplified the problems of historical memory. General Franco's army marched into Catalonia and the Basque provinces of Vizcaya and Guipúzcoa (not Alava or Navarre, which had fought on Franco's side) as if they were conquered territories. He was determined not only to outlaw nationalism but to wipe out all the public signs of a different identity in both regions and proscribe the use of the vernacular languages in public. From then on, it was easy for nationalists to depict this confrontation as the most recent and most serious in a long tradition of conflict between Spain and the regions, and yet another outbreak of central government's repression of local culture and self-government. It was not possible, however, to complain of the economic exploitation of these regions, for in fact they flourished. Industrial development since the 1950s brought in new waves of immigrants. They settled down permanently in Catalonia and the Basque country and in time became thriving communities. This influx, in turn, produced re-

sentment of the native residents, with the logical consequence of arous-
ing their nationalist sentiments.

By imposing its repressive policy, the Francoist state had laid itself
open to the nationalist interpretation. It also managed to alienate the
local clergy. Thus, when the state became less repressive in the 1960s, it
was faced with a new generation that was hostile, less easily intimidated
than were its parents by memories of the Civil War, and ready to take
advantage of any hint of freedom within the church or the universities
in order to organize and articulate their protests. It was done civilly in
Catalonia, and violently in the Basque country.

Francoism had brought the economic geography of the country into
a different balance: centers of economic modernization in Catalonia
and the Basque country were juxtaposed against Madrid and other
places that had well-developed services and industry. Furthermore, the
profound economic and cultural changes taking place led to the emergence of new middle classes with a new political orientation. They were
either Francoist-reformist or decidedly anti-Francoist, so they also dis-
tanced themselves from the extreme Spanish nationalism of the Franco
era. By the mid-1970s, this meant that the Catalan and Basque nationalists were dealing with a very different breed of politicians. The new
men claimed a modern mentality and a far more restrained Spanish
nationalism; an institutional understanding with them soon began to
seem possible. This in turn was to have favorable repercussions on the
attitudes of the immigrant population resident in Catalonia and the
Basque country, and on internal conflict in both regions, from which
the prewar antinationalist anarcho-syndicalism and socialism had disappeared (and memories of them grew dim).

In sum, our data illustrate an eventful map of a diversified human
landscape. The population was almost evenly divided into natives, immigrants, and people of mixed origin; a majority of the composite declared a sense of dual or shared identity. This fitted in well with the
coexistence of diverse linguistic practices. From the very beginning, the
regions' economies had overlapped the Spanish economy, for which
they had been the driving force and leader for decades. With Spanish
work force, demand and capital, and state assistance, the regions had
flourished. Under democratic rule, the two regions formed a political
mosaic which promoted a pattern of pragmatic compromise in order to
carry out any government task, notwithstanding the rhetoric of princi-

ples and intense emotions. Their past could be broken down into three historical eras: the period of a separate culture and tradition of self-government; the period of conflicts of the nineteenth and early twentieth centuries, leading to the Civil War and dictatorship; and the modern period, which invoked those earlier times, but put its emphasis on the more recent democratic experience.

The Nationalists' Support for the PP

The nationalists were naturally inclined to enlarge the range of their strategic opportunities (previously restricted to an understanding with the Socialists) after the 1996 elections. They found an affinity between their basic responses to the country's current problems (concerning Europe and the economy, the rule of law, and to some extent, even the national question) and those of the PP. Soon the inclination was translated into action: they signed a formal pact with the PP and the new government.

The economic policy favored by Catalan and Basque nationalists aimed at the development of a broadly based productive economy, integrated into the European economy and (thereby) into the world economy, with the mildest possible overhaul of the existing welfare state— aims compatible with their support of the PP. These policy orientations seem guided by the commitment to the apparently paramount objective of fulfilling the Maastricht criteria. Moreover, to have Spain join the nucleus of the EMU countries would contribute to accelerating the pace of European integration, which would bring the nationalist politicians closer to a very long-term political objective that was singularly attractive to them. Many nationalists hoped that once the European Union became consolidated, the relative importance of member nation states would be reduced in favor of some public authority of a supra-national nature. As all countries gained a broader European collective identity and their powers decreased, the relative weight of regions or smaller political entities would increase. This raised the hazy, but for some, exciting possibility of the relative independence of Catalonia and the Basque country vis-à-vis Spain in a shared situation of subjection and dependence vis-à-vis a larger European state.

Clearly, this vision would not materialize if the nation states made common cause, controlled the whole process, and maintained a supra-

national public authority. This is what has happened until now. Furthermore, even if there were a transfer of power from the nation states
upward, it does not follow that there would be devolution downward if
the supra-national authority considered that the governability of the
whole union required placing limits on centrifugal tendencies. The
member states would retain their autonomy and control the Europeanization process if their internal structures were strongly consolidated,
whether unitary in the French style or federal in the German style—as
Spain might turn out to be. Therefore the nationalist parties viewed the
uncertain future of European integration with mixed feelings of hope
and apprehension. In the meantime, they resisted policies aimed at the
clarification of their governmental jurisdictions within some sort of
federated Spanish state. Such a federation might treat all the regions
the same or give special status to Catalonia and the Basque country if
the other communities agreed (which is unlikely). Possibly too this
change would necessitate a hazardous all-Spanish referendum to
change the Constitution.[9]

As regards regional policy on cultural and economic matters, the
aims of the Catalan and the Basque nationalists differed somewhat. In
the second half of the 1990s, the Catalanists sought above all to solve
two immediate problems. They wanted the Spanish-speaking community of Catalonia and the rest of Spain to accept a language policy which
would encourage the learning and use of Catalan and to make the
schools *de facto* monolingual ("Catalan only"), in order to establish a
balance between Catalan and Spanish in a bilingual context. This rather
implausible argument was accepted by most of the local elite. So that
after many heated and confused debates on the subject, the problem
appeared to have been solved, if we are to judge by the verdicts of the
courts and the quasi-agreement of the political class. But in the long
run there is room for doubt. If the effect of such a policy is to displace
Spanish from schools, this *could* (logically) lead to the marginalization of
Spanish in the public sphere in due course. Then the problem would
not have been solved but simply shifted to a future date.

The second problem had to do with the problem of financing the
autonomous communities. Heretofore, Spain had been divided into
two communities: one, the Basque country and Navarre, was under a
fiscal regime of *conciertos* (agreements); the other, the rest of Spain,
was under a common tax regime. From the viewpoint of Basques and

Navarrese, the difference was owing to the existence of *fueros*, or traditional regional laws, which were upheld without interruption in Navarre and the province of Alava, but abolished, after the Civil War, in Vizcaya and Guipúzcoa, and later reinstated. These were their historic rights recognized by the Constitution of 1978, the Estatuto Vasco and the equivalent basic law for Navarre (Ley de Amejoramiento del Fuero Navarro).

The Catalan nationalists were ambivalent about disputing these claims. They expressed a desire to be on a par with the Basques, but suspected that would never happen—the issue would have to be discussed not just with Madrid but with all the other communities as well. Nevertheless, the Catalanists believed that the regions which operated under the *conciertos* enjoyed an economic advantage, and that their net contribution to what could be called the inter-regional solidarity fund was lower than everyone else's, thus increasing the burden upon the rest of Spain, including themselves. They felt, therefore, that the criteria for defining jurisdictions and allocating the corresponding public funds ought to be carefully examined; and they considered that so far no solution had been found for doing this in a reasonable way.

Until now, part of state spending went for central government and the other part to all the communities subject to the common tax regime. A preliminary calculation was made of the total amount which the communities would receive, based on the estimates of the cost of the services which the state must guarantee equally to all Spaniards (such as education, for example). The state collected taxes throughout Spain and, to the extent that taxes were progressive, the individuals with higher incomes contributed a higher proportion of their income to state revenues than did the rest; the richer regions thus contributed more than the rest. These funds were distributed according to the need for services in each region (for example, the number of school places), and it was the regional authorities that evaluated the needs and took charge of the services. The system was simple and redistributive, that is, it was based on the idea of fairness—not so much among the regions themselves as among the different strata of taxpayers. However, although no serious argument was raised over principles, the practical application was complex: accounts were far from clear, statistics for reference purposes were defective (there was no cost accounting for services, for example, so calculations were made on estimates), and continual adjustments were necessary. One of these adjustments dealt with the overall question of final authority and responsibility, which the Catalanists (and other regional governments not in nationalist hands) would like to see increased. The problem was that, so far, the system meant that transfers of funds went from the central government to the regions. The regional governments had little leeway in collecting the taxes and in deciding (and being held responsible for) what level of fiscal pressure they wanted to exert on their own constituencies. This situation favored a policy of public spending and indebtedness on the part of the Autonomous Communities that ran against the general economic goals of reducing public debt and deficit. The solution could be to promote joint fiscal responsibility by allowing the regions more freedom to decide their own fiscal policy—a position which was gradually accepted by the central government and brought in a measure of tax competition.

For the most part, the problem with these adjustments stems from the demands of the Catalan nationalists. Short of getting *de facto* fiscal independence like that of the Basques and the Navarrese, the Catalanists wanted more jurisdiction than any other region, and also argued that the transfers should have no ceiling. This had important implications not only for economic policy, but also for symbolic reasons and institutional policies. The symbolic or institutional importance of the Catalan nationalists' call for no ceiling on transfers was to leave the way open for unrestricted renegotiations of the limits to self-government. This, in the final analysis, could put into question the constitutional frame, place on the agenda a debate on the so-called right to self-determination, and lead toward the goal of an independent public authority, in the best tradition of classical state nationalist thought. Both nationalist groups subscribed to this theory, but while the Catalans were more discreet about it, the Basques were notoriously less so.

With this in mind, both Catalans and Basques held to a strategy of underlining "the differential fact" of their "historical nations," even though this cleared the way for recognition of the differential fact of other self-styled historical nations or nationalities such as Galicia— and perhaps also Andalusia, Aragon, Valencia, and the Canary Islands. Aware of this potential, the nationalists insisted that they were champions of a nation and not just a nationality, as the Constitution would claim. As a result, the Basque nationalists (and more than a few Catalanists, in an ambiguous way) persistently avoided speaking of Spain and only referred to a "Spanish state" or a "Spanish reality"; likewise, neither would accept an interpretation of Spain as a "nation of nations," and they rejected the admissions of the plural, dual, or shared identities of many Catalans and Basques as incoherent and unjustified irrelevancies.

The question of regional policy was, in turn, closely related to policies of public order and the fight against terrorism, and, through them, to the effective rule of law. This undoubtedly affected the Basque nationalists far more, and the matter needed some time for clarification. For a period, there had been indecisiveness (and for many, ambiguity) in the Basque nationalist attitude toward the nationalist-terrorist phenomenon, which was understood as legitimate in its ends although mistaken and even reprehensible in its means. Later, however, the feeling that there could be neither economic nor political development of Basque society in a climate of violence, and that it was Basque citizens and public officials who were both the main victims (mostly non-nationalists) and the ones primarily responsible for the state of violence (mostly nationalists), seemed to convince a majority of nationalists that there was no longer room for indecision and ambiguity on this question. In the social sphere many pacifist groups became active, and the majority of political forces converged around a common platform declaring against violence (the *Mesa de Ajuria Enea)*. Accordingly, the Basque government felt obliged to deploy its own security forces (for whose existence it had fought long and hard) *against* the terrorists, and started to pay the corresponding price in human lives. The question arose of how to carry out an effective policy with adequate coordination and sufficient respect for the rule of law (which, as the political scandals showed, had been systematically violated).

Long-Term Prospects and Sudden Choices

In the circumstances following the 1996 elections, the Catalan and to a lesser extent the Basque nationalists obviously found themselves in a position of extraordinary influence as the pivotal party or parties between the PP and the Socialists—and would be able to exert this influence on public policies of enormous importance for the future of Spain. Nevertheless, we should distinguish the medium-term from the long-term expectations.

To begin with, the nationalists signed a stable pact with the PP, which led to the investiture of José María Aznar as Prime Minister in May 1996. By early 1999 (at the time of this writing), the nationalists' parliamentary support has held firm for nearly three years. This has increased the range of their strategic options considerably from their choices under the Socialists. In 1996 they joined a center-right party whose right-wing component was conspicuous, and which had inevitable symbolic and emotional associations with Francoism and the Civil War. As a result, nationalist politicians found a way of looking back at their original aspirations prior to the Civil War, when the self-definitions of the peripheral, Catalan, and Basque nationalist movements were formed. It was almost as if the opportunity to broaden their horizons were inseparable from the opportunity to revise their historical memory; as if the more hopeful their future prospects appeared, the more easily they were able to view their past with equanimity.

By allying themselves with the PP (and governing with it shoulder to shoulder), the nationalists could now take a relativistic view of what once had appeared to be the absolute and definitive experience of their position in the Civil War (and, as a result, during Francoism), thus placing this experience within a larger context. More than that, the nationalists could return to an even earlier time, to their complex roots and to the first era (between the 1890s and the 1920s, more or less) when both Catalan and Basque nationalists repeatedly attempted to gain the support of the right or center-right. The two parties had much in common then, principally common Catholic roots (hence shared experiences), and a preference for market economy (hence a clear common interest). By this (relative) return to the past the nationalists, or at least the Catalans, were exploring once more the common ground of Cambó and Maura over eighty years ago (and adopting Francesc Cambó's call *"Per la concòrdia"* [For reconciliation]).[10] So the stage was set for a strategic agreement that counted on a gradual increase in mutual confidence and loyalty between the center-right and moderate nationalists, which might eventually culminate in a stable coalition.

So much for the medium term. In the longer term, this outcome is not the only possibility. In time the nationalists may finally be able to carry out a slow, gradual, in-depth revision of their overall position, far beyond mere circumstantial, tactical operations. They are growing increasingly aware of the changes occurring not only within the more limited framework of Spanish society, but within all Western societies.

And these changes are not only revising the importance of national sovereignty; they are placing the aspiring politician of the left or right in an ideological milieu different from any that has existed in Western political life for most of the twentieth century. It is only since the fall of the Berlin Wall in 1989 that Western European societies in general, and their political classes in particular, have been free of the millstone that resulted from the Bolshevik coup d'etat in St. Petersburg in October 1917.

Under the totalitarian regimes, the strategic options of nontotalitarian parties were relatively limited, and now they have been considerably enlarged. This is just as true for parties of the center-right as for those of the center-left; all of their strategies and programs gained in flexibility. Current developments do not lead to the hegemony of a single philosophy but to an opening of the public space, because the scope of discussion on matters of economic and social policy is greater. Previously, it had been distorted by the weight of collectivist arguments on public opinion; arguments which, one way or another, were linked to totalitarian referents. In the same way, the electorate has increased the scope of its preferences and increased its capacity to influence political activity. This, I repeat, can only encourage strategic flexibility on the part of all the parties.

In the long run therefore, after rushing into the strategic agreement with the PP, the nationalists may decide to prolong it, or they may be tempted to use their pivotal position to sway the balance of power toward the center-right or the center-left. Under certain circumstances, it could be reasonable and useful for the country if they did so: it could guarantee an alteration in the power structure, place limits on the possible excesses of a right-wing party, and reduce the likelihood of a Socialist party drifting into radical populism. (In other words, they could do the job the liberal party in Germany has been doing for such a long time.)

It is also possible, however, that if the nationalists ever got this far, they could overreach themselves or fumble and eventually find themselves confronted with a grand coalition of the PP and the PSOE. Such a coalition may sound inconceivable today, and there are certainly reasons which would make it inadvisable in general terms, since it could blur the identities of its member parties. But there are also objective reasons for many Spaniards to support some agreement between the PP and the PSOE: in order to stabilize the territorial structure of the state, for example, or to place a ceiling on the transfer of jurisdictions to the regions.[11]

A reappraisal of the political alignments (such as the one implied in the PP and the PSOE moving closer to each other) could take place if and when the nationalists were to understand the situation as one which enabled them to get substantially closer to their independist goals, and would therefore move to challenge the constitutional framework. This can happen at any time, as the unilateral declaration of a truce by ETA, in September 1998, and the subsequent events in the Basque country demonstrate. All of a sudden, a general expectation has been created that the end of three decades of terrorist violence is at hand, even though the situation remains open to a number of different outcomes.

The truce may be seen partly as the result of a *rapprochement* of all nationalists, moderate and radical (Herri Batasuna, later renamed Euskal Herritarrok, the *de facto* political representatives of the terrorist organization), who signed a joint declaration in Estella during the summer of 1998. In it they made a common plea for starting an open debate among all political contenders, to be followed by a decision-making process and a final decision. The assumption was that whatever was decided by the Basque political parties, both nationalist and non-nationalist, should be accepted by the Spanish political order as a whole— even if this decision entailed changing the Spanish Constitution. In exchange for this agreement, it was understood that ETA would give up killing its political opponents. ETA did in fact issue a *communiqué* declaring an indefinite truce.

Regional elections were held in October 1998. Nationalist parties obtained 54.6% of the vote, down from 56.4% in the regional elections of 1994 (compare to 46.2% in the national elections of 1996). Non-nationalists obtained 44.5%, up from 43.3% in 1994 (52% in the national elections of 1996). In other words, the political landscape remained almost the same (even though, within the non-nationalist camp, some realignment occurred as PP jumped to 20.1% from 14.4% in 1994). Seen in the perspective of the last nine years (from 1990 on), this suggests a near-equilibrium between nationalists and non-nationalists, with a slight tendency for the non-nationalist vote to rise gradually (as indicated by the rise of approximately 344,000 votes in the 1990 regional elections to about 559,000 in the regional elections of 1998, while the non-nationalist vote has oscillated around 670,000 votes).[12]

At the moment of translating these electoral results into politics, PNV would have to make a choice of joining a coalition government with the Socialist party, as it had done since the late 1980s, or participating in an all-nationalist coalition including Herri Batasuna. If the last were chosen, the situation might evolve toward a confrontation between a nationalist front and a non-nationalist one (in which PP and PSOE would join hands); and this might facilitate the transition of Basque terrorism from violence to politics.

But whatever choice the PNV makes in the end, the heart of the matter is that success in the task of solving the Basque problem depends less on elaborate political games and more on the twin issues of peace and assertion of the rule of law. The elites and the public need to focus on this subject and to engage in whatever debates on whatever topics and at whatever forums that will be useful for sorting out and explaining their political differences—always with the understanding that democratic procedures will be respected. The links between peace and the assertion of the rule of law had been clearly demonstrated in the course of the last few years as a result of three developments which, no doubt, had a bearing on the declaration of the truce by ETA in the first place.

First, the combined pressure from the judiciary and from the police, sustained for a number of years, has met with significant success. The Tribunal Supremo moved to imprison the whole central committee of Herri Batasuna (December 1, 1997), and the judge of Audiencia Nacional, Baltasar Garzón, decided to close the radical newspaper *Egin* (July 14, 1998). These proceedings revealed and documented the connections between the financial, propaganda, and political networks associated with the terrorist activities of ETA. The disclosures placed the terrorists and their political associates on the defensive.

Second, public sentiment in the Basque country gradually shifted away from an even-handed condemnation of both state-institutional violence and terrorism—a position once held by an influential part of the Basque clergy and the nationalists—toward an unconditional condemnation of terrorist violence. This was the cumulative effect of many years of terrorist assassinations (an average of about 40 a year in the last twenty years), but a critical threshold was reached in the last few years, when seven local councilors of PP were assassinated—and more particularly, when a young local councilor of Ermua, Miguel Ángel Blanco, was killed on July 12, 1997. This death provoked spontaneous manifestations of millions of people all over Spain and the Basque country against terrorist violence. It was an outburst of moral indignation that the more nationalist-minded Basque clergy tried to channel but could not contain.[13]

Third, the various political parties interpreted the situation as favoring the endeavor to end the violence. In general, it was clear that most Basques inclined toward a politics of compromise and accommodation (as shown, for instance, by their support of coalitions of nationalists and non-nationalists). The progress of PP should be interpreted in the light of this—particularly as the government had moved to reach a compromise with PNV on most matters, and to reformulate its commitment to a united Spain in terms of a "plural" Spain. The electoral gains of Herri Batasuna may also be seen as a reward for ETA's declaration of a truce. As for the PNV, it seems that it has decided to bet on the chance of achieving a lasting peace and has taken on the job of key player and broker between the main contenders.

The point is that, irrespective of the contingencies of political moves, countermoves, and unpredictable events, the hard data of the long-term prospects and the stability of the electoral results, plus the soft data of the evolution of the judiciary institutions and of public sentiment together suggest a frame of specific incentives for the various political parties to undertake what we may call the "civilization" of the Basque conflict—that is, the process of substituting politics (civil debate) for violence (war, or simply murder).[14]

CHAPTER EIGHT

Becoming a Civil Society by Trial and Error

AT VARIOUS INTERVALS in the course of, let us say, the last five centuries, Spanish society has been coming close to and moving away from (often very far away) a model characterized by the institutions of freedom—let us call it a "civil society."[1] Not a society organized around the paramount goal of the defense of a religious faith, nor around the collectivistic dream of a corporate or a social-revolutionary community, nor around a defiant self-assertion of that national community in the theater of the world; just one that provides the people who belong to it with the minimal and basic conditions for living together while pursuing their own goals. A civil society thus understood requires a consensus on rules and procedures. This in turn implies a minimal normative (or at least behavioral) consensus on substantive values, in the absence of which these rules cannot apply: namely, respect for individual freedom, rational persuasion, and a commitment to the community itself. But while a civil society does refer to a minimal normative consensus, it falls short of a complete definition of a good society, let alone of a good life. Simply, it does not address the questions of what is a good society and what is a good life, and so it cannot and should not be expected to answer them.

This civil society is a rather sophisticated and complicated institutional construct and therefore rather fragile; for its survival, as Charles Darwin might have suggested, it requires a certain favorable environment. Darwin reminds us that under relatively primitive conditions a complex living organism may not survive because its delicate constitution makes it more vulnerable to destruction, so that under harsh conditions life would revert or regress to an inferior form of organization (Darwin, 1957 [1859]: 96).

What We Can Learn from the Spanish Experience

In a previous work, I attempted to describe how this complex form of organization emerged in Spain roughly between the mid-1950s and the late 1970s, and here I have tried to explain how it has survived in the particular conditions of the last quarter of the twentieth century, and the transformations it went through. I chose to focus on the interplay between the choices made by the protagonists and the institutional and cultural framework in which they operated, on the assumption that this would shed light on the recent history. Such an examination should draw attention to the strengths of the institutional design and of the citizens' dispositions, as well as to those flaws and weaknesses which may prompt the democratic polity's regression to an inferior, uncivil form of social life. And it should provide a set of lessons to be drawn (successes to replicate, mistakes to avoid) for those who would like similar forms of organization to survive under other local conditions.

The immediate starting point was Spain's transition to democracy in the mid-1970s. But, of course, the complete historical cycle that serves as a background to that drama was larger and longer. It went back to the period in which the character of the protagonists, that is, the generation of 1956–1968, was formed, and back even further, to the crucial event that was the key to understanding the world this generation inherited and reacted to: the Civil War of 1936–1939, which was the antithesis of that civil society they were to bring about much later.

I indicated summarily how the Francoist regime attempted at first to perpetuate its victory and secure the results of the war for all time. But the pressure of outside influences and a gradual softening of its core authoritarian institutions began to tame Franco's Spain, so that by the time of his death, the population had already between one and two decades of experience with a relatively well-functioning and open market economy, a legal framework that allowed room for this market and for a plethora of voluntary associations, and a lively though uneven

debate that made possible the expression of diverse interests and political sentiments. This was the soil that provided nutrition, stimuli, and
opportunities to a new generation.

Then came the democratic transition itself. This experience allowed
the inchoate fragments of civil society that had begun to form during
the last period of Francoism to develop fully. The evolution took place
at the same time as the new regime was seeking its consolidation and
determining the quality of a liberal democracy, making its adjustment
to the new conditions of the world economy, and evaluating the relationship between central and peripheral nationalisms. The point is that
only a certain way of solving or managing these problems was compatible with the key tenets of an order of freedom. The successes and
pitfalls which comprise the drama of this book show how, and how well,
they were managed so as to preserve the fundamentals of that order.

Solutions compatible with an order of freedom are those compatible,
in the first place, with a system of governance by rules. This is not a
system of plebiscitarian democracy with a charismatic leader and a large
mass following, seeking to enact historic projects of a semi-collectivistic
character; it is a liberal order with division of powers, and with the
executive properly subject to the rule of law. It is not a system in which
a passive citizenry alternates between abstention and a massive vote to
political leaders barely accountable for their deeds, but one in which an
alert and discriminating citizenry debates public matters in a climate of
civility, is ready to trust its elected leaders (and parties), and also holds
them to account without false sentimentality if they infringe the rules,
let alone the basic laws.

An order of freedom also requires the proper functioning of free and
open markets which operate under the rule of law and in accordance to
additional specific rules (such as those that punish the corrupt practices
of insider trading and monopolistic collusions, not to speak of Mafia-
like arrangements). In Spain these continued to operate in the face of
macroeconomic imbalances, high unemployment, and pressing welfare
needs (which might require a prudent reassessment of the welfare system). A third, ongoing problem for the new democracy was to (re)de-
fine the community in such a way that the competing claims of nationalist feelings of diverse segments of the population would be somehow
reconciled, through a mix of institutional design, compromise, and the
assertion of the law. For this to be successful, a modicum of the civic

constitutional identity would have to be incorporated into the national
or multinational identity, to yield the generic sentiment that people
with different nationalistic feelings felt part of the same community,
and establish a basic reference point to regulate conflicts.

To arrive anywhere close to this "final destination," the people involved in the process of building the civil society had to be educated,
bred, tamed, civilized—you choose the label. And, in a sense, the Spanish story is one of a half-completed civic education: teaching a diversity
of parties and other associations, businessmen, unionists, and lastly citizens how to handle politics, the law, the markets, and public debate in a
free society. They had to be educated partly by the institutions that
framed their activities, and partly by having to face the consequences of
the choices they made, including most notably those of their own mistakes.

Sometimes, these lessons came the hard way. This was particularly
true for the political parties. UCD, the most successful one in its appeal
to the centrist voters, learned in the most painful manner what happens
when political leadership is careless in attending to the party organization and its internal tensions. After its second electoral (relative) victory, in 1979, UCD dreamed of staying in power until 2007. It woke
up by 1982. In the best tradition of "life is a dream," as Pedro Calderón de la Barca claimed in the seventeenth century, UCD went from
glory to nothingness and became a "dream of a dream" in less than five
years.

The lesson was not lost on the other parties. PSOE and (in time)
PP learned to combine an appeal to the center (the successful part of
UCD's strategy) with keeping a keen eye on organizational cohesive-
ness and firm assertion of party leadership. Hence PSOE was extremely
vigilant of its internal factions, and built up a powerful, disciplined
organization that confirmed its leaders in rubber-stamp congresses. So
much discipline, however, had a few drawbacks, particularly in light of
the "excess of success" in the electoral arena. By that I mean that the
disappearance of UCD created the extraordinary circumstance of leaving the PSOE in charge of the central government, most regional governments, and most governments in cities and big towns; it also had an
absolute parliamentary majority and an enormous influence, indeed the
upper hand, on the judiciary. That immense triumph contained the
seed of the Socialists' ruin.

From their peak, some of the Socialists may have thought that, as in one of Dostoevski's novels, everything was permitted. With no other powers to check them, they played games in foreign policy, first calling for neutralism when they thought it useful and then switching to Atlantism when the time came for a final decision. In economic policy, their games of half-measures allowed unemployment to reach enormous proportions. They got away from both games with a deceptive ease and without paying a proper price for it. But then, caught in the trap of hubris and a sense of impunity, they forgot about a minor set of incidents in the fight against terrorism—the GAL affair. Neither the government nor its friends realized the grave nature of those events until it was too late, and, much to their surprise and indignation, they found themselves in the hot spot. Finally, they had to pay a heavy price in loss of power, in jail sentences, and in loss of self-confidence. (All of this may be for the better in the long run, if these lessons serve to promote self-knowledge and some wisdom.)

The story ends with the PP and the nationalists as the protagonists of the next act: the next set of learners, so to speak. Fortunately for them (and for the country as a whole), they are not in a position of absolute power. The PP governs from a minority position with the nationalists' support, and the nationalists hold power in their own backyards under even more complicated circumstances. This state of equilibrium is actually helping to promote increasing complexity and diversity in society, together with the development of a system of rules that frame and channel the conflicts of interest and persuasion that are part and parcel of this process. The diversity stems from the development of a market economy as well as from the growing variety of associations and social networks, and of voices in the public sphere. The system of rules (and mechanisms for monitoring and sanctioning compliance) derives from an ongoing process of external and internal regulation (of the capital markets, for instance) and from the increasing assertiveness of the judiciary. But the prevalence of a pattern of governance by rules also benefits from coalition politics and institutional compromises (within the frame of the constitutional order) between the central, all-Spanish parties and the peripheral nationalist movements.

All this may or may not succeed in the next stage. As in a *commedia dell'arte*, the players are allowed to improvise and depart from a script which, of course, has not even been written.

Memories and Emotions in the Public Debate

Before parting company with my subject, two final touches need to be added to the picture: one has to do with memory, with self-appraisals and appraisals of antagonists, and the emotional tone of the public debate; another, with the relevance the Spanish story may have for other European countries.

Remembering and forgetting the past are important parts of the story just told. Thus it may be argued that the Civil War haunted the Spanish collective imagination at the time of the transition. The memory was all there, but at the same time a concerted effort was made to exorcise it—or to mention it only in a way that avoided putting the blame and the responsibility for it on anybody. Time helped: a new generation of political leaders was ready to take the helm of government and also of the opposition. The politicians associated with the past receded into the background, after a dignified yet brief appearance on the stage.[2]

This looked like good common sense during a difficult and ambiguous transition from one regime to another. Yet silences or mere allusions depleted memory, so long as nobody was responsible for the war and people avoided talking about supporting, living with, or fighting against Francoism. Though it made political sense, the reverse of the coin was that people got used to replacing true memories with fake ones.

There was a price to pay, however, for the denial of memory. One of the negative effects was that it put a premium on postponing the moment of reckoning with the consequences of past deeds, and therefore with matters of political responsibility when the time came for it. It also had a bearing on the distorted self-perception of several political protagonists of democratic Spain, and—this is the point I want to stress here—it encouraged a lack of toleration on their part to political criticism which, in turn, worked against a proper level of civility in public debates.

It has been suggested that people who have an inflated, unrealistic level of self-esteem which does not correspond to actual merits become impervious to external criticisms that question their self-appraisal.[3] Yet a civil society cannot exist without a lively public space in which criticism of public figures and political parties is taken and given before a critical audience. It is like a game which cannot go on unless certain game rules are followed. By this I mean basically the rules of truth-seeking and truth-testing, of reckoning with established facts and accepting responsibility for them.

If criticism is difficult to tolerate in general, it is more difficult for people who have allowed themselves (and their followers) to entertain unrealistic ideas about what they actually did in the past, thus blurring the line between reality and self-serving fantasies. Some people who had been Francoists made believe this was not so; and people who had run no real risks pretended they had fought Francoism tooth and nail. The danger of these fantasies lay not in making use of them for a modest biographical embellishment, but rather in setting a pattern of self-delusion. Thus a fake memory about freedom fighters and heroic deeds might find its natural continuity in a person's belief that he has extraordinary missions to fulfill and is the privileged bearer of the values of freedom and democracy. This memory and self-image could then be used as high ground on which to reject pertinent criticisms, to boil up feelings of moral indignation against the people who raised objections, and to introduce into public life a language of violence and stigmatization of the political adversary. This language was only a few steps short of the kind of symbolic violence which, in due time, could well lead to an uncivil society—in the same way in which the verbal and symbolic violence of Spanish politics in the 1930s contributed to the moral and emotional climate that was partly responsible for the Civil War.

To avert this dangerous development, the Spanish experience suggests the need for two complementary, but also, I must add, highly contingent processes. One is a process of channeling accusations through the judiciary institutions. The experiment here is an ongoing one, as manifest by the avatars of the GAL affair. This may help to tone down the political language from that of the Furies of Greek tragedy into that of the courts of law; justice tempered by a touch of pity.

The other process is that of the politicians going through a humbling experience. Unlike politicians in real life, the protagonist of a novel by Kazuo Ishiguro reflects on his involvement in authoritarian politics in Japan prior to World War II as follows: "I find it hard to understand how any man who values his self-respect would wish for long to avoid responsibility for his past deeds; it may not always be an easy thing, but there is certainly a satisfaction and dignity to be gained in coming to terms with the mistakes one has made in the course of one's life. In any case, there is surely no great shame in mistakes made in the best of faith. It is surely a thing more shameful to be unable or unwilling to acknowledge them."[4]

From One European Periphery to Another

Starting in the late 1980s, the history of most European countries can only be understood in the larger European context, and as a part of it. The decisive push to European unity resulted from the pressure of the internal market to join the European Monetary Union, and from the disintegration of the Soviet Union, which allowed the Eastern and Central European nations to choose their ways. They opted for rejoining Europe, eager to replicate the European experiment with liberal politics and markets and to be part of the European process.

Could the Spanish lessons be useful to these former Soviet bloc countries in their search for a well-functioning system of liberal politics, markets, and the accompanying institutions and cultural dispositions that go with them? In short, for a civil society in the large sense of the term? My first answer to such a big question is that of course other nations may eventually profit from the Spanish experience—Western European as well as Central and Eastern European ones. Let us remember that the phenomenon of detachment from and ambivalence toward political parties is prevalent in all of Western Europe. Likewise, political scandals and the complicated maneuvers by politicians, judges, and journalists to expose or cover up these scandals have happened in many European countries;[5] not a few, moreover, have had their own experiences with dirty tactics in dealing with terrorism. The issue of internal nationalist movements is far from being an exclusive Spanish problem: France, England, and Italy have also experienced it in one form or another. As for unemployment, it exists in Western Europe at a fairly high level (though lesser than the Spanish one) and seems to resist the usual economic remedies. Finally, procrastination in carrying out the necessary revision of the welfare state has been the preferred tactic of many Western European leaders in the last decade or so.

But coming back to countries such as Poland, Hungary, the Czech Republic and others—are there enough similarities between them and

Spain to make the Spanish lessons particularly relevant to them? The fate of these countries might have been that of Spain, had the Republicans won the Civil War, had the Communists then succeed in gaining control (with the help of a functional equivalent of the Soviet Army), and had the Western powers allowed all this to happen and to persist during the many decades of the Cold War. These three big "ifs" make the counterfactual seem quite unlikely, but not utterly unthinkable. The point helps to bring into sharp focus the fact that Francoist Spain was a much softer authoritarian regime than were its Communist counterparts in Central (and Eastern) Europe; also, the country was part of the Western world from beginning to end—and it is not irrelevant that the end came about ten years before the collapse of communism.

The legacy of communism was much harder to overcome, and its memories even more difficult to bear, than was the legacy of Francoism. The totalitarian system to which the Soviet bloc countries were subject may have had obvious and important limits, but compared to the Franco state, it required a much higher degree of subordination of the legal system, the economy, the social fabric, and the sphere of public debate—in short, of the entire culture—to the state and the party (not even when Franco's rule was at its worst, during the 1940s). As a result, the emergence of fragments of a civil society that took place in Spain during the 1950s, 1960s, and 1970s took place later and was weaker in those countries. Still, it was felt in Poland, Hungary, and Czechoslovakia. In some mitigated form, the "cunning of reason" was at work there too, and it fostered the development of private property and markets, autonomous forms of social organization, and spaces for debate.

In Poland, small peasant property had persisted all along. Later on, obstinate efforts were made to develop networks of mutual help in the fields of small production and services and to set up parallel distributive networks, in order to face the unusual circumstances of life under the military rule of General Jaruzelski. A parallel economy had developed in Janos Kadar's Hungary, encouraged (to a point) by the Communist government: a sphere of "small commodity production." The Communists allowed for an uneasy, unstable coexistence between mechanisms of bureaucratic and market coordination, and between public and private ownership (Kornai 1992, 106). Not much, perhaps, but possibly enough to provide a point of reference for the economic process to come after 1989. Another factor was the memory of life in the old days, before the disasters of the World War II, the German occupation, the Soviet occupation, and forty years of Communist rule. Those old days were only fifty years ago: ten years older than the memory of the Civil War. A second element was the continuous presence of the Western mode of life (private property and markets included) in the collective imagination of these peoples. This indirect experience should not be lightly dismissed: we know how important was that reference for the Spaniards through the entire Francoist period, particularly since the 1950s.

The importance of private property and markets was strengthened, also in an indirect but most powerful manner, by other aspects of social life: to begin with, by the way society functioned. It may be that subjection to a totalitarian rule, which tolerated no resistance and therefore sought to control all sorts of associations, kept society relatively divided and unorganized; certainly this was one of the state's and the party's most important goals. But the family persisted all along, and that was no small matter. It was the source of ever-renewed dispositions that permeated every field of life, from the lines of patronage (and corruption) of the Communist parties to the small commodity production of the Polish land holdings and the Hungarian "parallel" small firms. And then, there was the influence of the church: in Poland, the Catholic Church—again, no small matter. The party was forced to come to some accommodation with the church simply because the church was part of every aspect of society, including the cultural life.

Cultural debate was extensive and took place on several levels. In Poland, for instance, already in the 1950s many university students did not take the Marxist scriptures all that seriously (according to survey responses quoted by Pelczynski: 1982). The intellectual biographies of many Polish leaders include a variety of *rites de passage* that may start with the initial experience of membership in a Catholic association, pass through a long stay in the Communist party, go through a period of passionate interest in Marxist revisionism, and then enter a stage of ongoing dialogue with the exponents of various moral and intellectual positions: witness, for instance, the trajectory of Bronislaw Geremek (Geremek, Vidal 1997). Another story may feature an encounter between an intensely secular trajectory and a religious or quasi-religious experience, as in Jacek Kuron's autobiography (1991). All this takes place against a background of an older, rich, and complex tradition of cultural debates—in this case, the tradition of a positivistic Warsaw versus a more humanistic-oriented Cracow. In short, we are talking of established, culturally replete, and historically minded societies, and about people who are used to talking all day long (and possibly all night . . .) and, therefore, to create spaces where they might talk to each other.

These remarks point to a gradual emergence of quite significant elements of a latent civil society; they went beyond social movements and public debate, and pervaded the most diverse forms of social life, including the economy.[6] The various dimensions of that emergent civil society—the economy, the social fabric, and the public sphere—shared an important degree of consistency. The key lay in the development of polycentric orders which did not follow any pre-established program or script. Private ownership and markets, limited as they were, could not be strictly amenable to state control. Unions such as Solidarnosc and churches as well-organized as the Catholic Church could lead only to a point; mostly they could operate only as clearing houses for a number of initiatives, and their greater influence could only be achieved by following as closely as possible the sentiments of the people and the local organizations they were supposed to lead. The nostalgia of the Marxist revisionists or the democratic opposition for some sort of *avant-garde* that would replace the old revolutionary party as a privileged historical agent gradually faded away. Not even the working class could do the job, and certainly not the part of the working class that gathered around Solidarnosc, were it for no other reason than because the other part stayed with the Communist unions.

At the transitional moment, these fragments provided the basis for the development of a resilient form of liberal democracy and market economy, with a surprisingly unanimous social backing in the years that followed. Of course, political bargains (such as the round-table conversations in Poland) were of critical importance, and so were the new government's decisions to provide more solid legal and institutional supports to the market economy. But this did not mean that liberal democracy or capitalism were mere constructivist creations of the political elites.[7]

Political and economic freedoms were built upon a foundation of prior experiences, beliefs, feelings, and expectations. This explains the population's attachment to and deliberate use of these institutions in the decade after the transition, despite not a few disappointments during years of economic and political difficulties. The political uncertainties expressed themselves in high rates of electoral abstentionism (in Poland and Hungary: González 1996), in low levels of trust in the political parties (Sztompka 1998), and possibly as a result of this, in a surprising comeback, for a few years, of the Communists of the past, this time recycled as social-democrats.

The Spanish experience after the transition could be instructive to the former Soviet bloc countries. In the economic field, the gradualist way Spain handled industrial policy, plus the relatively high labor costs combined with rigid labor markets (with the resulting unemployment), would make for an ambiguous lesson. Spanish policy made sense at the beginning, as a way to create social consensus at a critical juncture; but beyond that point it made no sense at all as a way to handle Spain's human resources. The peculiar Spanish welfare system, based party on the family, partly on an expansion of the state sector, and partly on (a more recent) reliance on the private sector, is a hybrid that may suggest other peculiar accommodations for other countries—but it should be treated mainly as a *sui generis* case. At the same time, Spain's obsession with the European integration has been tempered lately by a growing awareness of the fact that the world is larger than Europe, and that it is increasingly important to compete worldwide. For Spain, this means, in the first place, to compete in Latin America. There may be a lesson here for these countries, too. But on the whole, we are referring to economies (those of Poland, Hungary, the Czech Republic, and some others) whose problems, by the late 1990s, "are no longer the problems of socialist economies in transition . . . but of dynamic, emerging economies."[8]

Spain has been able to handle the problem of her peripheral nationalist movements, so far—with the important caveat of having to suffer from Basque terrorism (and an average of about twenty political assassinations a year during the last ten years). The constitutional frame has eased the way for a number of political compromises, and may have provided some ground for a civic, constitutional collective identity to develop in time. The fact that the nationalist movements have to deal with the mix of people living in Catalonia and the Basque country has been also of crucial importance: no "ethnic cleansing" has taken place there. At the same time, the historical horizon of the European Union tends to soften the jurisdictional conflicts: it adds plausibility to a *modus vivendi* among all the competing political jurisdictions.

The Spanish experience might have been of more use to the former Soviet bloc countries if the complex Austro-Hungarian imperial pattern of lands and populations (of different ethnicities, religions, and cultural traditions) had been maintained. But the actual course of history since the end of World War I has moved toward artificial simplification of the old complexity—by way of deportations, mass extermination, ethnic cleansing (like in former Yugoslavia), or political split (like the one between the Czech Republic and Slovakia). Yet the Spanish experience may still be of some use for what remains of the old complexity: for the recognition of the rights of the minorities and for granting some degree of self-government to particular enclaves. It may have a larger field for application in the territories of the former Soviet Union.

Another point of similarity is the very delicate dilemma of forgetting or remembering the past. On the face of it, the tactful Spanish solution of selective remembering and of toning down the concomitant emotions seemed well suited to the needs of the democratic transition. Yet it has had its drawbacks, as I have suggested in this book. Anyway, formal committees for uncovering the truth are not a substitute for the civilizing process which the entire society has to go through and which may take years or decades of hard and daily work. I refer to the work of building the institutions of the rule of law, and the practices of honest and straightforward reporting, of accepting political responsibility and of learning and practicing the rules of living together in an order of freedom. All of these refer to the present and to current activities, but at the same time are bound to involve, sooner or later, a parallel work of reckoning with past misdeeds and deceptions. And one of the characteristics of totalitarian and authoritarian polities is that a great many of their members, in order to survive, have had to engage in opportunistic behavior. At least, this gives them a better chance to escape the danger of turning self-righteous when the time comes for them to live in a free society.

The Citizens' Turn and the European Union

Liberal politics depends on the relationship between politicians and citizens. For all their limitations, political parties and professional politicians are a crucial part of it. There is a need, then, for educating parties and politicians to do the job properly. This means, to begin with, parties should be strong enough to survive internal strife (by contrast with the UCD experience); determined and cohesive enough to govern; and open enough to public scrutiny by the public, the media, other politicians, and the courts of law. In this regard, no doubt the Spanish experience could inspire political life in the Eastern and Central European countries in a variety of ways. But the other side of the equation is an alert citizenry, which has learned to hold its leaders accountable for what they do and is also willing and able to hold itself (the citizens themselves, that is) responsible for what is going on in public life.

If we go back to the Spanish elections of 1996, we can argue that these results were a sort of answer to the previous three critical years. The voters indicated that they did not want the administration that brought them scandals and failures. They lost faith in the credibility of their rulers regarding the basic functioning of their institutions and the economy, above all the almost permanent deterioration in the level of employment. The elections were also a particular answer to a more complex question: what style of government did Spaniards want? And what did they expect from political parties, from their government, and from themselves as citizens? As I understand it, the answer to this last question touched on the relationship between political leaders and citizens, and this leads me to make one last point.

If Spanish voters imagine that agreements between parties would be enough to solve future problems, they would be just as mistaken as when they believed that the solution to the political scandals and unemployment of the three critical years depended only, or especially, on the political class. Such problems can never be solved without the active participation of the citizens themselves.

Indeed, the problems of a state apparatus reluctant to subject itself fully to the rule of law will never be solved unless the citizens themselves understand the importance of the principle of respect for the laws (and more generally, for the rules of the game), and then apply this principle to their daily behavior in a more or less consistent manner. We may suspect that a country cannot advance toward an economy capable of generating employment in reasonable conditions without the efforts of businessmen, union leaders and members, and the general public. All of them must be able to discriminate between demagogy and good argumentation when the time comes for supporting one public policy or another. By the same token, unless all sectors of society are prepared to build, rebuild, and constantly repair the foundations, the walls, the arches, the roof, the interior, and the embellishments of the social edifice, people cannot persuade themselves they inhabit a common home. The sense of that cannot rest upon the formal declarations of leaders but on the mutual confidence that can only come in the wake of an infinity of compromises, negotiations, meetings, conversations, and the joint actions of hundreds and thousands and millions of individuals. Neither will any foreign policy be meaningful if the people do not have a country with the strength and enthusiasm to export, to offer hospitality, to understand and communicate, and to fight when needed. These are tasks that require the broadest possible base of capable men and women, and their corresponding associations. And all of this has to grow and flourish (and *can* only flourish) from *within* society.

In the particular case of Spain, the dangers of leaving politicians too much room for maneuver and trusting too much in their problem-solving abilities have been clearly demonstrated. Many Spaniards now realize that it is imperative to keep both the state and politicians under strict control, not only when under electoral scrutiny but constantly, in the full glare of public opinion and before the courts when necessary, in order to limit abuses of power and rhetoric. Likewise, many people have learned to mistrust easy promises from politicians regarding solutions to unemployment. The mechanisms which the country has invented to cope with this situation demonstrate its ability to survive, its ingenuity, and (to some extent) its spontaneous social solidarity, but they fail to offer a bright future; rather it forces people to turn to the family for support, and to the underground economy. Even so, it seems obvious to many Spaniards that the solution to the vexing problems of providing and financing welfare services is not just a matter of state policy, but requires coordination among state agencies, families, firms, and nongovernment organizations (Pérez-Díaz, Chuliá, Álvarez-Miranda 1998). At the same time, Spaniards know that they live in an ever more open economy: by 1998 exports and imports combined represented 76.1% of Spain's GDP. And they also know about the revolution in communication technology and want to be part of it, as witness the sudden phenomenon of 2.2 million Spaniards connected to the Internet.[9] It is likely, too, that the country has learned to accept the complex, urgent, and inevitable challenges of regional and European politics with greater realism and flexibility.

In the world of today, politics is too important and, paradoxically, too complicated to be left to professional politicians. Although leaders, representatives, and officials have very important tasks to perform, the problems are too big for them alone. They need reasonable support and criticism from their fellow citizens and also constant reminders that they are the servants, not the masters, of free citizens. In order for these citizens to occupy center stage in the public sphere, however, normative appeals and rhetorical declamations are not enough. Citizens must have to want to be free and hence responsible for what happens in their country. At bottom, it is that simple. They have to decide for themselves. No one else can do it for them. All we know is that if they do not take up the burden of their freedom and civic responsibility, they lack justification to complain about the consequences which derive from their inaction.

In this predicament the Spanish citizens do not stand alone. In every European country, for example, solutions to the problems of the rule of law, unemployment, reform of the welfare system, development of the public space, the articulation of regional identities within the nation, and a sense of community will only come about when the citizens put their civic abilities into action. What this book tells us about Spain is (more or less) applicable to all, or almost all, of them: *de te fabula narratur*, and not only to each one individually but to the European Union as a whole. In some ways it is a question of deciding whether or not Europeans want a European civil society, in the sense of a community of European citizens who feel themselves to be such and act accordingly. It is not necessary to create it. If they achieve it, it will be the result of an act of freedom, or rather, of many individual acts of freedom.

But since pure freedom (or pure will) is, as Hegel would put it, a rather empty abstraction, it would help to look more carefully into the specific institutional mechanisms and the particular socioeconomic and political interests that shape and underlie the process of Europeanization, and thereby gain an insight into what the decisions made so far look like, and where they may lead. The fact is, the European process is open-ended and may progress in several directions, but it seems that, in view of almost forty years of accumulated experience, it moves more toward an order of liberty than toward a European state writ large, with a grand historical project to fulfill and an overly assertive political leadership. The main goals of the Europe-builders—those of sharing in the pleasure of living together, engaging in useful economic, social, and cultural exchanges, constructing a civil space beyond the boundaries of the Union, and so many others—intimate a kind of political leadership which is unobtrusive, conversant with and responsive and accountable to its fellow citizens (Pérez-Díaz 1998b: 12ff).

This is consistent with the way in which European public authority is organized: in the shape of a net or network of public authorities (Keohane and Hoffmann 1991: 13ff) including the Council, the Parliament, the Commission, and the High Court; a number of powerful independent agencies; plus a web of committees, all interconnected in ways that require continuous and massive inputs of goodwill and ingenuity to keep the system working. This implies an ongoing, multilayered conversation that mirrors, in its own way, the extraordinary and increasingly numerous exchanges in which Europeans in all walks of life engage—and which can be coordinated only when all subscribe to formal and abstract rules.

As a matter of fact, in the process of complying with the Maastricht criteria, both politicians and citizens have trusted the decision to abide by a set of formal, abstract rules, which are those of the open markets. Moreover, these rules will be monitored by a regulatory agency which is relatively independent of the political authorities. Thus both politicians and citizens have opted for a mode of governance which could be defined as governance by rules. This builds on the previous work done by the Court of Justice, and on the acceptance of the supremacy of European law by most European High Courts (Ludlow 1998: 2). It is reasonable to expect this mode will be reinforced by the acceptance of the rules of budgetary restraint in the stability pact.

The corollary of this governance by rules is a redefinition of political leadership that makes it second to and dependent on the emergence and development of an alert and discriminating citizenry. Though there may be plenty of room for politicians' leadership in matters European, there is none for the kind of leadership remotely resembling that of most rulers of the past—those who shaped the political expression of most European nation-states over several centuries, sometimes by means of friendly persuasion and covenants, but mostly by means of massive acts of violence and tribal enthusiasm, such as forced conscription into armies, forced submission to tax-extracting machinery, and punishment of those who protested. These activities were carried out with the help of thousands or millions of enthusiasts (functionaries, teachers, clerics, military officers) who shared a sense of mission and a common fate (Pérez-Díaz 1998b: 11).

At present, from the way the European institutions actually work it may be inferred that Europeans have put off building a new political association of that kind. But if this is so, it is a choice between two alternatives. One is to lead the European Union toward a sort of dual or two-layer polity, in which pan-European elites, horizontally stratified but sharing a common language, preside over vertically segmented communities able to communicate with their local elites but not with each other. The other alternative is to build, step by step, a more homogeneous political society. This requires the emergence and development of a public space where a debate can take place on the main topics of European politics, such as huge unemployment, and imposing the rule of law over the economic and political elites.

Notes

Introduction

1. For a more detailed discussion of unemployment (and unemployment figures) see Chapter 5 below.

2. In a more restricted, limited sense than the one used by Elias (1978). Here the emphasis is on one particular kind of sociopolitical institutional arrangements, and the dispositions that come with them.

3. I have dealt at length with the late Francoist period (roughly from the mid-1950s to the mid-1970s) and the democratic transition (and consolidation, which lasted until the early 1980s) in Pérez-Díaz 1993. In chapter 1 of that book I relate some of the problems of Spain's liberal democracy to the "institutionalization" of that political regime.

1. Spain's Transition to Democracy

1. For the relative importance of the different factors see Pérez-Díaz 1993, pp. 26–40.

2. On civil society as an "ideal character" and on the normative and analytical dimensions of this concept, see Pérez-Díaz 1995, 1997, and 1998a. I adopt a broad view of civil society (a generalist view) as opposed to a more restricted (minimalist) view that tends to reduce civil society to the realms of the social fabric and the public sphere. For a contrary view, see Alexander 1998.

3. For a more extended discussion of this and the next section, see Pérez-Díaz 1993.

4. For the way in which these experiences shaped the working class and its organizations at the time of the democratic transition, see Pérez-Díaz 1979 and Fishman 1990.

5. For a careful discussion of the evolution of the political language of the Francoist state with regard to the Civil War, see Aguilar 1996.

6. Chueca 1989, Huneeus 1985, Hopkin 1995.

7. Apparently, it grew even stronger as we pass from the 1980s to the 1990s. In the 1980s, about 70% of the respondents supported the statement that "democracy is preferable to any other form of government" (70% in June 1985; 71% in November 1987; 68% in January 1989); the rate of favorable responses oscillated around 80% in the 1990s (80% in December 1990; 79% in December 1995; 82% in June 1997). Source: CIS (Centro de Investigaciones Sociológicas [Center for Sociological Research]), *Revista Española de Investigaciones Sociológicas*, 48 (1989) and 56 (1990), *Boletín de Datos de Opinión*, 3 (1996), and *Estudio 2252—barómetro de junio* (1997).

8. I leave aside the sizable number of Spaniards who do not usually answer this type of question.

9. Data for Spain from 1980 to 1993, and international data from Montero (1994). Data for Spain in 1998 (April) are from CIS, *Estudio 2285—Distribuciones marginales, barómetro de abril* (at the CIS webpage: cis.sociol.es).

10. An interesting account of the process from the viewpoint of those who were critical of Suárez can be found in Herrero 1993.

11. Data for 1996 in CIS, *Datos de Opinión*, 4, 1996; from CIS 1998 at the CIS webpage: cis.sociol.es. Data for 1998 from ASP (Analistas Socio-Políticos, Research Center), Survey 98.013, carried out in July 1998.

12. In fact membership has gradually risen in PSOE and even more so in PP during the 1990s. When the PSOE held its primary in the spring of 1998 to choose its presidential candidate for the next national election (see below), official membership in the party was 383,462 affiliates. At the Thirteenth Congres of February 1999, the PP claimed 584,341 affiliates.

13. *El Mundo*, Feb. 27, 1994, and March 27, 1994.

14. On this point see Bobbio 1995 (which I criticize in Pérez-Díaz 1997, 116–131).

15. Data for CIS 1996 in CIS 1996. Data for 1998 from Analistas Socio-Políticos Research Center 1998c.

16. This diagnosis may apply only partially to Western European parties at large. For a somewhat different view, see Mair 1998.

2. The Socialists Rule

1. I borrow this expression from Murray Edelman's book title (1988).

2. For two different views of the crisis of UCD see Martín Villa 1984, and Herrero 1993.

3. According to a postelectoral survey of CIS, about 30% of past UCD supporters voted PSOE, 25% gave their votes to Suárez's new party (CDS), and 18% voted AP. UCD received only 6.5% of the total vote and did not survive to the next election. It is quite likely, however, that the survey results contained a significant hidden vote for AP which did not show up in the responses (CIS 1996d: 11–12).

4. The liberalization went further for banks (because of external pressure by foreign banks wanting to come in); it did not go so far in telecommunications and energy (where the external pressure was weaker, and the domestic lobbies from within the public sector and from friendly private interests were stronger). In the

areas of retail trade and real estate it was a yes-but-no kind of policy (a balancing act that depended on electoral support).

5. A discussion of this experience of coalition politics in the Basque country may be found in Pérez-Díaz, Mezo 1998.

6. On the first steps of AP see Gunther, Sani, Shabad 1988, and on subsequent development the reader may find a record of the events until 1989 in Palomo 1990, and an interesting (and controversial) interpretation in Herrero 1993.

7. According to Robert Skidelsky's proposed defintion of the term; see 1995: 17ff.

8. European Commission data in *Instituto de Estudios Económicos* 1993a.

9. World Bank data in *Instituto de Estudios Económicos* 1993b.

10. Rubio was sent to jail without a trial at a time when the government was anxious to distance itself from cases of political and economic corruption, and was released after a few weeks. The allegations of tax fraud were corroborated, but it was too late to prosecute them. The allegations of inside trading could not be proved.

11. This case is still pending (August 1998). The chairman of BANESTO, Mario Conde, was brought to trial for his role in a dubious operation in which 600 million pesetas were missing. He claimed that this money was given to a lobbyist in order to influence the government—to no avail, since the court sentenced him to four years in jail.

12. *The Wall Street Journal*, Feb. 3, 1994; *Financial Times*, Feb. 2, 1992; *The Economist*, Feb. 29, 1992.

13. Data for 1994, according to estimates published by *The Economist*, May 5, 1997: 76.

14. For instance, the Rural Employment Plan provided months of subsidies to rural workers in Andalusia and Extremadura who managed to work just a few weeks (often for local council offices).

15. On the concept of "social capital of a civil kind" see Pérez-Díaz 1998d.

16. On the role of the family in the Spanish welfare system see Pérez-Díaz, Chuliá, and Álvarez-Miranda 1998.

3. The Two Faces of a Generation

1. A lucid observer of economic and political affairs of the seventeenth century, Cellorigo, used to refer to Spain as a country of *gentes encantadas:* people living under a magic spell (Elliott 1990). On the public sphere in Spain from the sixteenth through the eighteenth centuries see Pérez-Díaz 1998b.

2. On the relationship between the Falangist circles and the student movement see Ruiz Carnicer 1990.

3. Apparently with some success; even though the top positions of the Socialist party eluded him, he landed the job of mayor of Madrid, and got a solemn show of respect and public recognition at the time of his death. At the same time, we may recall that his position was difficult in Spain in the years immediately after the Civil War. On Tierno and his image see Alonso de los Ríos 1997.

4. Popper 1968 [1934], 82ff.

5. To their "informed" eyes Solidarnosc looked politically incorrect: see the testimony of Carlos Semprún 1998.

6. My interest in applying a generational perspective and my emphasis on the interrelated concepts of habits, dispositions, and moral character had been greatly stimulated by a Spanish tradition of moral and political philosophy that includes José Ortega y Gasset 1959a [1921] and José Luis Aranguren 1958.

7. The age breakdown for the entire 1977 Congress is: 5.4% were under 30 years old; 33.4%, 30–39 years old; 34.0%, 40–49 years old; 17.5%, 50–59 years old; and 9.7%, 60 years old or more (Huneeus 1985: 173).

8. As a participant and a witness in these debates, I remember we followed rather closely the parliamentary procedures similar to those codified in the classic manual of *Robert's Rules of Order* 1978 [1907]; but then, the study of law in the Spanish universities of the 1950s required a careful (and often sympathetic) reading of foreign (and Spanish, old and new) public as well as private procedural laws.

9. Before the government took away his chair at the University of Madrid, in 1965, for his participation in a street demonstration organized by the student movement.

10. This aspect of the moral and emotional mood of the student body in the 1950s (including its detachment from the political regime) comes out rather clearly in the testimony of two thoughtful witnesses: Pinillos 1982 [1953] and Laín 1982 [1955].

11. In a sense, this evolution suggests a continuity between the moral opportunism of a critical segment of this generation and the moral opportunism that underlay the survival tactics of their parents. Therefore it suggests a moral and emotional regression on their part. It may well be, then, that at the moment of truth (as the range of their political and economic opportunities expanded, and this was followed by a series of scandals), they were unable to overcome a "crisis of integrity," to use Erik Erikson's terms 1962: 254ff. This would explain their proclivity to use the language of magical realism and their unwillingness to take responsibility for their actions. But I cannot pursue this idea here.

4. Public Drama and the Rule of Law

1. *El Mundo*, Jan. 3, 1996.

2. For a sympathetic presentation of this self-image of the Socialist leaders as modernizers, see Feo 1993 (on Felipe González's first years in office) and Fernández-Braso 1983 (based on a series of conversations with Alfonso Guerra. Guerra was second in command in the PSOE and in the government until the early 1990s).

3. GAL stands for Grupos Antiterroristas de Liberación (Antiterrorist Liberation Groups).

4. See, for instance, Jung 1964.

5. With a few remarkable exceptions; see in particular Miralles and Arqués 1989.

6. *El Mundo*, Jan. 12–13, 1995; May 11, 1995.

7. The text may be found in *El País*, August 22, 1995.

8. The text of Móner's *auto de instrucción* may be found in *El Mundo*, Jan. 25, 1996.

9. *El Mundo*, Sept. 7, 1995.

10. *El País*, Dec. 24, 1995.

11. As if to make up for this misinformation, Roldán started working for a Master's degree in Political Science at the Open University, from jail.

12. *El País*, Dec. 24, 1995.

13. See a particularly insightful treatment of this political scandal in Jiménez Sánchez 1995.

14. On the Urralburu case see the allegations collected by different journalists in *El Mundo* (by Antonio Rubio and Manuel Cerdán, October 11, 1996), *ABC* (by Isabel Durán and José Díaz Herrera, April 4, 1997), and *El País* (by José María Irujo, March 2, 1998).

15. See Marino Barbero's explanation of his difficulties, years later, in *ABC*, Nov. 16, 1997, pp. 28–29.

16. *El País*, Jan. 29, 1995.

17. *El Mundo*, April 25, 1995.

18. See Enrique Gimbernat's argument in *El Mundo*, August 2, 1995.

19. More on the CESID documents in Chapter 6.

20. But before rushing into conclusions (and unfair comparisons of southern Europeans with their northern counterparts), the reader should be aware that until now, the Swiss system of justice has seemed particularly sensitive to these matters in cantons such as Geneva (where most Latin European political and economic figures have traditionally played games with their secret or half-secret accounts). See Robert 1996 (especially the author's interview with Bernard Bertossa in pp. 91–160).

21. In this regard, the reader may consult Miralles and Arqués 1989, the books by Díaz Herrera and Durán 1996, 1996b, 1997, and Cerdán and Rubio 1995.

22. We may add a further qualification: people acted as if they did not know and did not want to know whether such counterterrorist activities were already actual policy of the Spanish state. Rumor had it that a counterterrorist organization, the Basque-Spanish Battalion or Batallón Vasco Español (BVE), had been set up by the last Francoist governments. The BVE was active during the first years of the democratic transition. But the democratic governments of the transition have always claimed that they had nothing to do with these counterterrorist activities; they said they were barely able to control the armed forces and the security apparatus and point to the military coup of February 1981 to corroborate their assertions.

23. These words were supposed to have been pronounced by Felipe González, and indeed they were attributed to him by José Luis Aranguren in his Prologue to Miralles and Arqués 1989 (p. 21).

24. *El Mundo*, Feb. 12, 1995.

25. *El Mundo*, Jan. 1, 1994.

26. Published by late May 1994: *El Mundo*, May 21, 1994.

27. *El Mundo*, May 19, 1994.

28. *El Mundo*, Nov. 13, 1994.

29. *El Mundo*, Jan. 8, 1995.

30. *El País*, Jan. 11, 1995.

31. *El Mundo*, July 23, 1995.

32. These conditions apply generally, and they have certainly done so in the case of the impeachment procedures of U.S. presidents Richard Nixon and William Jefferson Clinton in the early 1970s and the late 1990s. More in particular, in both

cases we witness a struggle to define the central issue as being one of respect for the rule of law rather than one of partisan politics—the outcome of the struggle depending on the merits of the case and on the ability of the contenders, but also on the disposition and the ability of the public to focus its attention on the main points and to see through the tactics of the different parties. On the other hand, a word of caution about social learning may be appropriate. In the Spanish case (as we will see later in Chapter 6) the Socialists insisted on a strategy of denial, were defeated by a narrow margin in the next election, and many of them stuck to their line of defense even in the face of the courts' final sentences; in so doing they have enjoyed the support of a sizable part of their constituency.

33. *El País*, Dec. 18, 1994.
34. *El Mundo*, June 11, 1995.

5. *Unemployment*

1. Employment and unemployment figures in Spain are debatable and vary according to the source. For instance, total employment in 1997 was 13.2 million workers according to National Accounting Statistics but only 12.9 according to the Labor Force Surveys (*Encuesta de Población Activa*, or EPA). The most quoted figure for unemployment is that of EPA (19% in 1997), but different sources may give different unemployment and work force figures and percentages. Alcaide (1998) makes the most recent and probably the most serious attempt at reconciling these figures (while taking into account estimated underground employment). For Alcaide, total employment was 14.2 million in 1997, and unemployment would account for 15% (out of an active population slightly larger than the one given by EPA).

2. For a more extended discussion, which includes other complementary factors such as training and educational policies, see Pérez-Díaz 1999a.

3. See also Barea 1995 for the devices the government used to overcome budgetary restrictions, and Fuentes Quintana and Barea 1996: 99–102 on the loss of credibility of official budget figures, particularly for the period 1989–1993.

4. In 1990, elections for works councils reached a coverage of just over half the potential voters, that is, workers in firms with more than 5 employees; the coverage was of 70% in the industrial sector, and much lower in the service sector: 44% (Pérez-Díaz 1999a).

5. *The Economist* estimates, Feb. 12, 1994.

6. On the issue of the division of work and responsibility between the genders see Pérez-Díaz, Chuliá, Álvarez-Miranda 1998, and Pérez-Díaz 1998c.

7. A more extended discussion on family and the welfare system is in Pérez-Díaz, Chuliá, and Álvarez-Miranda 1998; on women's roles in the family and the labor market, see Pérez-Díaz 1998c.

8. A 1996 survey directed by myself as part of a study of attitudes toward the pension system took in a sample of 3,520 Spaniards older than 19 years of age (which allowed for a subsample of 1,060 salaried workers) and cast the results of 22% of the salaried workers belonging to a union (19% of private sector workers; 28% of public sector ones). The union affiliation rates are as follows: men, 26%; women, 15%; people aged 20–29, 12%; aged 30–39, 18%; aged 30–39, 31%; aged

50 and more, 34%. Men aged 40 and over seem to show the highest percentages, around 36% (Analistas Socio-Políticos, Survey 96.005).

6. A Political Shift from Left to Right

1. On water policies see Pérez-Díaz, Mezo, and Álvarez-Miranda 1996.
2. Apparently Pujol was not ready to forget the attempt made by some of the Socialists to involve him in the Banca Catalana scandal in the mid-1980s, which put him in danger of going to jail in 1987.
3. *El Mundo*, Nov. 1, 1995.
4. *El Mundo*, Nov. 23, 1995.
5. *El País*, June 18, 1992.
6. As I have argued with regard not only to the Spanish public but to the European public at large, on the basis of my analysis of survey data collected in late 1995 in Pérez-Díaz 1998d.
7. Data corroborated by two ASP recent surveys four years later (ASP Surveys 98.012 and 98.013, the fieldwork for which was done in March and July 1998): 33% and 19% respectively.
8. For a more extended discussion of both European and Spanish public opinion concerning the European Union as a political association and its main policies (in 1995), see Pérez-Díaz 1998b.
9. The reader may find several assessments of the PSOE's first steps along this road: a detached view in Gillespie 1988 and Craig 1993; a critical appraisal in Gutiérrez and de Miguel 1989, and a more sympathetic understanding in Maravall 1981.
10. González's political rhetoric was still fairly radical as late as in 1976: see for instance Aguilar 1996: 322.
11. On the referendum and, in general, on the avatars of Spanish foreign policy until 1986 see Pérez-Díaz and Rodríguez 1997.
12. *El País*, June 15, 1993.
13. Several surveys published by the media had given the PP an advantage of between 5 and 10 points over the Socialists, though the final vote was, of course, very much closer. Some of the disparity was probably the result of using samples which tended to under-represent the rural sector; using incorrect substitutes for people who refused to be interviewed; and, especially, making over-hasty estimates of the voting intentions of the undecided. All these technical defects may have been accentuated by the "snowball effect" of some estimates on others as they were being published; the sense of security grew out of the apparent congruence between the estimates and the trends apparent in the voting in legislative, autonomous, local, and European elections from 1993 to 1996.
Not all of the problems were technical, however. Estimating the final vote requires a careful interpretation of the disposition of the sample that declares itself undecided at the time of the interview. In turn, this calls for taking into account not just one or two but a number of interconnected questions, as well as sociodemographic and economic factors within the local context of the interviewees. Likewise, it is important to monitor the voting tendency throughout the temporal sequence, starting from the moment of the interview up to the time of voting. This

process gains depth when the survey explores the reasoning processes of interviewees and tries to interpret what effect the anticipation of the likely aggregate results of the election may have on the individual voters. A certain number of voters may consider the vote estimates provided by opinion polls before deciding. They may choose to jump on the majority bandwagon, even if that party was not their first choice, in order to strengthen its victory. Alternatively, they may opt for casting a vote for a party which was not originally their first preference either, in order to prevent an overwhelming victory by another (which they wish to win, but not to such an extent).

Post-electoral surveys suggest, however, that the number of such reflective (and polls-sensitive) voters was rather low. Though 69% of the people interviewed said they had been aware of the polls, and 44% thought the polls had an effect on the voting, only 9% admitted that the polls have had an effect on *their own* voting—and of these, only 8.6% conceded that they changed their vote from one party to another as a result; CIS 1996c.

Conversely, we may speculate that respondents tend to downplay anything that may suggest that they are too easily influenced by polls (or campaigns, for that matter), whereas professional politicians and observers strongly believe that campaigns do matter. Given that electorates tend to be increasingly educated and sophisticated, it may be expected that they will identify less closely with a single party in the long term. Hence the importance of campaigns as instruments used to persuade a discriminating electorate will tend to increase. It seems quite plausible, therefore, to infer that the PP's margin of victory would have been greater with a different campaign.

Other explanations for the divergence between opinion poll forecasts and the results may be found in articles by Amando de Miguel, José Ignacio Wert, and Carlos Malo de Molina in *ABC*, March 8, 1996, *El País*, April 5 and 6, 1996, and *El Mundo*, March 10, 1996.

14. This was a failed attempt to create an all-Spanish liberal party led by a Catalanist politician.

15. For instance, the investigation into the death of Ramón Oñaederra or the alleged abuses of reserved (public) funds, the case against Gabriel Urralburu, and others. In September 1998, former President of the Autonomous Community of Navarra Gabriel Urralburu, a Socialist, was sentenced to 11 years in jail for "continued crimes of bribery involving eight construction companies, and for two crimes against public finance of Navarra" (*El País*, Sept. 8, 1998).

16. A summary of the sentence is in *El Mundo*, Oct. 29, 1997.

17. A summary of this sentence is in *El País*, Feb. 27, 1998.

18. The complete text of this sentence can be found in *El Mundo*, July 30, 1998.

19. Including documents proceeding from the CESID, which were brought to bear on the case only after a protracted legal battle that only ended in March 22, 1997.

20. See the Sentence by the Supreme Court, First Part ("Proven Facts"), section of "Analysis of the Proof," clause 1, paragraph D (in *El Mundo*, July 30, 1998).

21. Source: ASP 1998b and 1998c; the fieldwork was done in March and July 1998.

22. See the White Paper of Consejo General del Poder Judicial (1997).

23. With a participation rate of 54.3%: about 200,000 votes out of a census of 383,000 party members.

24. See OECD report on Spain (1998).

7. The Challenge of Nationalism

1. I elaborate this argument in Pérez-Díaz 1998b.

2. In my opinion Gellner overrated the importance of its economic preconditions and underplayed the role of ideological politics. See Kedourie 1993: 142.

3. In the early 1980s, only 4% of the population of Alava spoke Euskera, and in and around Bilbao the figure was under 7%; Mezo 1996.

4. This seems corroborated by the finding that 71.4% of the Basques interviewed said they were "proud of being Spaniards when they compared themselves with people of other countries." Source: ASP Survey 98.015, October 1998.

5. A more extended discussion is in Pérez-Díaz and Mezo 1998.

6. ASP Survey 98.014, July 1998.

7. Ibid.

8. Curiously enough, the earliest known texts written in Castilian and Basque have been found together, next to each other in the same manuscript.

9. Nationalist resistance occurs in spite of the medium-term advantages which could accrue from federalization, an arrangement that could minimize or prevent any competition which a center-right party like the PP might offer the nationalist parties on their own territory. When UCD was in power, the possibility of such a political formation in Catalonia was discussed. Their possible voters would have been invited to support Catalan nationalism, within the framework of a stable alliance between UCD and the nationalists, along the lines of the one between the German CDU and the Bavarian CSU. Perhaps in the long term such an arrangement is conceivable, but at present Catalan nationalists fear that to agree to it would mean losing part of their freedom of maneuver and their capacity to attract the most intensely nationalist sector of their own electorate.

10. See Cambó 1986 [1923/1927].

11. As was demonstrated in the early 1980s, when a centrist party and the Socialist party supported the LOAPA: a law intended to put a ceiling on the ruling powers of the regional governments; see Pérez-Díaz 1993: 203ff.

12. In regional elections, the nationalist vote (in thousands) was 776 in 1986, 671 in 1990, 575 in 1994, and 679 in 1998; the non-nationalist vote (in thousands) was 367 in 1986, 344 in 1990, 444 in 1994, and 559 in 1998. Rates of participation were 69.6% in 1986, 60.9% in 1990, 59.6% in 1994, and 70.6% in 1998.

13. One year after the assassination of Miguel Ángel Blanco, 70% in a representative sample of the Basque population declared that the social reaction to this killing "was truly extraordinary, because many people either changed their attitude (toward political violence) or expressed their feelings publicly as they had never done before." Source: ASP Survey 98.014, July 1998.

14. For a more extended discussion of recent developments in the Basque country from the viewpoint of "civilizing" normative conflicts, see Pérez-Díaz 1999b. A factor which played a role in shaping political and popular expectations in the Basque country was the process leading to the end of political violence in Northern Ireland.

8. *Becoming a Civil Society by Trial and Error*

1. For a discussion about Spain moving closer to and away from some forms of civil society between the sixteenth and the eighteenth centuries, see Pérez-Díaz 1998a.

2. By the mid-1980s these politicians were out, or on the fringe of the action. Thus Santiago Carrillo came back from exile to cheers and then to retirement; something like that happened to Manuel Fraga, a prominent figure from the Francoist side, who has ended as a respected yet peripheral name in PP and a regional leader in his native Galicia.

3. Such individuals may become quite aggressive when someone points out that their self-appraisal is unrealistic; see Bushman and Baumeister's experimental studies on undergraduates (1998).

4. From Kazuo Ishiguro, *An Artist of the Floating World* 1989: 124–125.

5. I would just like to mention one of the latest political scandals in Western Europe: on December 23, 1998, Belgium's highest court sentenced the former secretary-general of the North Atlantic Treaty Organization, Willy Claes, to a three-year suspended prison term for corruption. Other high political figures were also involved. Source: *International Herald Tribune*, Dec. 24–25, 1998.

6. This is not the current understanding of civil society in Polish intellectual circles, which tend to reduce the concept to the sphere of public debate and the social movements, and exclude the markets from being an integral part of it (Szacki 1995: 100ff.). This minimalist notion of civil society in the intellectual climate of the 1970s and 1980s in Poland may reflect the combined influence of Marxist revisionism and Catholic corporatism—two semi-collectivistic views of society with a blind spot for the market economy.

7. For a contrary view (and a most interesting and thoughtful discussion of the cultural issues involved in the Polish experience) see Szacki 1995.

8. From Paul Hofheinz's column in the *Wall Street Journal*, August 3, 1998, p. 1. This was already the general conclusion reached by the "Survey on Business in Eastern Europe," *The Economist*, Nov. 22, 1997.

9. For data on exports and imports, see Ministerio de Economía y Hacienda 1999; and for connections to the Internet see Analistas Socio-Políticos 1999.

Bibliography

Aguilar, Paloma. 1996. *Memoria y olvido de la Guerra Civil española*. Madrid: Alianza Editorial.

Alcaide, Julio. 1995. "La alta tasa de paro española y sus expectativas a plazo medio." *Cuadernos de Información Económica*, 105 (December): 21–28.

——— 1998. "Evolución del empleo y del paro en 1997 y sus expectativas para 1998." *Cuadernos de Información Económica*, 131 (February): 20–26.

Alexander, Jeffrey. 1998. "Introduction. Civil Society I, II, III: Constructing an Empirical Concept from Normative Controversies and Historical Transformations." In Jeffrey Alexander, ed., *Real Civil Societies: Dilemmas of Institutionalization*. London: Sage.

Alonso de los Ríos, César. 1997. *La verdad sobre Tierno Galván*. Madrid: Anaya & Mario Muchnik.

Álvarez Blanco, Rafael. 1995. "El concepto de deuda pública según el protocolo de déficit excesivo. La deuda pública española." *Cuadernos de Información Económica*, 104 (November): 59–63.

Álvarez-Miranda, Berta. 1996. *El sur de Europa y la adhesión a la Comunidad. Los debates políticos*. Madrid: Centro de Investigaciones Sociológicas.

Analistas Socio-Políticos. 1999. *Cambio social y tecnologías de la información*. Madrid: ASP.

Analistas Socio-Políticos Research Center (ASP). 1996. *Survey 96.005*.

——— 1998a. *Survey 98.011*.

——— 1998b. *Survey 98.012*.

——— 1998c. *Survey 98.013*.

——— July 1998. *Survey 98.014. Encuesta sobre visión de presente y futuro del País Vasco*. Madrid: ASP.

——— October 1998. *Survey 98.015. Encuesta de opinión pública sobre la tregua declarada por ETA*. Madrid: ASP.

——— February 1999. *Survey 98.018. Encuesta de opinión pública sobre el XIII Congreso del PP, y otras cuestiones de actualidad*. Madrid: ASP.

Anuario El País. 1997. Madrid: Ediciones El País.

Aranguren, José Luis. 1958. *Etica*. Madrid: Revista de Occidente.

——— 1989. "Prólogo." In Melchor Miralles and Ricardo Arqués, *Amedo: El Estado contra ETA*. Barcelona: Plaza-Janés.

Aristotle. 1941. *Rhetoric*. In *The Basic Works of Aristotle*, Richard McKeon, ed.; trans. W. Rhys Roberts. New York: Random House.

Azaola, José Miguel de. 1988. *El País Vasco*. Madrid: Instituto de Estudios Económicos.

Banco de España. 1993. *Cuentas financieras de la economía española*. Madrid: Banco de España.

Barea, José. 1995. "Los agujeros del Presupuesto." *Cuadernos de Información Económica*, 100 (July): 75–85.

Barea Tejeiro, José and J. F. Corona Ramón. 1996. "La reforma de la empresa pública." In Fundación FIES y Asociación Española de Economía Pública. *Documentos de trabajo*, 121.

Blanchard, Olivier and Juan F. Jimeno. 1995. "Structural unemployment: Spain versus Portugal." In FEDEA: *Documentos de trabajo*, 95–104.

Bobbio, Norberto. 1995. *Derecha e Izquierda*. Trans. A. Picone. Madrid: Taurus.

Bushman, Brad and Roy Baumeister. 1998. "Threatened Egotism, Narcissism, Self-Esteem, and Direct and Displaced Aggression: Does Self-Love or Self-Hate Lead to Violence?" *Journal of Personality and Social Psychology*, 75, 1: 219–229.

Cambó, Francesc. 1986 [1923–1927]. *Por la concordia*. Madrid: Alianza Editorial; Barcelona: Enciclopèdia Catalana.

Campo, Salustiano del. 1995. *La opinión pública española y la política exterior. Informe INCIPE 1995*. Madrid: Instituto de Cuestiones Internacionales y Política Exterior.

Castillo, Pilar del (ed.). 1994. *Comportamiento político y electoral*. Madrid: Centro de Investigaciones Sociológicas.

CECS. 1994. *España 1993. Una interpretación de su realidad social*. Madrid: Fundación Encuentro.

Cerdán, Manuel and Antonio Rubio. 1995. *El "caso Interior."* Madrid: Temas de Hoy.

CIRES. 1993. *Identificación supranacional*. Diskette.

——— 1994. "Orientación hacia el trabajo." *Boletín CIRES*, October.

——— 1995. *Identificación supranacional*. Diskette.

CIS (Centro de Investigaciones Sociológicas). 1989. *Revista Española de Investigaciones Sociológicas*, 48.

——— 1990. *Revista Española de Investigaciones Sociológicas*, 56.

——— 1995. *Datos de Opinión*, 1. Madrid: CIS.

——— 1996a. *Datos de Opinión*, 3. Madrid: CIS.

——— 1996b. *Datos de Opinión*, 4. Madrid: CIS.

——— 1996c. *Estudio 2210* (May). Madrid: CIS.

——— 1996d. *Datos de Opinión*, 5. Madrid: CIS.

——— 1997. *Estudio 2252*. Madrid: CIS.

——— 1998. *Estudio 2285*. Madrid: CIS.

Chueca, Fernando. 1989. *Liberalismo: Ideas y recuerdos*. Madrid: Dossat.

Consejo General del Poder Judicial (CGPJ). 1997. *Libro Blanco de la Justicia*. Madrid: CGPJ.

Craig, Patricia. 1993. "The Spanish Socialist Party: Ideology and Organization in a Contemporary Social Democratic Party." Ph.D. diss., Yale University.

Cruz, Raúl de la. 1994. "An Examination of the Traditional Rural Vote in Spain (1977–1989)." M.A. Thesis, Louisiana State University.

Cuadernos de Información Económica, 135. 1998 (June).

Darwin, Charles. 1957 [1859]. *El origen de las especies.* Trans. J. Marco. Mexico: Grijalbo.

Della Porte, Donatelle, and Yves Mény. 1995. *Démocratie et corruption en Europe.* Paris: Découverte.

Díaz Herrera, José and Isabel Durán. 1996a. *El saqueo de España.* Madrid: Temas de Hoy.

——— 1996b. *Pacto de silencio.* Madrid: Temas de Hoy.

——— 1997. *El secuestro de la Justicia.* Madrid: Temas de Hoy.

Edelman, Murray. 1988. *Constructing the Political Spectacle.* Chicago: The University of Chicago Press.

Edo, Valentín, Laura de Pablos, and Aurelia Valiño. 1994. "El control presupuestario del gasto público." *Cuadernos de Información Económica*, 91 (October): 39–45.

Elias, Norbert. 1978 [1939]. *The Civilizing Process 1: The History of Manners.* Trans. E. Jephcott. New York: Pantheon Books.

Elliott, J. H. 1984. *La España imperial. 1469–1716.* Barcelona: Vicens Vives.

Elster, Jon. 1986. *Ulysses and the Sirens.* Cambridge: Cambridge University Press.

Elzo, Javier, Francisco A. Orizo, Pedro González Blasco, and Ana I. del Valle. 1994. *Jóvenes españoles 94.* Madrid: Fundación Santa María.

Enzensberger, Hans Magnus. 1995. *La grande migration* (and *Vues sur la guerre civile*). Trans. B. Lortholary. Paris: Gallimard.

Erikson, Erik. 1968. *Identity, Youth and Crisis.* New York: Norton.

Feito, José Luis. 1995. "La reforma del mercado de trabajo." Mimeo.

Feo, Julio. 1993. *Aquellos años.* Barcelona: Ediciones B.

Fernández-Braso, Miguel. 1983. *Conversaciones con Alfonso Guerra.* Barcelona: Planeta.

Fishman, Robert. 1990. *Working-Class Organizations and the Return to Democracy in Spain.* Ithaca: Cornell University Press.

Fuentes Quintana, Enrique. 1995. "El modelo de economía abierta y el modelo castizo en el desarrollo económico de la España de los años 90." In Enrique Fuentes Quintana, ed., *Problemas económicos españoles en la década de los 90.* Barcelona: Galaxia Gutenberg/ Círculo de Lectores.

Fuentes Quintana, Enrique and José Barea. 1996. "El déficit público de la democracia española: El carácter estructural del déficit presupuestario." In *Papeles de Economía Española*, 68: 86–191.

Fundación FIES. 1984. *Estadísticas básicas de España, 1971–1980.* Madrid: Fundación FIES.

Gangas, Pilar. 1995. *El desarrollo organizativo de los partidos políticos de implantación nacional.* Madrid: Centro de Estudios Avanzados en Ciencias Sociales, Instituto Juan March.

García Ferrando, Manuel, Eduardo López-Aranguren, and Miguel Beltrán. 1994. *La conciencia nacional y regional en la España de las autonomías.* Madrid: CIS.

García Pereda, Pilar and Ramón Gómez. 1994. "Elaboración de series históricas de empleo a partir de la Encuesta de Población Activa (1964–1992)." In Banco de España, Servicio de Estudios, *Documento de Trabajo 9409.*

Gellner, Ernest. 1983. *Nations and Nationalism.* Ithaca: Cornell University Press.

Geremek, Bronislaw and Juan Carlos Vidal. 1997. *Bronislaw Geremek en diálogo con Juan Carlos Vidal.* Madrid: Anaya & Mario Muchnik.

Gillespie, Richard. 1988. *The Spanish Socialist Party: A History of Factionalism.* Oxford: Clarendon Press.

Gimbernat, Enrique. 1995. "Sobre suplicatorios e inmunidades," *El Mundo*, August 2, 1995.

González Blasco, Pedro, Francisco A. Orizo, José J. Toharia, and Francisco J. Elzo. 1989. *Jóvenes españoles 89.* Madrid: Fundación Santa María.

González Enríquez, Carmen. 1996. "Transición y consolidación democrática en Europa del Este." In Carmen González and Carlos Taibo, *La transición política en Europa del Este.* Madrid: Centro de Estudios Constitucionales.

Gunther, Richard and José Ramón Montero. 1994. "Los anclajes del partidismo: Un análisis comparado del comportamiento electoral en cuatro democracias del sur de Europa." In Pilar del Castillo, ed., *Comportamiento político y electoral,* Madrid, CIS.

Gunther, Richard, Giacomo Sani, and Goldie Shabad. 1988. *Spain after Franco: The Making of a Competitive Party System.* Berkeley: University of California Press.

Gutiérrez, José Luis and Amando de Miguel. 1989. *La ambición del César: Un retrato político y humano de Felipe González.* Madrid: Temas de Hoy.

Hayek, Friedrich von. 1978. *New Studies in Philosophy, Politics, Economics and the History of Ideas.* London: Routledge and Kegan Paul.

Herce, José A. and Víctor Pérez-Díaz. 1995. *La reforma del sistema público de pensiones en España.* Barcelona: La Caixa, Servicio de Estudios.

Herrero de Miñón, Miguel. 1993. *Memorias de estío.* Madrid: Temas de Hoy.

Hopkin, Jonathan. 1995. "Party Building and Democratic Transition: The Union of Democratic Centre and the Transition to Democracy in Spain." Ph.D. diss., European University, Institute Florence.

Huneeus, Carlos. 1985. *La Unión de Centro Democrático y la transición a la democracia en España.* Madrid: Centro de Investigaciones Sociológicas.

Instituto de Estudios Económicos (IEE). 1993a. *Documentación* (November). Madrid: IEE.

——— 1993b. *Documentación* (July). Madrid: IEE.

Instituto Nacional de Estadística (INE). 1992. *Contabilidad nacional de España: Serie enlazada 1964–1991, base 1986.* Madrid: INE.

——— 1998. *Boletín de estadísticas laborales,* 152 (June).

Ishiguro, Kazuo. 1989. *An Artist of the Floating World.* New York: Random House.

Jiménez Sánchez, Fernando. 1995. *Detrás del escándalo político: Opinión pública, dinero y poder en la España del siglo XX.* Barcelona: Tusquets.

Jung, Carl. 1964. "Approaching the Unconscious." In Carl Jung, ed., *Man and His Symbols.* New York: Dell Publishing.

Kedourie, Elie. 1993 [1960]. *Nationalism.* Cambridge, Mass.: Blackwell.

Keohane, Robert and Stanley Hoffman. 1991. *The New European Community: Decisionmaking and Institutional Change.* Boulder, Col.: Westview Press.

Kirchheimer, Otto. 1966. "The Transformation of West European Party Systems." In J. LaPalombara and M. Weiner, eds., *Political Parties and Political Development.* Princeton: Princeton University Press.

Kissinger, Henry. 1994. *Diplomacy.* New York: Simon & Schuster.

Kornai, Janos. 1992. "The Affinity Between Ownership and Coordination Mechanisms: The Common Experience of Reform in Socialist Countries." In Kasimierz Poznanski, ed., *Constructing Capitalism: The Reemergence of Civil Society and Liberal Economy in the Post-Communist World.* Boulder, Co.: Westview Press.

Kuron, Jacek. 1991. *La foi et la faute: A la rencontre et hors du communisme.* Trans. J. Y. Erhel. Paris: Fayard.

Laín Entralgo, Pedro. 1982 [1955]. "Informe sobre la situación espiritual de la juventud española." In Roberto Mesa, *Jaraneros y alborotadores: Documentos sobre los sucesos estudiantiles de febrero de 1956 en la Universidad Complutense de Madrid.* Madrid: Editorial de la Universidad Complutense.

Laparra, Miguel, Mario Gaviria, and Manuel Aguilar. 1995. "Peculiaridades de la exclusión en España: Propuesta metodológica y principales hipótesis a partir del caso de Aragón." Mimeo.

Linz, Juan. 1978. "From Great Hopes to Civil War: The Breakdown of Democracy in Spain." In Juan Linz and Alfred Stepan, eds., *The Breakdown of Democratic Regimes: Europe.* Baltimore: The Johns Hopkins University Press.

Ludlow, Peter. 1998. *The EU on the Eve of the 21st Century: Governance, Leadership and Legitimacy.* Brussels: Centre for European Policy Studies.

Machin, Howard. 1990. "Changing Patterns of Party Competition." In Peter A. Hall, Jack Hayward, and Howard Machin, eds., *Developments in French Politics.* New York: St. Martin's Press.

Mair, Peter. 1998. "Representation and Participation in the Changing World of Party Politics." *European Review,* 6, 2: 175–190.

Malo de Molina, Carlos. 1996. "En defensa de los sondeos políticos." *El Mundo,* March 10, 1996, p. 11.

Maravall, José María. 1981. *La política de la transición (1975–1980).* Madrid: Taurus.

Martín Villa, Rodolfo. 1984. *Al servicio del Estado.* Barcelona: Planeta.

McDonough, Peter, Samuel H. Barnes, and Antonio López Pina. 1998. *The Cultural Dynamics of Democratization in Spain.* Ithaca, N.Y.: Cornell University Press.

Melville, Herman. 1992. *Moby Dick: Or, the Whale.* New York: Random House.

Mezo, Josu. 1996. *Políticas de recuperación lingüística en Irlanda (1922–1939) y el País Vasco (1980–1992).* Madrid: Centro de Estudios Avanzados en Ciencias Sociales, Instituto Juan March.

Miguel, Amando de. 1995. *La sociedad española, 1994–95. Informe sociológico de la Universidad Complutense.* Madrid: Editorial Complutense.

Miguel, Amando de, Roberto-Luciano Barbeito, Javier Castillo, and Iñaki de Miguel. 1996. "Informe de Tábula V. Por qué se han equivocado las encuestas electorales." In *ABC,* March 8, 1996, pp. 53 and 54.

Ministerio de Economía y Hacienda. 1993. *Síntesis mensual de indicadores económicos: Series.* Madrid: Dirección General de Previsión y Coyuntura. Diskette.

—— 1995. *La negociación colectiva en las grandes empresas en 1994.* Madrid: Ministerio de Economía.

—— 1999. *Síntesis de indicadores económicos.* Madrid: Ministerio de Economía y Hacienda.

Ministerio de Educación y Ciencia. 1995. *Curso escolar 1995/96.* Madrid: Ministerio de Educación y Ciencia.

Ministerio de Trabajo y Seguridad Social. 1996. *Boletín de estadísticas laborales*, 131 (March).

Miralles, Melchor and Ricardo Arqués. 1989. *Amedo: El Estado contra ETA*. Barcelona: Plaza-Janés.

Montero, José Ramón. 1994. "Sobre las preferencias electorales en España: Fragmentación y polarización (1977–1993)." In Pilar del Castillo, ed., *Comportamiento político y electoral*. Madrid: CIS.

OCDE. 1994. *Perspectivas del empleo 1994*. Madrid: Ministerio de Trabajo y Seguridad Social.

——— 1998a. *Informe sobre España 1997*. Paris: OCDE.

——— 1998b. *Estudios económicos de la OCDE 1997–98: España*. Paris: OCDE.

Ortega y Gasset, José. 1959a [1921]. *La España invertebrada*. Madrid: Revista de Occidente.

——— 1959b [1933]. *En torno a Galileo: Esquema de las crisis*. Madrid: Revista de Occidente.

Pallarés, Francesc, coord. 1991. *L'electorat català a les eleccions autonòmiques de 1988: Opinions, actituds i comportaments*. Barcelona: Fundació Jaume Bofill.

Palomo, Graciano. 1990. *El vuelo del halcón: José María Aznar y la aventura de la derecha española*. Madrid: Temas de Hoy.

Pelczynski, Z. A. 1982. *Poland: The Road from Communism*. Oxford: Pembroke College.

Pérez-Díaz, Víctor. 1979. *Clase obrera, partidos y sindicatos*. Madrid: Instituto Nacional de Industria.

——— 1993. *The Return of Civil Society: The Emergence of Democratic Spain*. Cambridge, Mass.: Harvard University Press.

——— 1995. "The Possibility of Civil Society: Traditions, Character and Challenges." In John Hall, ed., *Civil Society. Theory, History, and Comparison*. Cambridge, Eng.: Polity Press.

——— 1997. *La esfera pública y la sociedad civil*. Madrid: Taurus.

——— 1998a. "State and Public Sphere in Spain during the Ancient Regime." In *Daedalus*, 127, 3 (summer): 251–279.

——— 1998b. "Putting Citizens First: The Tasks Facing Europe; Her Public Sphere and the Character of Her Public Authority." *ASP Research Papers*, 22(b). The French version of this paper is "La cité européenne," *Critique Internationale*, 1.

——— 1998c. "Ancianos y mujeres ante el futuro," *Claves*, 83 (June): 2–12.

——— 1998d. "From 'Civil War' to 'Civil Society': Social Capital in Spain, 1930s–1990s." *ASP Research Papers*, 23(b).

——— 1999a. "The 'Soft Side' of Employment Policy: The Spanish Experience." In Paul Heywood, ed., *Politics and Policy in Democratic Spain*. London: Frank Cass Publishers.

——— 1999b. "Iglesia, economía, ley y nación: La civilización de los conflictos normativos en la España actual." In Peter Berger, ed., *Los Límites de la cohesión social: Conflictos y mediación en las sociedades pluralistas. Informe de la Fundación Bertelsmann al Club de Roma*. Barcelona: Galaxia Gutenberg (forthcoming).

Pérez-Díaz, Víctor, Elisa Chuliá, and Berta Álvarez-Miranda. 1995. "El Pacto de Toledo: Un punto de partida problemático," *Economistas*, 13, 68: 49–54.

——— 1998. *Familia y sistema de bienestar: La experiencia española con el desempleo, las pensiones, la sanidad y la educación*. Madrid: Fundación Argentaria y Visor.

Pérez-Díaz, Víctor and Josu Mezo. 1998. "El horizonte del País Vasco." Unpublished.

Pérez-Díaz, Víctor, Josu Mezo, and Berta Álvarez-Miranda. 1996. *Política y economía del agua en España. Criterios, alternativas y proceso de aprendizaje.* Madrid: Círculo de Empresarios.

Pérez-Díaz, Víctor and Juan Carlos Rodríguez. 1997. "From Reluctant Choices to Credible Committments: Foreign Policy and Economic and Political Liberalization: Spain 1953–1986." In Miles Kahler, ed., *Liberalization and Foreign Policy.* New York: Columbia University Press.

Pinillos, José Luis. 1982 [1953]. "Actitudes sociales primarias: Su estructura y medida en una muestra española." In Roberto Mesa, ed., *Jaraneros y alborotadores: Documentos sobre los sucesos estudiantiles de febrero de 1956 en la Universidad Complutense de Madrid.* Madrid: Editorial de la Universidad Complutense.

Polanyi, Michael. 1962. *Personal Knowledge: Towards a Post-Critical Philosophy.* Chicago: The University of Chicago Press.

Popper, Karl. 1968 [1934]. *The Logic of Scientific Discovery.* New York: Harper.

Prieto Lacaci, Rafael. 1993. "Asociaciones voluntarias." In Salustiano del Campo, ed., *Tendencias sociales en España (1960–1990),* vol. I. Madrid: Fundación BBV.

Puell de la Villa, Fernando. 1997. *Gutiérrez Mellado: Un militar del siglo XX (1912–1995).* Madrid: Biblioteca Nueva.

Putnam, Robert. 1995. "Foundations of Democracy: Bowling Alone, Revisited." *The Responsive Community* (spring issue).

Robert, Denis. 1996. *La justicia o el caos.* Trans. M. Wazcquez. Barcelona: Muchnik Editores.

Robert, Henry. 1978 [1907]. *Robert's Rules of Order: The Classical Manual of Parliamentary Procedure.* New York: Gramercy Books.

Ruiz Carnicer, Miguel Angel. 1990. "El Sindicato Español Universitario (SEU) y el surgimiento de la oposición estudiantil al régimen." In Javier Tussell, Alicia Alted, and Abdón Mateos, eds., *La oposición al régimen de Franco,* Vol. 2. Madrid: Universidad Nacional de Educación a Distancia (UNED).

Ruiz Olabuénaga, José Ignacio, and María Cristian Blanco. 1994. *La inmigración vasca: Análisis trigeneracional de 750 años de inmigración.* Bilbao: Universidad de Deusto.

Semprún Maura, Carlos. 1998. *El exilio fué una fiesta: Memoria informal de un español de París.* Barcelona: Planeta.

Skidelsky, Robert. 1995. *The Road from Serfdom: The Economic and Political* Consequences *of the End of Communism.* New York: Penguin Books.

Szacki, Jerzy. 1995. *Liberalism after Communism.* Trans. C. A. Kisiel. Budapest: Central European University Press.

Sztompka, Piotr. 1998. "Mistrusting Civility: Predicament of a Post-Communist Society." In Jeffrey Alexander, ed., *Civil Societies: Dilemmas of Institutionalization.* London: Sage.

Tezanos, José Félix. 1992. "El papel social y político del PSOE en la España de los años ochenta: Una década de progreso y democracia." In Alfonso Guerra and José Félix Tezanos, eds., *La década del cambio. Diez años de gobierno socialista 1982–1992.* Madrid, Sistema.

——— 1993. "Continuidad y cambio en el socialismo español: El PSOE durante la transición democrática." In José Félix Tezanos, Ramón Cotarelo, and Andrés de Blas, eds., *La transición democrática española.* Madrid: Sistema.

Turner, Victor W. 1986. "Dewey, Dilthey and Drama: An Essay in the Anthropology of Experience." In Victor Turner and Edward Bruner, eds., *The Anthropology of Experience*. Urbana: University of Illinois Press.

Valle, Victorio. 1996. "La hacienda pública de la democracia española: Principales rasgos." *Papeles de Economía Española*, n. 68, pp. 2:26.

Weber, Max. 1958 [1919]. "Politics as a Vocation." In H. H. Gerth and C. Wright Mills, eds., *From Max Weber*. New York: Oxford University Press.

Wert, José Ignacio. 1996. "El retorno de los brujos," *El País*, April 5 and 6, 1996.

Wert, José Ignacio, José Juan Toharia, and Rafael López Pintor. 1993. "El regreso de la política. Una primera interpretación de las elecciones del 6-J," *Claves de razón práctica*, 34 (July/August): 32–42.

Whitehead, Lawrence. 1986. "International Aspects of Democratization." In Guillermo O'Donnell, Philip C. Schmitter, and Lawrence Whitehead, eds., *Transitions from Authoritarian Rule: Comparative Perspectives*. Baltimore: The Johns Hopkins University Press.

Ysmal, Colette. 1989. *Les partis politiques sous la Ve République*. Paris: Montchrestien.

Newspapers and periodicals:

ABC
Financial Times
El País
El Mundo
La Vanguardia
The Economist
The Wall Street Journal

Index

Accountability, 2, 4, 7–8, 12, 31, 56, 70–71, 87, 95–103, 114, 186, 189–190
Acuerdo Económico y Social (AES), 110, 116
Agriculture, 10, 55, 107, 127, 137–138, 155
Ajuria-Enea conference (1988), 157, 167
Álava, 156, 159, 161, 165
Albero, Vicente, 130
Algeria, 57, 83
Alianza Popular (AP), 22–23, 26, 36, 38, 135–136
Almunia, Joaquín, 146–147
Álvarez, Francisco, 80–82
Amedo, José, 79–84
Andalusia, 49, 85, 111, 129, 138–139, 155, 166, 195n14
Anguita, Julio, 83
AP. *See* Alianza Popular
Arabs, 159
Aragón, 159, 166
Aranguren, José Luis, 61
Aristotle, 101
Army, 9, 15, 19, 22, 37, 79
Asunción, Antoni, 85, 130
Audiencia Nacional, 79–80, 171
Audiencia Provincial de Madrid, 143–144
Austria, 148
Austria–Hungary, 185
Aznar, José María, 38, 75, 125, 136, 142, 148, 168

Baader–Meinhof gang, 83
Banca Catalana scandal, 199n2
BANESTO affair, 45, 92, 195n11
Bank of Spain, 44, 111, 148
Barbero, Marino, 86–87
Barcelona, 43, 111, 137
Baroja, Pío, 62
Barrionuevo, José, 79, 81–82, 144–146
Basque language (Euskera), 154, 158
Basque country, 85, 87, 201n14; violence in, 2, 15–16, 18, 20, 45, 72, 79, 91, 125, 157, 167,

170–172, 184; nationalism in, 3, 6, 18–19, 29, 32, 37–38, 45, 123–124, 141–142, 148, 151–172, 184; sociopolitical conditions, 16, 125–126, 153–156, 163–164, 166–167; political parties in, 20, 29, 37–38, 124–126, 129–130, 142, 151, 156–158, 167–172; and GAL affair, 72, 78–79, 81, 145; economy of, 155–156, 164–166; history of, 158–163
Batallón Vasco Español (BVE), 197n22
Belgium, 148, 202n5
Belloch, Juan Alberto, 80, 84, 90
Benegas, "Txiqui," 81
Berlin Wall, 169
Bilbao, 125, 137, 141, 157, 160
Blanco, Miguel Ángel, 171, 201n13
Boletín Oficial del Estado, 85
Bolsheviks, 169
Borrell, José, 147
Bourbons, 159
Brandt, Willy, 134
Britain: elections in, 20; political parties in, 22, 24, 109; economy of, 43, 104, 107, 149; and terrorism, 83; nationalist movements in, 180
Budgetary policy, 41–42, 44, 71, 109, 111–112, 123, 148, 189
Business, 9, 17, 19, 24, 39–40, 50, 56, 116, 127, 136, 155–156
BVE (Batallón Vasco Español), 197n22

Calderón de la Barca, Pedro, 176
Calvo-Sotelo, Leopoldo, 36
Cámara Sindical, 60
Cambó, Francesc, 168
Canada, 149
Canary Islands, 166
Capitalism, 10, 15, 26, 44, 55, 57, 64, 77, 131–132
Carlists, 159–160
Carlos, Don (brother of King Ferdinand VII), 160
Carrillo, Santiago, 202n2

Castille, Castillian, 18, 155, 159
Castro, Fidel, 57
Catalán (language), 153–154, 158, 164
Catalonia, 144; nationalism in, 3, 6, 18, 29, 32, 37–38, 123–125, 141–142, 148, 151–169, 184; political parties in, 22, 27, 29, 37–38, 75–76, 124–126, 129–130, 142, 151, 156–158, 167–169, 201n9; economy of, 111, 124, 155–156, 164–166; sociopolitical conditions, 153–156, 163–164, 166–167; history of, 158–163
Catholic Church, 15, 57, 182–183; in Francoist state, 9–11, 55, 60, 62, 64, 99; in Basque country, 16, 160, 168; current influence of, 24, 49–50
Cayman Islands, 68
CCOO (Comisiones Obreras), 17, 28, 115
Centro Democrático Social (CDS), 23, 36, 194n3
Centro de Investigaciones Sociológicas (CIS), 92–93
Centro Superior de Información para la Defensa (CESID), 81, 87, 130
Cervantes, Miguel de, 54
CESID (Centro Superior de Información para la Defensa), 81, 87, 130
China, 57
Chirac, Jacques, 79
CIS (Centro de Investigaciones Sociológicas), 92–93
CiU. *See* Convergència i Unió
Civil society, 1–2, 4–9, 12–13, 20, 31, 34–35, 47, 51–52, 67, 69, 71, 87, 100, 173–181, 188
Civil War, 7–14, 16, 18–19, 54, 56, 62, 64, 71, 100, 140, 143, 161–163, 165, 168, 174, 178–179, 181–182
Claes, Willy, 202n5
Clinton, William, 197n32
Coalition politics, 123–126, 142, 149, 157–158, 168–169, 177
Cold War, 131, 181
Collective bargaining, 11, 24, 50, 112
Comisiones Obreras (CCOO), 17, 28, 115
Communications, 68–69, 111, 149, 187–188
Communism, 14, 181–184
Communist party (PCE), 22–24, 28–29, 132, 135
Comunidades Autónomas, 18, 143, 147, 151, 164, 166
Concha, Manuel de la, 45
Conciertos, 164–165
Conde, Mario, 195n11
Consejo General del Poder Judicial, 41. *See also* Council of Judiciary Power
Conservative democracy, 135
Constitution (1931), 15

Constitution (1978), 15–16, 18–20, 26, 30, 32, 135, 151, 158, 164–166, 170
Constitutional Court, 18–19, 41, 89, 125, 144
Convergència i Unió (CiU), 22, 27, 75, 87–88, 103, 123–124, 126, 137, 142, 157
Corcuera, José Luis, 84–85, 89, 130, 144
Corruption, 72, 75–78, 84–90, 93–94, 97, 100, 129, 144–145, 175
Council of Judiciary Power, 81, 87, 89
Coup by military (1981), 19, 22, 37, 79
Cracow, Poland, 183
Craxi, Bettino, 134
Crime rate, 45–46
Critical realism, 54
Cuba, 57
Cultural nationalism, 151
Czechoslovakia, 181
Czech Republic, 180, 184–185

Darwin, Charles, 173–174
Democracy, 9, 13, 40, 60, 77, 83, 90, 158, 174, 178–179, 194n7; period of consolidation, 1–2, 63, 67, 79, 97, 114, 116, 135, 140; transition to, 4–5, 7–8, 11, 14–18, 20, 22, 24–25, 32–33, 53, 61, 71, 73, 79, 101, 104, 108, 115–116, 123, 128, 137, 140, 175, 185; liberal, 7–8, 30–31, 34–35, 38, 52, 76, 87, 90, 122–123, 134, 183; conservative, 135; and nationalism, 162–163, 171
Denmark, 22, 67
Diario 16, 90, 92
Domínguez, Michel, 79–84
Dostoevski, Feodor, 177

EA (Eusko Alkartasuna), 125, 157
Economic growth, 107, 109–110
Economy/economic policy, 2–3, 162, 165–166; of Francoist state, 10–11, 60, 64–65, 155, 184; during 1970s, 17–18, 42–43, 107–108, 114–116; during 1980s, 22, 37, 43–44, 47, 68, 72, 104, 108–113, 115–118, 177; during 1990s, 43–45, 56, 67–69, 71, 103–108, 110–115, 117–118, 121–124, 127, 129–130, 143, 147–150, 156, 163–164, 177, 187. *See also* Market economy; Underground economy; Unemployment; Welfare state/system
Education, 11–12, 43, 48–49, 63–64, 118, 138–139, 176
Egin, 171
Elections, 24, 30, 32, 35, 102, 172; in 1977, 20–22; in 1979, 20–23, 176; in 1982, 20–23, 39, 135–138, 176; in 1986, 20–21, 23, 37, 136; in 1989, 20–21, 23, 37, 130, 136–138, 141; in 1993, 20–21, 23, 75–76, 123–124, 129, 137, 141; in 1994, 129–130, 170; in 1995, 129–130; in 1996, 20–21, 23, 76, 82,

93–95, 122–123, 137–138, 140–142, 156, 167, 170, 186; in 1998, 147, 156, 170. *See also* Parties, political
El Mundo, 90–92, 97
El País, 91
El Periódico, 90
EMU. *See* European Monetary Union
Ermua, 171
Estatuto Vasco, 165
Estella declaration (1998), 170
ETA. *See* Eusaki Ta Askartasuna
EU. *See* European Union
European Commission, 114, 127, 189
European Community. *See* European Union
European Council, 147–148, 189
European High Court, 189
European Monetary Union (EMU), 1–3, 33, 71, 103, 110–111, 114, 142–143, 147–148, 163, 180
European Parliament, 130, 189
European Union (EU), 3, 6, 19–20, 32, 67–68, 71–72, 101, 111, 114, 126–131, 151, 153, 163, 184, 188–190
Euskadi Ta Askatasuna (ETA), 79, 81, 85, 87, 91, 170–172
Euskal Herritarrok, 170
Euskera (Basque language), 154, 158
Eusko Alkartasuna (EA), 125, 157
Extremadura, 87, 138–139, 195n14

Falange, 55
Family, 25, 48–49, 55, 63–64, 67, 117–118, 120–121, 184, 187
Fascism, 13–14
Fascist party, 55
Fernández Ordóñez, Francisco, 36
Ferdinand V ("the Catholic"), 159
Ferrer, Ana, 85
FILESA affair, 45, 73, 78, 86–88, 90, 104, 143–144
Fisheries, 127
Foreign policy, 2, 20, 32–33, 72, 103, 127–128, 131, 135, 177, 187
Fraga, Manuel, 38, 135–136, 202n2
France, 10, 57, 117, 128, 140, 164; economy of, 11, 43, 90, 104, 107, 149, 161; elections in, 20; political parties in, 24, 77, 86, 109; and terrorism, 78–79, 81–83, 91, 145; nationalist movements in, 180
Franco, Francisco, 4–5, 7, 9–13, 16–19, 34, 46, 53, 56–57, 59, 61, 64, 71, 109, 135, 137, 140, 161–162, 174, 181
Francoism/Francoist state, 8–14, 16, 18, 25, 36, 39, 55, 60–61, 65–66, 74, 93, 108–109, 123, 132, 135–136, 140, 155, 159, 162, 168, 174–175, 178–179, 181–182
Fueros, 165

GAL. *See* Grupos Antiterroristas de Liberación
Galicia, 18, 129, 136, 158, 166
García Damborenea, Ricardo, 80–83
García Vargas, Julián, 87, 130
Garzón, Baltasar, 75, 79–81, 83, 88–89, 94, 97, 102, 145, 171
GDP. See Gross domestic product
Gellner, Ernest, 152
General Strike (1988), 50, 91, 136
Generation of 1898, 62
Generation of 1956–1968, 54, 59–69, 174
Geremek, Bronislaw, 182
Germany, 10, 14, 45, 112, 140, 164, 182; elections in, 20, 22; political parties in, 24, 77, 169; economy of, 43, 104, 107, 148–149, 161; and terrorism, 83
Gibraltar, 83
Gómez de Liaño, Javier, 83, 89, 143
Gomulka, Wladyslaw, 57
González, Felipe, 2, 34, 41, 56, 72–76, 81, 87, 91, 93–94, 102–104, 122, 124–125, 129–131, 133–134, 140, 146–147
Gracián, Baltasar, 54
Gramsci, Antonio, 47
Granados, Carlos, 84
Greece, 19
Gross domestic product (GDP), 43, 45, 105, 111, 113, 118, 124, 148–149, 187
Grupos Antiterroristas de Liberación (GAL), 72, 75, 78–84, 88–95, 102–104, 143, 145, 147, 177, 179
Guardia Civil, 84–85, 144–145
Guerra, Alfonso, 41, 85, 131, 133, 196n2
Guerra, Juan, 73, 85, 90, 92
Guevara, Ernesto (Che), 57
Guipúzcoa, 154, 156, 159, 161, 165

Hapsburgs, 159
HB (Herri Batasuna), 157, 170–172
Health care, 43, 49, 117
Hegel, G. W. F., 114, 188
Hernández, Eligio, 80, 84, 87
Hernández Mancha, Antonio, 38
Herrero, Miguel, 36, 38
Herri Batasuna (HB), 157, 170–172
Holy Week *fiestas*, 49
Homeless people, 117
Huelva, 141
Hungary, 57, 180–182, 184

IBERCORP, 45
Imperialism, 132
Industrialization, 155–156, 160–161, 184
Inflation, 17, 37, 44, 103, 106, 108, 111, 115, 127, 148
Inquisition, 160

Interest rates, 103, 108–109, 112, 148
Internal Security Law, 89
International Monetary Fund, 64
Internet, 187–188
Investment, 43–44, 68
Ireland, northern, 201n14
Isabel I, 159
Isabel II, 160
Ishiguro, Kazuo, 179
Italy, 10–11, 14, 17, 20, 24, 38, 77, 90, 104, 107, 149, 157, 180
Izquierda Unida (IU), 23, 83, 122, 132

Jansenism, 99–100
Japan, 44, 77, 179
Jaruzelski, Wojciech, 181
Jesuits, 57, 99
Journalists. *See* Media
Juan Carlos, King, 2, 14, 16, 19, 31, 73, 87, 93, 97, 125
Judiciary, 1, 18–19, 40–41, 58, 72, 76, 78–90, 94–96, 112, 139, 143–147, 171–172, 176, 179
Jung, Carl, 78
Justo, Juan de, 79–81

Kadar, Janos, 57, 181
Kissinger, Henry, 134
Kuron, Jacek, 182
Kuwait Investment Office (KIO), 45

Labor. *See* Workers
Laos, 85
Lasa, José Antonio, 82, 143
Latin America, 184
Law. *See* Rule of law
León, 159
Ley de Amejoramiento del Fuero Navarro, 165
Liberal democracy. *See* Democracy, liberal
Lockheed scandal, 90
López, Antonio, 58

Maastricht Treaty, 3, 67, 71, 103, 126–128, 148, 163, 189
Madrid, 19, 54, 58, 75, 117, 125–126, 137, 140, 155, 162, 165, 195n3
Madrid Stock Exchange, 45
Mafia, 175
MALESA, 86
Marey, Segundo, 72, 80, 82, 143–145
Market economy, 4, 8–10, 12, 34, 37, 42, 70, 123, 131–132, 134, 147, 149, 151, 168, 174–175, 177, 180, 189
Martínez Torres, Jesús, 88
Marxism, 16, 26, 41, 57, 62, 64, 99, 133, 182–183
Maura, Antonio, 168

Media, 58, 76, 79, 83–84, 87, 90–93, 96, 114, 118, 138
Melville, Herman, 35, 69
Mesogovernment, 17, 32
Middle Ages, 158–159
Middle class, 9, 40, 55, 63, 65, 161
Ministry of Interior; Ministry of Justice and Interior, 79–82, 84–85, 90, 98, 130, 145–146
Ministry of Labor, 118
Mitterrand, François, 134
Modernizing state nationalism, 152
Moncloa Pacts, 17, 116
Móner, Eduardo, 81, 145
Monetary policy, 44, 71, 109, 111, 123, 148
Montesquieu, baron de (Charles-Louis de Secondat), 41
Morality, 63–66, 76, 86, 92, 94–102
Morocco, 68, 127

Nationalism, 1, 3, 6, 54, 103, 175–176, 184; during transition to democracy, 15–19, 26, 29, 32; under Socialist rule, 37–38, 45; under Francoist state, 60, 66, 161–163; and political shift to right, 123–126, 141–143, 149, 163–167; types of, 151–153; social/economic background, 153–156; political context, 156–163; contemporary issues, 167–172. *See also* Terrorism
Nationalists, 64, 66
NATO. *See* North Atlantic Treaty Organization
Navarre, 49, 85, 159, 161, 164–166, 200n15
Navarro, Carlos, 87, 144
Netherlands, 22, 148
New York City, 117
Nixon, Richard, 197n32
Nomocratic order, 8
North Atlantic Treaty Organization (NATO), 23, 26, 33, 37, 75, 86, 109, 123, 131, 133–135, 202n5

Older people, 115–117
Ollero, Manuel, 85
Olympic Games (1992), 43, 67, 111
Oñaederra, Ramón, 200n15
Ordóñez, Gregorio, 125
Organization for Economic Cooperation and Development, 64
Ortega y Gasset, José, 46, 62–63

Palme, Olaf, 134
Pandillas, 24–25, 49
Papandreou, Andreas, 134
Paris, France, 117
Parliament, 9, 34, 37, 40–41, 59–60, 75, 81, 84, 87–89, 91, 102, 124, 134, 144

Parliamentary procedures, 196n8
Partido Comunista Español (PCE). *See* Communist party
Partido Nacionalista Vasco (PNV), 88, 124–125, 137, 156–158, 171–172
Partido Popular (PP), 20, 23–24, 26–28, 75–76, 88, 122–123, 125–126, 129–130, 135–138, 140–142, 148, 157, 163, 167–172, 176–177, 194n12, 199n13, 201n9
Partido Reformista, 142
Partido Socialista Obrero Español (PSOE). *See* Socialist Party
Parties, political, 185–186; during transition to democracy, 15–17, 20–32; under Socialist rule, 34, 36–40, 44, 49–50; and political shift to right, 122–126, 129–131, 133, 135–142; and nationalist movements, 151, 167–172. *See also specific parties;* Coalition politics; Elections
PCE (Partido Comunista Español). *See* Communist party
Peasants, 9–10
Pensions, 116–117
PER. *See* Plan de Empleo Rural.
Planchuelo, Miguel, 80–82
Plan de Empleo Rural (PER), 138
Plato, 54
PNV. *See* Partido Nacionalista Vasco
Poland, 57, 149, 180–184, 202n6
Polanyi, Michael, 57
Political nationalism, 151–152
Political parties. *See* Parties, political
Popper, Karl, 56
Portugal, 19, 68, 107–108, 148
PP. *See* Partido Popular
Press. *See* Media
Privatization, 149
PSOE (Partido Socialista Obrero Español). *See* Socialist party
Public authority, 95–96, 99–100, 102, 164
Public debate, 8–9, 12, 53–54, 75, 95, 103, 123, 172, 175–176, 178, 190
Public debt, 103, 108–109, 111, 124, 127, 148, 166
Public opinion polls, 139–141
Public spending, 42–43, 110–112, 114, 123
Public sphere, 4–6, 8–9, 12, 34, 177
Public trust, 2, 40, 100
Pujol, Jordi, 75–76, 124–126, 199n2

Railroads, 111, 149
Rato, Rodrigo, 148
Recession of 1992–1994, 103, 112–113
Redondo, Nicolás, 133
Redressive rituals, 70–71
Regional movements. *See* Nationalism

RENFE, 111
Republicans, 64
Responsibility. See Accountability
Ridruejo, Dionisio, 16
Roca, Miguel, 142
Rodríguez Ibarra, Juan Carlos, 87
Roldán, Luis, 78, 84–85, 88, 90, 92, 130, 143–145
Rosa, Javier de la, 45
RTVE, 111
Rubio, Mariano, 44–45, 73, 90, 92, 130, 195n10
Rule of law, 1–2, 4, 6–8, 12, 34, 44–45, 70–71, 87, 100, 123, 132, 142–143, 146, 151, 163, 167, 171, 175, 177, 189
RUMASA affair, 41, 78
Rural Employment Plan, 195n14

Sala, José María, 87, 144
Salanueva, Carmen, 85–86
Sancristóbal, Julián, 80–82, 89–90, 145
San Sebastián, 125, 157
Sartre, Jean-Paul, 91
Scandals, 1–2, 5, 30, 38, 44–45, 56, 63, 67, 70–104, 122–124, 129–130, 133, 141, 143–147, 167, 177, 180, 186
SEAT, 45
Second Vatican Council, 11
Serra, Narcís, 81, 87, 130
Severance payments, 106, 108
Seville, 43, 111, 141
Slovakia, 185
Social capital, 24–25, 46–51
Social class, 65–66
Social-democratic outlook, 41, 56
Social-Democratic party, 16
Socialism, 5, 56–57, 184
Socialist party (PSOE): during transition to democracy, 19–20, 22–24, 26–30, 32–33; and nationalist movements, 19, 38, 124–126, 157–158, 163, 167–171; and NATO, 23, 26, 33, 37, 123, 131, 135; apparatus/administration of, 27–28, 176, 194n12; and scandals, 30, 38, 45, 72–98, 133; rule by, 34–51, 59, 65; slogan, 36, 40; and economy, 37, 42–44; and terrorism, 37; authoritarian behavior, 39; ideology, 40–41, 47, 131–133; leadership, 54–56, 59–60, 133–134, 196n2; and unemployment, 103–104, 109, 113, 116; fall of, 122–126, 129–147, 150, 199n13; loss of direction, 130–134, 177; persistent support for, 139–141
Social security, 110, 112, 118
Sociocultural nationalism, 151
Sofia, Queen, 86
Solana, Javier, 75

Solbes, Pedro, 148
Solidarnosc, 57, 183
Soviet Union, 14, 57, 112, 169, 180–182, 184–185
State nationalism, 152
Strikes, 11, 17, 24, 50, 91, 110, 136
Student movements, 11–12, 60–61
Suárez, Adolfo, 2, 14–16, 18, 22–23, 36, 39, 73, 134
Subsidies, unemployment, 106, 108, 110, 112
Supreme Court. *See* Tribunal Supremo
Switzerland, 80, 90, 197n20

Taxation, 42–44, 149, 164–166
Teleocratic order, 8
Term contracts, 106, 108–110, 117
Terrorism, 2, 6, 15–16, 18, 20, 22, 37–38, 45, 72, 76, 78–84, 91, 94, 98, 125–126, 139, 145, 157, 167, 170–172, 177, 180, 184
Tierno Galván, Enrique, 55, 195n3
Time Export, 86
Toledo Pacts, 112
Tomás y Valiente, Francisco, 125
Tourism, 10, 68
Tribalism, 53–54, 58, 67, 95–96, 139
Tribunal de Cuentas, 41, 88
Tribunal Supremo, 81–82, 87–89, 143–147, 171
Turner, Victor, 70

UCD. *See* Unión de Centro Democrático
UGT. *See* Unión General de Trabajadores
Underground economy, 45, 56, 67–68, 117–118, 120, 187
Unemployment, 1, 3, 5, 17–18, 37, 43–44, 47–49, 67, 70–71, 101, 103–122, 124, 129, 139, 141, 148–149, 156, 175, 177, 180, 184, 187, 198n1
Unión de Centro Democrático (UCD), 15–16, 18, 20, 22–23, 25–26, 31, 36–37, 39, 42, 59–60, 93, 104, 109, 123, 135, 137, 142, 176, 186, 194n3, 201n9
Unión General de Trabajadores (UGT), 17, 28, 45, 115

Unions, 11, 17, 19, 23–24, 45, 49–50, 69, 109–111, 114–116, 118, 148
United States: pacts with, 10; unemployment in, 47, 105, 107; and corruption, 90; homeless people in, 117; impeachment procedures, 197n32
Universities, 11–12, 40, 43, 60–61, 63–64, 73–74
University of Madrid, 60, 73–74, 196n9
University of Seville, 74
Urba affair, 86
Urralburu, Gabriel, 85, 197n14, 200n15

Valencia, 49, 159, 166
Vatican, 10–11, 159
Vera, Rafael, 79–81, 145–146
Vietnam, 57
Virgin Islands, 68
Vizcaya, 80, 84, 145, 154, 156, 159, 161, 165
Voluntary associations, 8–9, 12, 24–25, 49–50, 174, 177

Wages, 17–18, 37, 106, 108–109, 111, 115, 117
Warsaw, Poland, 183
Wars of Succession, 159–160
Weber, Max, 92
Welfare state/system, 37, 40, 42, 75, 116–117, 121, 131, 136, 139, 149, 175, 180, 184, 187
Wittgenstein, Ludwig, 114
Women, 47, 106, 115–116, 121
Workers, 10–11, 17–19, 24, 37, 40, 42, 45, 47, 50, 55, 65–66, 70–71, 103–121, 139, 148
Workers' Statute (1980), 17, 116
World Bank, 64
World Fair (1992), 43, 67, 111
World War I, 140, 185
World War II, 10, 14, 182

Young people, 106, 115–121
Yugoslavia, 29, 57, 126, 185

Zabala, José Ignacio, 82, 143